THE BEST GAME EVER

THE BEST GAME EVER

Pirates vs. Yankees: October 13, 1960

JIM REISLER

CARROLL & GRAF PUBLISHERS
NEW YORK

THE BEST GAME EVER
Pirates vs. Yankees: October 13, 1960

Carroll & Graf Publishers
An Imprint of Avalon Publishing Group, Inc.
11 Cambridge Center
Cambridge, MA 02142

AVALON
publishing group incorporated

First Carroll & Graf edition 2007

Library of Congress Cataloging-in-Publication Data

Reisler, Jim, 1958-
  The Best game ever : Pirates vs. Yankees : October 13, 1960 / Jim Reisler. — 1st ed.
    p. cm.
  Includes bibliographical references.
  ISBN 13: 978-0-7867-1943-3
  ISBN 10: 0-7867-1943-5
  1. World Series (Baseball) (1960) 2. Pittsburgh Pirates (Baseball team)—History—20th century. 3. New York Yankees (Baseball team)—History—20th century. I. Title.

  GV878.4.R45 2007
  796.357'646—dc22

                                                    2007015513

9 8 7 6 5 4 3 2 1

Interior Design by Maria E. Torres

Printed in the United States of America

For Tobie and Julia, and in memory of my father.

A portion of this book's royalties will go to the Western Pennsylvania Sports Museum at the Senator John Heinz Pittsburgh Regional History Center.

"They set all the records and we won the Series. Let 'em stuff that on their mantelpieces."

—Gino Cimoli

CONTENTS

PREFACE

EVEN MY MOTHER remembers where she was when the Pirates won the 1960 World Series. She was pulling into a gas station in our old hometown of Cornwall, New York, just as a roar emerged from inside the station, where a group of men huddled around a black-and-white television set watching Game 7.

When the attendant emerged, he had a question: "Aren't you moving to Pittsburgh, Mrs. Reisler?" he asked.

"Yes, we are," Mom said, "Later this month."

"Well, you'll be happy to know that the Pittsburgh Pirates just beat the Yankees to win the World Series," the attendant said.

My mother, never a sports fan, doesn't remember how she responded. Nor do I—I had just turned two years old, so at least I have an excuse. But in time, even Mom would come to realize what the 1960 Pirates meant to the city of Pittsburgh.

So we moved to Pittsburgh, where my father had been transferred by Gulf Oil. Unlike Mom, my father was a true sports enthusiast, an all-round athlete who had played college baseball. My father, who had been in Pittsburgh for several months by the time the rest of us arrived, had already been many times to see the Pirates play at Forbes Field and was well on his way to developing an abiding affection for the team of his new hometown.

We didn't move into Pittsburgh right away, but to Bakerstown in the northern suburbs. Six years later, we moved into the city—to a section of town called Squirrel Hill, which borders Oakland, where the Pirates played. Our house was exactly one mile from Forbes Field—so close that we could hear the crowd noise from the back patio. To get to the ballpark, we walked across the campus of Carnegie Mellon University, then Carnegie Tech (or just "Tech"), into Schenley Park, a parkland setting just beyond the left-field wall at Forbes Field, and over the Panther Hollow Bridge, arriving in about twenty minutes.

At the time, it didn't occur to me how fortunate we were to be so close to Forbes Field, or for that matter, to crummy old Pitt Stadium, the soulless concrete bowl atop Cardiac Hill where the Steelers played from the mid-1960s until 1970. Indeed, there were no tears shed when Pitt Stadium was demolished. But in the end there were tears for disheveled old Forbes Field, which was comfortable in a familiar way, like a well-worn basement den or a favorite pair of jeans. Forbes Field featured clogged aisles, rows of obstructed-view seats, bathrooms that smelled like a circus, and few concessions beyond watery Coke, peanuts, and popcorn. But Forbes had loads of character, much of it drawn from the surrounding neighborhood, including the green splendor of Flagstaff Hill, the centerpiece of Schenley Park that you could see from much of the second and third tiers. The imposing Carnegie Library loomed beyond left field, across the parking lot. And along Boquet Street, which paralleled the first base side of the park, was a line of row houses whose residents turned their small, square front yards into parking lots and then sat back to loaf on their front porches and listen to the game on KDKA radio.

Built in the middle of the dead-ball era when home runs were a rarity, Forbes Field featured an enormous outfield and fences that, except for right field, were far, far away. No pitcher ever threw a no-hitter at Forbes Field, where even the weakest banjo-hitter could usually find some part of the spacious green to drop a base hit. The left-field wall was 365 feet from home plate—the National League's deepest—and was topped by a 25-foot scoreboard. People prowled about inside the wall, putting numbers in the slots to show inning-by-inning scores from other games. Center field was the league's most spacious as well, with the wall a whopping 457 feet from the plate, an expanse so vast that a tractor was stored in a cage *on the field*. On the other hand, right field, the National League's shortest, offered a tempting target to left-handed batters: The wall was only 300 feet from home plate. But it was topped by a 25-foot chain-link fence, which in its day absorbed a lot of line-drive doubles—or singles, when Roberto Clemente was playing right.

It was all so long ago—a vanished world where men wore felt hats to games and smoked cigars, where home plate umpires wore suits and sported bulky, handheld chest protectors, and where policemen outside the ballpark called you "Mac" or "Buddy." It was an age when the Reds weren't just from Cincinnati, but from Russia and China, too, as in a *Pittsburgh Press* article from the early '60s about the U.S. missile base in Omaha with the headline: "If the Red Phone Rings," a reference to the Cold War's Communist threat. Ballparks, too, were more basic back then, and at Forbes Field, already the National League's oldest park in 1960, there were no such things as luxury or loge boxes—just boxes, reserved, general admission, and bleachers. Nor were there ads on the field's ivy-covered red-brick walls, exploding scoreboards, or any major street signs telling you how to get there. No need—people knew where Forbes Field was and generally arrived by streetcar, bus, or on foot, since parking was limited. About the only adornment I remember was the bold letters painted on the back side of bleachers along Sennott Street: "Home of the 1960 World Champions," it said in black against the background of yellow brick—the team colors.

A decade later, when the Pirates hadn't returned to a World Series, that big sign was a reminder of a special moment in the city's history, an enduring symbol of an underdog 1960 team that the experts had said couldn't win, but did—beating the powerful Yankees, no less. It would have been one thing to have taken on the Orioles, White Sox, or Tigers, but it was something else entirely to beat *them*—the dynastic, regal Yankees of Mickey Mantle, managed by Casey Stengel, and winners of twenty-five pennants in forty years.

The 1960 team became the standard by which future Pirates teams would be judged. Though the Pirates were often competitive—the 1966 season, when I went to my first game, comes to mind—they were forever dogged by one question: "Could this be '*another 1960?* " Alas, 1966 was not—the Pirates led the NL for some of the season, but then faded to third place—and no year since has ever quite measured up in the eyes of Pirates fans. In contrast to the great teams of the 1970s, or even to the Steelers Super Bowl teams, the 1960 Pirates triumphed over limited expectations. "It was just one of those times in baseball when it was our turn," says Gino Cimoli, an outfielder with the 1960 Pirates. "It had also been a long time, so when we did it, the people of Pittsburgh went crazy. It was a magical season."

Like a lot of people who grew up in Pittsburgh, the dawning of my baseball awareness was centered around listening to Pirate games on KDKA Radio, which was usually playing somewhere in our house, sometimes on several radios blaring at once. Don Hoak, the third baseman of the 1960 Pirates, was a member of the broadcast team when I started listening, and I distinctly remember my father pointing him out in the press box at Forbes Field. As much as my father admired Roberto Clemente and other members of the '60 Pirates, he revered Hoak, a fellow Marine who had fought at Okinawa. Hoak was nicknamed "Tiger" by the head broadcaster, Bob Prince, who was known as the "Gunner" for his rapid-fire cadence. The third broadcaster was Jim "Possum" Woods; I remember thinking how natural it seemed for a group of generally sober adults to refer to one another by animal names.

On a bookshelf at home, I found a 1960 World Series Game 6 program and ticket stub ($11 for Roof Box 354, Seat 8) that my father had saved, a souvenir of seeing Whitey Ford shut out the Pirates. At the ballpark, my father would often recall the night in 1960 he saw Dick Groat fouling off ball after ball to protect the plate. "Could somebody actually do that?" I asked. "Dick Groat could," my father said. Pittsburghers admired Groat and Hoak, and everyone worshiped Roberto Clemente and his thunderbolt of a right arm. My first hazy memory of Clemente was watching him field a routine single in right field and fire the ball on a laser *into first* to prevent the runner from even thinking about taking the extra base. The runner slid back, barely, but it was the kind of play you'll never see on an ESPN retrospective. Even at the advanced age of eight, I knew I was seeing greatness.

I vividly remember the moment I learned that Clemente had been killed in a plane crash off the coast of Puerto Rico. It was early in the morning on New Year's Day 1973 when my father, having just heard the news on the radio, woke me up to tell me in halting language about the terrible event. That his emotions got the better of him was an extraordinary occasion, the only time I remember him having trouble getting out his words. In retrospect, his reaction spoke to the reverence people in Pittsburgh felt for Roberto Clemente.

By then, Forbes Field was gone. Its last game was in June 1970—a doubleheader sweep of the Cubs in which Bill Mazeroski had the ballpark's final base hit—and I hauled home a third-base rooftop box seat, my reward from the postgame pillaging. The Pirates' new park was bland Three Rivers Stadium, where the team won the 1971 World Series, with Clemente giving the world a clinic, playing the game better than anyone else on the planet. "Now everyone knows how Roberto Clemente plays baseball," he told Bob Prince in the crowded locker room after the game. Speaking in the third person would be boasting for most people, but it wasn't for Clemente, who was being honest. That Series was like a switch going off in the national media, which suddenly woke up to pronounce Clemente a special player. In Pittsburgh, we'd known that for years.

I remember watching the last out of that '71 Series—a ground ball to Steve Blass, who threw to first. I jumped on my bike and raced out to bond with people in cars racing through the streets in triumph. I ended up at Forbes Field because, well, it just seemed appropriate. So did a lot of other people, spontaneously popping up along Sennott Street to celebrate. It was like sharing a bit of the joy with an old friend. Apparently, Clemente felt the same way: the following day, he too stopped by the old park.

So it went growing up with the Pirates in Pittsburgh. I went to a lot of games, and by the age of twelve had acquired a profound appreciation for the rhythms and character of big-league baseball. I admired Clemente, of course, as well as Willie Stargell and Al Oliver, but I rooted especially hard for shortstop Fred Patek because he stood only 5'4"—my height at the time. Along with my friends, I developed a particular affinity for Charlie Sands, the third-string catcher in 1971, for no other reason than that third-string catchers deserve support. I wore my Pirates hat from Cap Day 1967 so much that my sister said I had a permanent case of "helmet hair." Watching games on TV, I developed a curious ritual—if I was sitting or lying in a certain way when a Pirate hit a home run or the team turned a big double play, I'd have to remain in the same position for the rest of the game, as if I were telepathically transmitting good karma. For variety, I'd tune in late at night and listen to Jack Buck broadcasting the Cardinals on radio station KMOX from faraway St. Louis. And on Saturday afternoons when I wasn't at the ballpark, I seldom missed the NBC *Game of the Week* with Curt Gowdy and Tony Kubek. Subscriptions to the *Sporting News* and *Sports Illustrated* completed my baseball world, in which the Pirates were very much at the core.

Bob Prince, who always seemed to be talking out of one side of his mouth, was the team's most visible symbol, its ambassador. When we would see him dressed in a garish sport jacket during the winter, headed to a Penguins hockey game, my father would always belt out, "Good evening, Gunner!" to which Prince, who didn't know my father from Adam, always returned a hearty greeting. About four hundred others would do the same, all the way from the corner of Centre Avenue, where white-gloved "Candid Camera" cop Vic Cianci directed traffic, into the arena. No wonder I always think of Bob Prince when I think of going to both baseball *and hockey* games with my father.

I have an enduring image of my father at Game 6 of the 1960 World Series. He is thirty-four years old, looking natty in a sport coat, smoking a pipe, and chatting with the people around him on an Indian summer Wednesday afternoon. As a native New Yorker, he had grown up a Giants fan, but he had really taken to the team of his new hometown. My father would have been disappointed at the Yankee blowout that day but also happy just to have been there. Too bad he wasn't at the park the next day, Thursday, October 13, when the Pirates and the Yankees played Game 7. But I know that he and the rest of America would have found it hard to put in much of a workday, feeling compelled to take in every pitch—each one more pressure-packed than the last. Bravo for him; it was baseball's best game ever.

PROLOGUE

NOTHING LIKE IT had ever happened before—or has ever happened since. Many World Series have gone seven games—thirty-five of them, in fact—some with dramatic, nail-biting finishes. Take the 1991 Series, in which Game 7 went scoreless until the Twins finally broke to beat the Braves 1-0 in ten innings, with warhorse Jack Morris outdueling John Smoltz. The 1955 Series ended dramatically when Johnny Podres pitched the Brooklyn Dodgers to a win in Game 7 for the Dodgers' only Series title. Much further back, Game 7 of the 1924 Series went twelve innings, with the great Walter Johnson shutting down the Giants in relief to give the Washington Senators their only title and unleash a memorable celebration that no inaugural bash could ever match. There was 1912—Game 8, actually, since one of the games had ended in a tie—when Tris Speaker and the Red Sox took the Giants in ten innings, thanks to the celebrated muff by center fielder Fred Snodgrass of a routine fly to center. The miscue helped turn a slim Giant lead into the winning Sox rally and haunted Snodgrass the rest of his days: "Hardly a day in my life, hardly an hour, that in some manner or the other the dropping of that fly doesn't come up," he told an interviewer in 1940. "On the street, in my store, at my house. . . . It's all the same. . . . They always ask." Even death didn't spare him—"Fred Snodgrass, 86, Dead, Ball Player Muffed 1912 Fly," was the headline of his 1974 obituary in the *New York Times*.

The 1960 World Series is the only time that Game 7 was decided by a walk-off home run—a homer on the final pitch of the game—even though the term "walk-off" wasn't used back then. It capped the most dramatic finish to the most improbable World Series ever. Some eight and a half innings into Game 7, the Yankees had outscored the Pirates by twenty-nine runs—winning their three games by a combined 38-3 and sending the Pittsburgh pitching staff's ERA to a stratospheric 6.79. The Pirates, on the other hand, had clawed their way to three wins by a combined six runs—spacing timely home runs, rally-killing outfield catches, and stellar relief pitching from Elroy Face to somehow, improbably, pull the teams even at three wins apiece.

It was Thursday, October 13, 1960—a week in which John Kennedy and Richard Nixon prepared for their third televised debate leading up to the closest presidential election in memory, and America had had a look at a hot new TV program, *The Andy Griffith Show.* In New York, it had been only two weeks since Soviet Premier Nikita Khrushchev had given a jolt to the Cold War by banging his shoe on the podium at the United Nations, and a former curveball specialist turned revolutionary, Fidel Castro of Cuba—a lefthander, of course— bolted the stuffed shirts at the U.N. for the Theresa Hotel in Harlem, where he and his party roasted chickens on the fire escape.

If all of this was preoccupying New Yorkers, people in Pittsburgh were focused instead on something central to their core—the out- come of their Pirates' first World Series appearance in thirty-three years, a stark contrast to the performance of the Yankees, who seemed to be there most years. In fact, Senator Kennedy had campaigned in Pittsburgh earlier in the week—wisely on Monday, while the teams were in New York. Warmly greeted in an open motorcade that stretched from the streets downtown all the way to a rally at the Syria Mosque in Oakland, Kennedy struck the right tone for people in Western Pennsylvania: Greeting a whooping crowd on Centre Avenue in the Hill District, he slyly cautioned them, "I'm not Roberto

Clemente." The following day, the *Pittsburgh Press* put the senator's appearance in context for the city's baseball fans, running a simple one-column headline covering his speech, "Kennedy Rips Nixon in Jobs Here," next to a bold-faced, uppercase, six-column headline: "BOB FRIEND RARIN' TO GO."

Long accustomed to lousy baseball, Pittsburghers were reveling in their good fortune—their team of overachievers had become the heart and soul of the city. Pittsburgh was baseball-mad in 1960, having packed Forbes Field all season with fans humming along to the song that had become the city's mantra, "The Bucs Are Going All the Way," by Benny Benack and the Iron City Six. When the Pirates arrived from New York at Greater Pittsburgh Airport on a United Airlines charter after taking a 3-2 lead after the fifth World Series game, fifteen thousand of the faithful were there to meet them. "The ghost was walking and it was a very live ghost," Arthur Daley wrote in the *New York Times*. "Now their magic number is one. That's all these astonishing young men need for a World Championship, one more victory." The sudden attention didn't escape the notice of the Yankee players: "When we flew back to New York after Game 2, four young teenage fans and our wives met us," says Bobby Richardson. "Going back to Pittsburgh, there were thousands to meet them."

From the get-go, this World Series had been a struggle of contrasts. *Sports Illustrated* got it right, contrasting "the stiletto-like skills of the singles-hitting Pittsburgh Pirates (against) the bludgeoning home-run power of the New York Yankees." As the improbable series played out, the contrasts widened, with sportswriters playing up the Series as a test of the loose, irreverent Pirates facing the regal, snooty Yanks who usually found a way to win in the end. By Game 7, the 1960 World Series was being portrayed in socio-economic terms—with the Pirates perceived as lunch-pail underdogs and the Yankees as bland, button-down, corporate men. It was as if the Pirates had become the 1960 version of the old Brooklyn Dodgers: a raffish, colorful bunch in their own right, the perpetual underdogs who usually came up just a little short. Blue collar versus blue blood, as the story line went. Stanwix Street against Wall Street. Pierogies versus filet mignon. "The Yankees are big moguls sitting in overstuffed chairs with big cigars in their mouths," said Las Vegas bookmaker Maury Schwartz at the outset of the Series, "(whereas) the Pirates are hungry."

Willing to overlook 7-to-5 odds favoring the Yankees, Schwartz had said at the outset that the Pirates had a legitimate shot at a win. "Some group in the East made these prices," he said. "They don't reflect the true situation. Over the last ten or twelve years, the Yanks have always been able to come up with a rally. (But) I personally expect (the Pirates) to take the Series in five to seven games. Remember, you heard it from Maury." Another contrarian was *Sports Illustrated* baseball writer Roy Terrell, who predicted the Pirates to triumph in six, maybe even five: "No matter what the bookmakers say . . . the Pirates have been ignoring the odds all year." Mickey Mantle, however, was optimistic that his Yankees would win, saying the team's sluggers would like hitting at Forbes Field, where the outfield dimensions were similar to Yankee Stadium. Mantle knew what he was talking about, having played two exhibition games at the Pittsburgh ballpark, including his first, back in April 1953, when he launched a shot of more than 500 feet that landed on the right-field roof.

Thanks to television, forty million people—in gas stations (like the one in Cornwall, New York), bars, offices, factory lounges, VFW halls, and living rooms—would be watching Game 7. In less than a decade, television had revolutionized baseball, removing it from the province of radio broadcasters, who, no matter how deftly they described the action, couldn't match the power of images of real ballplayers flickering across the TV screen. It was a phenomenon for people far from big-league cities to be able to watch as Joe DiMaggio wound down his career and Mickey Mantle, the most telegenic athlete of the age, started his.

In fact, baseball fed television's astounding rise across America. In the postwar generation, Americans focused on consumerism, on raising families and letting go after the deprivation and hardship of the war years. Overnight, TV made Milton Berle a star, as it did Ed Sullivan, Sid Caesar, and Imogene Cocoa. In 1946, Americans owned seventeen thousand TV sets. A year later, nearly four million people, mostly in bars, watched the Yankees play the Dodgers in the first televised World Series; the event, broadcast only to New York City, Schenectady, Philadelphia, and Washington, D.C., demonstrated the power of this new technology. That '47 Series was the biggest televised event to date—drawing more than *twenty times* the number who had watched Harry Truman give that year's State of the Union Address. By 1950, there were 4.4 million sets; in 1952, nearly 20 million; and by October 1960, Americans owned more than 50 million sets, creating vast changes in how people took their news, how they shopped, and what they wore and ate.

For Pirate fans, the World Series capped an emotional couple of months. On September 6, with the Pirates leading the National League by a comfortable six-game margin, all of Pittsburgh gasped when shortstop and team captain Dick Groat—batting .325 at the time, second best in the league and some 6 percentage points back of the Dodgers' Norm Larker—was drilled on his left wrist by an inside pitch from Milwaukee's Lew Burdette. The Pirates' physician, Dr. Joseph Finegold, set the wrist in a cast and said a break of that sort usually took a month to heal. Could the Pirates hang on without the team's leading batter? Many thought they could not. But in stepped utility shortstop Dick Schofield, who promptly went 3-3 the rest of that September 6 game to spark a 5-3 win for the Pirates, pushing their lead to seven games over second-place St. Louis and seven and a half over the Braves. The next day, Schofield had a base hit, and he kept on hitting—.414 the rest of the season. The Pirates, like a team on automatic pilot, maintained their lead. When Vernon Law beat the

Reds on September 18 for his twentieth win of the season, the Pirates'
lead was six games and the race was as good as over. Afterward in the
Crosley Field locker room, fiery third baseman Don Hoak pronounced
that "the National League is dead." He was right. A week later on
Sunday, September 25, in Milwaukee, the Pirates clinched their first
pennant in thirty-three years, and Pittsburgh celebrated with gusto.

Though the Pirates lost their third straight game to the Braves
that day, 4-3 in ten innings, the flag was ensured when the Cubs beat
the second-place Cardinals at Wrigley Field. Leaving the field, the
Pirates players shook hands and trooped silently past the television
cameras that had been posted there all weekend to capture the
moment, and into the County Stadium clubhouse. Then they let
loose, mindful they had just been swept in the three-game series and
still without Groat, but satisfied at their accomplishment. "We had a
letdown in Milwaukee," acknowledged Pirates manager Danny Murtaugh, "but any team that can win ninety-two games doesn't back
into the pennant." Then ace reliever Elroy Face doused him in a
champagne bath, and the celebration was on: General Manager Joe
L. Brown got a bath, as did Pirates radio announcer Bob Prince.
With mischief on his mind, outfielder Gino Cimoli commandeered
the hat of longtime *Press* reporter Les Biederman; soaking the hat in
champagne, he turned it inside out, thrust it on his head, and, still
clothed, hit the showers.

"Time stood still, money grew on trees and Santa Claus arrived
three months early," the *Pittsburgh Press* reported of the scene back
home on Sunday, September 25. It was the city's "biggest pow-wow
. . . since the days of . . . the French and Indian War, an emotional
binge in which half the population of the City participated." At the
exact moment of the clinching—4:45 PM Eastern Standard Time—
people throughout Western Pennsylvania sprang from front porches,
out of bars, or wherever else they were, into spontaneous celebrations. Car horns blared and one fan, thirty-two-year-old Walter Klinek

of McKeesport, grew so exuberant that he tossed a wooden board through the plate-glass window of a neighbor, Myrtle Galloway, sending shards of flying glass through her living room. At Weinstein's Restaurant in Squirrel Hill, news of the clinching was announced over a loudspeaker and greeted with a wall-rattling roar from several hundred diners. Kitchen worker Eddie Sims of Hazelwood became so worked up that he dropped a trayload of soup plates worth $14.85, but things being as they were, he was spared the expense. "Any other day, we'd have charged him for that," restaurant owner Larry Weinstein said, "but not today."

Touching down at Greater Pittsburgh Airport at 10:20 PM, the Pirates were met by fifteen hundred people, including Mayor Joe Barr and Governor David Lawrence, who was the former mayor and a Pirates season-ticket holder. The players piled into a bus, and all along the Parkway West toward downtown Pittsburgh, crowds lit railroad flares, waved, and honked horns as they passed. Emerging from the Fort Pitt Tunnel, the players met their wives and got into the backseat of convertibles for the real celebration: a torchlight parade snaking through the narrow streets of downtown Pittsburgh before a crowd estimated at five hundred thousand, the biggest turnout since President Eisenhower had toured the city at rush hour in the '56 campaign. Cobbled together quickly by the Chamber of Commerce, the parade featured bands and floats, including one, a gallows with a Brave and a Cardinal suspended from ropes, and a sign predicting a similar fate for the Yankees, which that afternoon had clinched the American League pennant. Serving as grand marshal was beloved Pirates Hall of Famer Pie Traynor, who had been the team's slick-fielding third baseman the last time they'd been to the World Series, way back in 1927.

"This town resembles a pressure cooker that has just flipped its lid," the *Pittsburgh Press* dutifully reported. "This is the hour of fulfillment for Pirates fans everywhere who have waited patiently for thirty-three years." Lights in downtown buildings blazed through the night. Fans brandished all makes of homemade signs, proclaiming everything from "Beat Them Yanks" to "Yippee!" the single yet meaningful word borne on a baseball-shaped balloon flying high above a department store. Vendors had a field day—except for a man stuck with $150 worth of "Pittsburg" Pirates pennants, an antiquated spelled without the "h," dating back to the turn of the twentieth century. Surveying the crowd, Pirates catcher Smoky Burgess mirrored the sentiments of many: "Wouldn't it be nice," he said, "if all these people could come out and see the Series?"

Many did, and when in the end it became apparent that the Series might go the full seven games, the Pittsburgh School Board considered its options: Why not shut down the schools on Thursday, October 13, rather than endure wholesale absenteeism? With the Series down to a single game—"a one-game series," as Yankee manager Casey Stengel put it—who could get any school work done? In the end, the School Board decided to keep classes going. But any Pittsburgh native old enough to remember the events of that memorable afternoon realized soon enough that it would be hard paying attention to anything by baseball that afternoon. Many called in ill; others took personal days and floating holidays. In schools, offices, bars, diners, and TV sections of department stores, people gathered around flickering black-and-white TV sets or listened to the game by radio, with the tension growing every inning.

* * *

Baseball Commissioner Bud Selig often cites attendance figures, television ratings, and marketing revenues to argue that interest in major-league baseball is today at an all-time high. That's certainly true if you want to rely on statistics, but in a whole other sense, baseball just mattered more in the less-cluttered sports landscape of 1960. Emmy Award–winning broadcaster Bob Costas calls America's connection to the game a half century ago a "kind of fondness" that can be hard these days to replicate: "That fondness didn't have to do with your fantasy team or the angle of sports talk radio. It was a different kind of connection—and something that cannot be quantified. Take ten baseball fans now and then, and the way they related to the game would be somewhat different."

The 1960 World Series itself kicked off just two days after the close of the regular season, offering an immediate, jarring climax to the day-in, day-out pressure of getting to that point. Just two teams left standing, the best in each league and ready to do battle—so different from today's mind-numbing series of playoffs where "wildcards" stand a fighting chance and the Series batting averages are lumped together within a single postseason statistic. There was another big difference to the World Series back then: Until 1971, it was played in the afternoon, in the sunshine, as God and Alexander Cartwright intended. Today's Series night games may be better for ratings, but how many kids do you know who, on school nights, make it to the end of games that often grind on past midnight? Series baseball in the day, buttressed by all those memorable archival images of the fall shadows enveloping the infield at Yankee Stadium—was indicative of a more orderly sports universe in 1960—one without the competition of Monday Night Football, the X Games, endless salary news, and Skating with the Stars.

Indeed, baseball, football, basketball, and hockey comprised most of the sports world in 1960, though big-league hockey extended to only six cities, two of them in Canada. There were a handful of college bowl games, and there were no such things as iPods, cell phones, Xboxes, and other technological gizmos that today hijack whole childhoods. In that less cluttered world, kids were freer to improvise—playing baseball in vacant lots or stickball in the streets. Games tended to be pickup and played during honest-to-goodness unsupervised time. It was an era when boys lovingly oiled their mitts and rode, at most, a three-speed bike. For baseball news, they might read the sports pages and, if they were real fans, subscribe to the *Sporting News* with its weekly stats on the majors *and* the minors. And what kid didn't collect baseball cards? Chances are they traded away the cards of players from teams they didn't like or separated the cards into teams and stored them in shoeboxes—not for a moment thinking of the investment value, even after Mom threw out the cards. Those with a eye on somebody else's collection could flip for it—going for broke in pitching their cards against a wall or a stoop until the corners were rounded and the card so bent that they no longer sailed against their target. They probably even chewed each pack's pale-pink, rectangle-shaped bubble gum that was guaranteed to be stale, sugary, and tasteless.

In 1960, big-league teams played 154 games—a balanced schedule in which teams, eight in each league, played every other team twenty-two times. With only sixteen big-league teams, half the amount of today, Groat believes the depth of talent and quality of play were better than today. "I'm not saying that the athletes were better then, but put everyone now in a pool and have sixteen teams, and you'd see the quality go right back up," he says. "There are just too many teams today. You watch the pitchers and can't believe how many hanging curveballs and hanging sliders they're throwing. These are kids who should still be in the minor leagues learning how to pitch, but because teams are so short of major-league talent, you have double-A– and triple-A–quality players in the big leagues."

If baseball's overall quality was better, the game itself was considerably more basic in 1960, particularly on the mound. Pitchers were either starters or mop-up men, or were relegated to the bullpen, which for the most part was composed of over-the-hill veterans trying to hang on. There were no setup men, and coaches did not keep pitch counts. If a pitcher was dragging, a manager took him out. "We were expected to go nine innings," says 1960 Pirates pitcher Bob Friend. "It's a game of specialists today. Relief pitching wasn't emphasized the way it is today."

One would think this would translate to a benefit for the hitters, but in 1960, batters did not compile the kinds of power numbers they do today. National Leaguers belted 1,042 home runs in 1960, and the American League just twenty-four more, whereas today the numbers are nearly twice that in this age of bulked-up hitters, a lot of suspect pitchers, and nearly twice as many teams. The era was chock full of marvelous sluggers, though—Ernie Banks of the Cubs outdistanced the rest of the 1960 National League in homers with 41, trailed by Milwaukee's Hank Aaron with 40, and Eddie Matthews with 39, after which the NL power numbers fell off considerably. That the Pirates' leading power hitter was the erratic Dick Stuart with 23 home runs was typical for an era marked by bigger ballparks and, as Groat suggests, more consistent pitching.

Off the field, there was little talk of money in 1960. Long before free agency, salary caps, or agents, players generally negotiated their contracts themselves and earned salaries commensurate with a middle-management white-collar worker. Players held out occasionally, but their options were limited, since the reserve clause bound them to the teams with whom they had signed. Groat says he and Bill Virdon roomed together for nearly eight years but never once discussed their salaries. The same goes for another old teammate, Jerry Lynch, with whom Groat has owned a golf course outside Pittsburgh for more than forty-five years. "I have no idea what either Bill or Jerry ever made," Groat says. "You signed your contract and that was it, a closed chapter, and players never discussed it."

Yet for all the differences on the baseball landscape of 1960, the modern era was beckoning. Making its debut that year was the lively new television show *The Gillette Home Run Derby*—the same one still shown occasionally on late-night cable television—in which the game's top sluggers squared off in contests of long-ball hitting. The creation of former Reds' broadcaster Mark Scott, this contest was shot over the winter months at Wrigley Field in Los Angeles. All the big names showed up—Hank Aaron, Ernie Banks, Mickey Mantle, Willie Mays, Frank Robinson, and Harmon Killebrew among them— with two players paired against one another in an elimination-style tournament in which any ball not clearing the fence was an out. Mantle earned the distinction of winning the final episode of *Home Run Derby*, beating Jackie Jenson of the Red Sox, but Aaron won the overall crown, taking six of seven games for a total of $13,500. While the show provided lots of forgettable commentary—"I really got a hold of that one," seemed to be its most penetrating analysis— it spawned some marvelous, unscripted moments. When a foul ball hurtled back toward the announcing table, as often happened, Scott turned to Dick Stuart of the Pirates, seeking his protection in mock fear. "Sorry, I didn't bring my glove today, Mark," the notoriously poor-fielding Big Stu quipped—which, as one wise guy noted, encapsulated his entire career. Sadly, Scott passed away that July of a heart attack, but the legacy of his creation lives on through the popular All-Star Game home-run contest.

Meantime, baseball marched ahead in other ways. When the Birmingham Barons folded in 1960, that was it for the Negro Leagues, the end of a truly sorrowful chapter in baseball history. In August, ninety-seven-year-old Fred Clarke, a onetime Pirates manager who many in Pittsburgh still remembered and who was the oldest member of baseball's Hall of Fame, passed away in Kansas—ironic, some said, with the Pirates on the verge of taking the pennant. On September 28, just days before the start of the World Series, the great Ted Williams, who had started his career during the Roosevelt Administration, bowed out with an appropriate drama: Facing Baltimore's Jack Fisher in the eighth inning on a dank, overcast afternoon at Fenway Park, Williams drilled a 1-1 fastball into the right field bleachers for a home run, his 521st and last. Rounding the bases with his head bowed, Williams ducked into the dugout and was implored to go out and acknowledge the cheers of the crowd. He never did—an acknowledgment of the tempestuous relationship with Boston fans throughout his nineteen-year career. This end was fitting, as John Updike wrote in his memorable *New Yorker* essay: "Gods don't answer letters."

But for all the endings came beginnings, too. On the field that day for Baltimore was their twenty-three-year-old third baseman Brooks Robinson, already the team's anchor, who was about to earn the first of his sixteen consecutive Gold Glove Awards. In the days after Williams' retirement, baseball fans fondly recalled how many of the great Red Sox slugger's finer displays of batting seemed to happen against hapless opponents like the St. Louis Browns and Philadelphia A's, both of which had recently found new homes. After a half century of relative franchise stability, baseball teams like the Browns, now in Baltimore as the Orioles, and the A's, relocated to Kansas City, were in transition during the early '50s, chasing the country's demographics to new urban centers with growing populations. Change was afoot in the National League as well, with the Braves leaving Boston for Milwaukee and both New York teams resettling in California.

In February 1960, a wrecker's ball painted with red stitching to look like a baseball took its first swing at dismantling Ebbets Field in Brooklyn. It was a symbolic finale to baseball's old days, a final reminder of how the sport had driven a stake into the heart of Brooklyn while opening up baseball to a truly nationwide audience. Looking on, Dodger great Roy Campanella, wheelchair-bound after a car accident had severed his spine, accepted his old locker and an urn of ballpark dirt. But former Dodger pitcher Preacher Roe boycotted the event: "I couldn't have taken it," he said.

Both Ebbets Field in Brooklyn and upper Manhattan's Polo Grounds, where the Giants had played, were aging structures with little parking space available in declining neighborhoods. Attendance at both parks was sagging when the teams left in 1957. Both team owners were vilified for their decision to leave New York, but the Giants' owner Horace Stoneham summarized his thinking: "I feel sorry for the kids," he said, "but I haven't seen too many of their fathers lately."

By 1960, in the sunshine of California, both teams were enjoying almost double the crowds of their last days in New York. The Dodgers' new home was the enormous 90,000-plus–capacity Memorial Coliseum, as they awaited the completion of Dodger Stadium. In April, the Giants inaugurated their brand-new $15 million stadium, the 43,765-seat Candlestick Park, before a capacity crowd. Among them was Vice President Nixon, who called it "the finest ballpark in the country." It took about a week for the complaints to begin—from the players about the swirling winds that kept them from hitting home runs, and from the fans about frigid nighttime temperatures that would often plummet into the 40s.

Back in Brooklyn, an apartment complex shot up on the site where the Dodgers once played—the suitably named "Ebbets Field Apartments." Visiting the site these days, one will find a plaque that commemorates the former park, and across the street, the Jackie Robinson Intermediate School, named for the Dodger pioneer who had integrated the major leagues. Although in 1960, it had been more than a dozen years since Robinson's stunning debut, big-league teams were only starting to benefit from the talents of truly exceptional black players like Mays, Banks, Aaron, and Frank Robinson, who still faced discrimination at some spring training sites in the Deep South, as well as from the boorish behavior of the odd teammate or two. Teams—such as the Dodgers and Cardinals—eager to sign top black players would benefit immensely; for others like the Red Sox, in 1959 the last big-league team to integrate, the reluctance to bring in nonwhite talent would cost them dearly.

* * *

You needn't have lived in New York or Pittsburgh to care passionately about who won the 1960 World Series. As the showcase of America's most popular sport, the Series occupied conversations around water coolers, lunch counters, and dinner tables. It divided classrooms, with some kids rooting for the Yankees and others for the Pirates (or, in many cases, whoever opposed the New Yorkers). Then as now, the Yankees inspired intense feelings of loyalty or hatred—beyond New York, usually the latter, throwing considerable public support from around America to the underdog Pirates. "When those weekday World Series games were on, there would be a definite buzz, a grapevine kind of thing, around school," recalls Bob Costas. "Somebody always had a radio, and you would hear scraps of detail about the game. During recess, we'd listen to the games on transistor radios, or you'd ask for a pass to the boy's room to go and get the score."

In Kansas City, the Rotary Club, knowing that any guest speaker would be told to sit down and be quiet if he interfered with the World Series, resorted to Plan B for Game 7—hauling in six of the old TV sets with rabbit ears so members could watch. At Shawnee Mission North High School in Kansas, the game's radio broadcast was piped into classrooms as a means of preventing the massive "flu epidemics" that mysteriously afflicted students at Series time in past years. And in Redondo Beach, California, Costas, an eight-year-old third-grader, refused for the second day in a row to attend school so he could stay home and watch Game 7 on his family's set. A Queens native who had grown up in Long Island as a colossal Yankee fan, Costas had moved the previous month to the West Coast, where his father, an electrical engineer, was transferred. "I told my parents that you can send me, but between home and school, I'll find a place where I can watch the game," says Costas.

So what was a parent to do? "They just said, 'He loves this too much,' and let me stay home," as they had the previous day for Game 6, says Costas. "I was a good student, so it wasn't a goof-off thing.

They knew that it really meant something to me and they acquiesced. In retrospect, what I learned and what I remember today from that time did me a whole lot more good than whatever it was they were teaching in elementary school."

The 1960 World Series had already been a memorable time for a Cedar Rapids, Iowa, clothing store called the Syndicate—a result of its sale on suits, topcoats, sport jackets, and slacks with prices set according to the total runs scored in each game. During the Yankees' 16-3 blowout in Game 2, customers had flooded the store, forcing the Syndicate to quickly take on five extra clerks and admit only twelve to fifteen customers at a time. Slashing prices on suits and topcoats to $1 for every run, and on slacks to only 50 cents a run, business boomed. "It was our most phenomenal (sale) in our eighty-six-year-history," said store manager Herbert Levin.

If people in Kansas and Iowa were excited, Pittsburghers were downright giddy by Series time. Having waited so long for a pennant, most of southwestern Pennsylvania seemed to be suffering from a prolonged case of hyperactive overdrive at the realization their Bucs were at long last atop the National League. "Here we were playing the Yankees, a team that *was* baseball, and had won for years," said Bill Virdon, a one-time Yankee farmhand. "Combine that with the fact that Pittsburgh hadn't won for so many years and add the way our club had come from behind for so many times during the year, and the fans just got wrapped up in it. As it turns out, they couldn't have asked for more."

TV repairmen scooped up overtime pay to fix errant aerials and wires, to insure that people not lucky enough to make it to Forbes Field wouldn't miss a pitch. City school officials announced a zero-tolerance policy for students—but "without a doubt," the *Press* predicted, "more grandmothers will be buried in Pittsburgh this week than ever before." Those who couldn't watch, listened—and resorted to ingenious measures to do so. At Lincoln Junior High in Ellwood City, Pennsylvania, some 40 miles northwest of Pittsburgh, seventh-grader Ed

McConnell used the time-honed method of keeping up with the action by concealing his transistor radio in his shirt pocket and running the chord up his sleeve and into his ear. Another radio listener, Sister Carmen, who taught at St. Paul's Cathedral Grade School on Craig Street in Pittsburgh, pulled a similar stunt by putting her radio inside her flowing robes. Like a lot of people, she caught parts of the weekday afternoon games as best she could.

Meanwhile, the city basked in the national spotlight as a baseball "who's who" streamed into town. The Pittsburgh Hotels Association reported that all forty-two hundred rooms in the city were gone. Most of the baseball bigwigs, including the Yankees, stayed at the downtown Hilton, sharing the lobby with the members of the Pennsylvania Kiwanis, who had gathered for their state convention. Crosstown at the Pittsburgher Hotel, a group of retired big-league umpires shared Series predictions during their annual reunion: Retired ump Beans Reardon gave the edge to the Yankees. "But (Vernon) Law is the key man," he said. "If he can pitch a big Series, the Pirates will win it."

Anticipating traffic tie-ups, city officials urged fans to leave their cars at home and take the streetcar to Forbes Field. Expecting steep parking fees of up to $5 per car in the scattered lots around Oakland, the Port Authority added extra lines to the Wilkinsburg, East Liberty, and Homestead routes to the east. Meantime, the police department worried about pickpockets, gamblers, and ticket scalpers and stationed 220 extra officers, some undercover, to mingle with the crowds converging around Forbes Field. Others, like Samuel Strauss, a prosecutor in the Allegheny County District Attorney's Office, worried about the area's collective attention span. Strauss requested and received a postponement in the trial of Paul Hamilton of Monroeville, charged with murdering his wife. Readily agreeing to the decision was Judge Loran Lewis, who dismissed the jury for two days despite a backlog of five hundred cases, saying that "this seems an appropriate time to salute baseball."

Those who couldn't score a coveted ticket to Games 1 and 2 at Forbes Field planned accordingly. Western Penitentiary announced that some one thousand prisoners would be allowed to watch the Series on TV. In the Hudson River Valley town of Ossining, New York, prisoners at Sing Sing, most of them presumably Yankee fans, got television privileges as well. In the Pittsburgh suburb of Bethel Park, Mrs. Robert Maloy developed the novel idea of a World Series Luncheon Club—a gathering of homemakers to watch the games. "There were just two prerequisites for the girls to get in this club," Mrs. Maloy said: They had to like both entertaining and baseball. "We don't want to sit and gab," she said. "We want to watch the ballgame."

The night before Game 1, several dozen collegians gathered outside the downtown Hilton where the Yankees were staying and belted out the Pirates' fight song as loud as they could—all in an effort, as one singer said, "to keep (them) up all night." Just then, the authors of the fight song, Benny Benack and his Iron City Six, who had been entertaining all year before games in and around Forbes Field, pulled up in their trademark skimmers and nifty bowties to play the tune themselves, over and over.

On the eve of Game 1, Forbes Field felt more like a carnival than a ballpark. Police guarded the new NBC color-TV camera, which was mounted on a platform atop the center-field fence. Many in those more formal days dressed in coats and ties to attend the game but topped off their attire with silly hats plastered with a "Beat 'Em Bucs" bumper sticker. *Life* magazine's Arthur Rickerby snapped a photo of two local gents in shiny Pirates regalia, including eye patches and pointy hats, which made them look like they were headed to a Klan rally rather than a baseball game. A bumper sticker circulating around town read, "Remember '27: Beat the Yankees."

Ticketless and trying to collect on a bet, Jack Heatherington of McKeesport resorted to desperate measures. With Game 1 about to begin, he hired a plane, strapped on a red parachute and leapt from the plane as it circled Forbes Field. But as he drifted down toward his target, home plate, Heatherington was carried by a sudden gust of wind across Sennott Street and landed on top of the former Board of Education warehouse. The throng inside the ballpark roared at the spectacle, but Police Superintendent James Slusser was not amused, saying Heatherington could have caused mayhem had he collided with a high-tension wire. Plucked from the rooftop, Heatherington was booked for disorderly conduct but seemed more upset about missing the action than about breaking the law. "The thing that hurts me is that I missed the game," he said.

Tickets to Pirates home games for the Series had been gone, long gone, since mid-September—having sold out via mail order in just days. So many ticket orders were sent—120,000 in all—that the Pirates placed ten secretaries at two long tables to sort through the duffle bag–size sacks of envelopes. It didn't matter that the prices—$11 for box seats, $7.70 for the grandstand, $4.40 for standing room, and $2.20 for the bleachers—were steep for many. Forbes Field was guaranteed to be rollicking through the Series.

Those lucky enough to have scored tickets were turning down offers of $100 apiece. Desperate to attend, one Pittsburgh sportswriter called his friends at the *Chicago Daily News* to see if they could fix him up with a ticket. Among the lucky ones was Ralph Belcore of Chicago, first in line for standing-room tickets for his twentieth Series in a row. Belcore had lined up by the Schenley Park bleacher entrance the previous Wednesday evening—*131 hours* prior to Game 1—whiling away the time by sitting on a milk crate, eating and reading the newspaper as if he were in his living room. "It was a breeze," Belcore said upon receiving the coveted ticket. "I've stood in line eight days before." Also finding tickets were most members of Pittsburgh's judiciary, so many of them that the Allegheny County courts shut down at noon for the Series games. Pennsylvania governor David Lawrence, the state's longtime political kingmaker, was another fortunate soul, a passionate baseball fan who in mayoral days had spent a lot of time watching the Pirates from his seat in Box 209 at Forbes Field. For the World Series, Lawrence was a man with his priorities in order—refusing to campaign with vice presidential candidate Lyndon Johnson until the World Series was finished. Recognizing he was no match for baseball, Johnson postponed his campaign trip to Pennsylvania.

Lawrence threw out the ceremonial first pitch at Game 1—"a bloop" as the newspapers described it. But he had to miss Game 7 to attend a luncheon of the Distinguished Daughters of Pennsylvania in Harrisburg. For the first three innings, a state trooper dispatched a batter-by-batter account to the governor. Mercifully watching the next three innings on television, Lawrence caught most of the final few innings on radio while traveling to a ceremony in Kutztown. Arriving at the ceremony just as the game reached its climatic finish, the crowd roared—not for the governor, but for the game's improbable finish.

Like a lot of people on October 13, 1960, Governor Lawrence would sweat out all the pitches, base hits, and other details of Game 7. So would Ralph Belcore, the man who liked standing in line for tickets: Recognizing the historical importance of this game, he had lined up by the box office during the second inning of Game 6— waiting twenty-two hours this time. It was well worth the effort for an event that held America spellbound, a game in which every move was magnified, even Casey Stengel's endless trips to the mound, and each big play was broken down and debated for years afterward. The postgame party—a spontaneous explosion of joy after thirty-five years of frustration—was the greatest in the history of Pittsburgh. So was the game—climatic from the get-go and filled with lead changes, massive momentum swings, and not just one epic moment but several. Yes, there was the big home run to end the game, but there was another home run, in the eighth inning, which was nearly as big— ranking it as perhaps the most forgotten "big" homer in baseball history. Put it all together and Game 7 of the 1960 World Series was the wildest and arguably the most electrifying of the more than fifteen thousand major-league games ever played.

That's right. Babe Ruth's supposed called shot in the '32 Series, Bobby Thomson's 1951 "Shot Heard 'Round the World" and Carlton Fisk's 1975 World Series home run in Game 6 are storied baseball moments, dripping with mystique and lore. They were exclamation points to memorable games, and though the stakes were high in every one of those games, none were a part of *Game 7*. For a time, it seemed that Fisk's demonstrative efforts to keep his home run fair would help the Red Sox overcome their inability to win a World Series, but the team would in fact take another twenty-nine years to do so. Remember Kirk Gibson's homer in the 1988 World Series, when the injured Dodger golfed the game-winning shot into right field and limped around the bases? An extraordinary moment in *Game 1*. Likewise, the Mets' improbable comeback when the ball rolled by Boston's Bill Buckner in the Series of 1986 was in *Game 6*. That Bill Mazeroski became the unlikely slugging hero in Game 7 of the 1960 Series, a game featuring Mickey Mantle and Roger Maris, was enough of a surprise; the Pirate second baseman had hit all of eleven regular-season home runs that year. Had he not hit the big homer, Game 7—with its gut-wrenching lead changes, stream of pitchers (nine in all), controversial managerial moves, improbable plays, and unlikely ebb and flow—would still have been one for the ages.

To be sure, there have been other Game 7 classics. That 1924 Senators win in twelve innings, the Brooklyn triumph in '55, and the 1-0 Yankee win in '62 come to mind. So do more recent games: the Twins-Braves in '91, Florida's 3-2 edging of the Indians in '97, Arizona's two-run rally in the ninth, capped by Luis Gonzalez' ninth-inning broken-bat bloop off Mariano Rivera, to beat the Yankees in 2001. All were tight games defined by clutch pitching, crisp fielding, and timely hits, making them memorable, but not *completely different* from games seen before. No question, those games were great, but none can match Game 7 of the 1960 World Series, which stands out as a game with more—more twists, more turns, and more big moments than a Hollywood script writer could invent, and for all nine innings. Was this game the "greatest" ever? Debatable. But the best for pure baseball drama through all nine innings? You bet. That the game was played in a small market and is still considered a fluke by Yankee purists detracts from its true magnificence.

Game 7 of the 1960 World Series stands out for a host of other reasons. For a game in which a bushel full of runs were scored off a gaggle of pitchers, it had plenty to admire, from smooth fielding—there was only one error, Roger Maris's harmless outfield bobble—to memorable at-bats and, believe it or not, stretches of good pitching. Today, a game with nineteen runs and seemingly endless managerial jaunts to the mound would take four hours or more to play, but Game 7 in 1960 was surprisingly brisk, a testament to short TV time-outs and fast-working pitchers who threw strikes and challenged batters early in the count. That the Pirates—a team of experienced major leaguers who believed in themselves and had overachieved all season—had made it this far was a great story; how they won, besting a team that on paper should have clobbered them, was epic.

Nearly a half century later, Bill Mazeroski's big home run has no spiffy nickname. The ball has disappeared and the ballpark where it happened was torn down long ago. At least the great glove man, the best of his generation, is finally in the National Baseball Hall of Fame, though he had to wait a long time—too long—to get there. Mazeroski reached Cooperstown in 2001, elected by the Veterans Committee in his final year of eligibility after fifteen years on the regular ballot. New York fans, most of whom had never seen his play, whined that a life-time .260 batter didn't belong in the Hall—choosing to ignore the fact that fellow Hall of Fame infielders Phil Rizzuto and Pee Wee

Reese hit only .273 and .269, respectively. Maybe Maz's pop should be called "the Shot-Heard-'Round-the-'Burgh"? Pirates fans, used to underdog status, wouldn't mind. As with Pearl Harbor, the day that Kennedy was shot, landing on the moon, and the Twin Towers falling, they remember where they where and what they doing at 3:36 PM, Thursday, October 13, 1960. Here is how it happened.

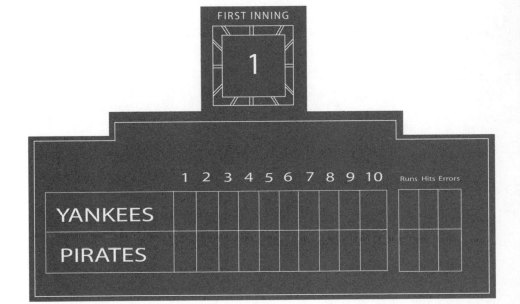

IT HAD BEEN apparent since the big left-field Longines clock at Forbes Field struck 2 PM the previous day that there would be a Game 7. That was about the time Bobby Richardson of the Yankees rifled a third-inning triple off Pirates starter Bob Friend into another of the ballpark's spacious outfield gaps, this one between right and center. The blow—Richardson's eighth base hit of the Series—drove home a boatload of Yankee runners: Mickey Mantle, Yogi Berra, and Elston Howard, who had all singled. It put the New Yorkers up 6-0 in Game 6 and sealed another lopsided loss for the seemingly over-matched Pirates. By the time the day's bloodletting had ended, the Yankees, behind Whitey Ford's complete-game, seven-hit shutout, had won a rout, 12-0. The shellacking was typical of the way the Yanks had banged around Pirates pitchers most of the series, now tied at three apiece.

When the Yankees won games in the 1960 World Series, they won by a lot. Through six games, the Yankees had created a new standard of excess in their three lopsided wins—bludgeoning the Pirate pitching staff almost at will by smashing home runs and extra base hits to distant parts of both Yankee Stadium and Forbes Field. In addition to the 12-0 pummeling in Game 6, the Yankees had won 16-3 in Game 2 and 10-0 in Game 3—outscoring the Pirates in the routs by thirty-five runs overall. Through six games, the New Yorkers had scored forty-six runs to the Pirates' sixteen, batted a collective .341—100 percent ahead of Pittsburgh—and walloped eight home runs, several of them tape-measure shots, to the Pirates' lone long ball, in Game 1, from second baseman Bill Mazeroski. More telling were the troubles of the normally dependable Pittsburgh pitching staff—a group reliant on sinker-ballers—whose sinkerballs weren't sinking, which ballooned the team's ERA to 6.79. Given the ridiculous bulge in the three Yankee wins, Red Smith of the *Herald-Tribune* posed the obvious question, and the answer, too: "What are the jokers still hanging around for?" he asked of the Pirates. "Why haven't (the Yankees) wrapped it up and gone fishing? The answer is that Vernon Law was Pittsburgh's starting pitcher in two games and Roy Face was Pittsburgh's reliever in three."

After Game 6, the writers almost seemed blasé about the latest case of Yankee excess—in this case, seventeen hits and twenty-seven total bases before the third en route to chasing Friend, an eighteen-game regular-season winner and the Series' hard-luck case. Baffling to many pundits was how the Pirates had somehow hung in there all the way to Game 7 by winning the close games, in what the *New York Daily News* called "the most extreme, up and down Series ever played." Even Mantle, not normally given to introspection, admitted that all those runs didn't mean much when you lost the close games: "I wish I could have saved them for a time when they meant something," he said, referring to his two home runs after Game 2, which the Yankees won by 13. For Red Smith, "It became painfully apparent today that if baseball is ever going to catch on in Pittsburgh they've got to bring in Lindsay and Crouse or Brendan Behan or maybe even Walt Disney to freshen up the script."

Taking the lordly Yankees to a seventh game was a Pirates team that was good, but hardly great. No Pirate had driven in one hundred runs or hit twenty-five home runs. Their collective power numbers were exceedingly average and they stole few bases. Some of them didn't even look much like ballplayers, especially the squat catcher Smoky Burgess, who looked barely fit enough to make the Moose Lodge softball team. Sure, the Pirates had future Hall of Famers Roberto Clemente and Bill Mazeroski, but their stars were still some years away. "The remaining players were mostly competent-to-very-good major leaguers," writes Pirates historian Bob Smizik. "But they came together."

Did they ever. The first six games of the 1960 World Series were a microcosm of the Pirates' entire year. Blown out in those three losses, they had scratched and clawed to three close wins with good pitching when it counted, solid defense, timely hitting, and aggressive base running. As in the regular season, the Pirates just hadn't gone away. They were a team with a major dose of mojo and a new hero just about every day. In Game 1, on October 5 at Forbes Field, Law and Face had held down the big Yankee bats, while Mazeroski nailed his home run, a two-run shot, and center fielder Bill Virdon, a one-time Yankee farmhand, robbed Yogi Berra of a two-run double and maybe more by making a spectacular catch against the 407-foot center-field wall to ensure the 6-4 win. "That stunt in center wrecked us," said Stengel. But Games 2 and 3 were so lopsided in favor of the Yankees that bettors rewrote the odds to make the Yankees 5-to-1 favorites to take the Series. United Press International reported that some bookies were so confident of a New York blowout that they were refusing any more wagers.

But in Game 4, the Pirates bounced back just as they'd done all year. At Yankee Stadium, Law and Face again combined to quiet the big, booming New York bats, and Bill Virdon made another sensational run-saving catch and drove in a couple with a single in the team's three-run sixth. The final was 3-2 Pirates, evening the Series at two games each. Then in Game 5, Harvey Haddix, with relief help from who else but Face, paced the Pirates to a 5-2 win to send Pittsburgh back to Forbes Field ahead, somehow, three games to two.

While the first six games of the Series had been a showcase for Yankee firepower, they had also exposed each team's deficiencies.

Beyond Whitey Ford, the Yankees had little pitching depth, particularly among the starters. Nor did the Pirates get a chance to display what had really defined them in 1960—a gritty knack to win by coming from behind, which they had done in their final inning at bat an absurdly high twenty-three times, including twelve times with two outs in the ninth. "We just never, ever thought we were out of it," says Groat.

At that point, the Series had been far from a classic, with the Yankees' three blowout wins so uneven and anticlimatic "that pity for the Pirates was the predominant emotion," wrote Roy Terrell of *Sports Illustrated*. "If suspense existed in the three early Pirate victories, it was there merely because of an awareness of what the Yankee hitters might do, not because of what they did." While Law and Face had pitched like they could, the Series had been a bitter disappointment for Bob Friend, the Pirates' bulldog of an eighteen-game winner, who had been on the losing side in Games 2 and 6.

With the Series down to Game 7, the bookmakers were still adjusting the odds—this time, installing the Yankees as 7-to-5 favorites to prevail. These *were* the Yankees, after all—the team of Casey Stengel, Mickey Mantle, and Yogi Berra, the team with history on its side, the team that was sports' longest-running dynasty. The Yankees had dominated the 1950s—taking eight pennants and six world titles—and ruled the '40s, '30s, and '20s, too. It was as if Mantle, Joe DiMaggio's successor in center field, had inherited the aura and mythology of all the legends who preceded him. "Ruth, Gehrig, Huggins—someone throw the ball!" Stengel yelled one day, as he implored a Yankee outfielder to find the ball that landed near the Yankee Stadium monuments.

The Pirates? Sure, they'd been decent once upon a time, but it had been thirty-three years since they'd even been to a Series, an era marked by lean times and a reputation for lousy baseball. Even team co-owner Bing Crosby couldn't resist a dig. "Do they still have Pirates in America?" Dorothy Lamour asked him in the 1952 film,

Road to Rio. "Yeah, but there's nothing to worry about," Crosby cracked. "They're probably hiding in the cellar somewhere."

* * *

The best that Pirates Manager Danny Murtaugh could offer after Game 6 was a shrug and the obvious commentary that "they beat the heck out of us." But then he caught himself and in the same breath said, "If I'm not mistaken, I believe the score is 3-3 right now."

Murtaugh was resorting to spin, of which he was a master. "A lot of times, you make good pitches and they hit them," he said, referring to Friend, who had absorbed two of those three lopsided losses. "This thing pays off on games won and lost. Maybe that's the way it should be. Two pretty good clubs tied three and three."

The Pirates' skipper had taken a page from Big-League Managing 101: It's a long season, so move on, don't look back, and keep plugging away. Murtaugh had turned forty-three on October 8, the day the Pirates were thrashed in Game 3, but the worst he'd say about it was, "The way things turned out, I don't feel any younger." That evening, he and his wife, Kate, saw *My Fair Lady* on Broadway in an effort to make something of the day. Murtaugh had been a smooth-fielding National League shortstop for nine years but developed a potbelly in retirement, seldom smiled, and looked a least a decade older than he was. But he was in fact an upbeat, soft-spoken man—milk and cookies was his favorite snack—whose quiet motivation relaxed and inspired his players.

Standing near Murtaugh in the Pirate locker room after Game 6, Dick Groat let it be known that his team was neither intimidated nor finished. "My, my, don't those Yankees make it look easy when they win?" he said. "They murder mediocre pitching, but they can be stopped. I think we've shown the world that much." Added Virdon, "We had a lot of good exercise chasing those balls in the outfield today; it will loosen us up for tomorrow."

Other Pirates barely acknowledged how they had been hammered. "We looked like a minor-league club today," conceded Roberto Clemente, who had two of Pittsburgh's seven hits in Game 6, and hit safely in every Series game. "But tomorrow, Law is pitching and I think we'll beat these Yankees."

Outfielder Gino Cimoli didn't even care to discuss the result—it was yesterday's news already. All he was wanted to know was who would be the Yankee pitcher for Game 7.

"(Bob) Turley," a reporter said. "Or (Bill) Stafford."

"What the hell do you care who's pitching?" suggested fiery Don Hoak.

"Right," Cimoli said. "We'll beat 'em both—unless Ford comes back again and they get twelve more runs for him."

Word that Pirate first baseman Bob Skinner had been cleared to play the next day was welcome news for the Pittsburghers, giving them a real advantage for Game 7. The twenty-nine-year-old Skinner, a .273 regular-season hitter, was a loping 6'4" left fielder with a long, lethal swing and an uncanny ability to hit in the clutch. He had jammed his left thumb in when sliding into third in Game 1 of the Series and had been out ever since—giving him "the most publicized thumb since Jack Horner," as Jimmy Powers wrote in the *Daily News*. Skinner's injury made a starter out of Dick Stuart but had depleted the Pirates of its core of reliable left-handed batters on the bench. The situation became so dire that Murtaugh had been forced in Game 6 to use a lefty pinch-hitter, Rocky Nelson, against the left-handed Ford, a baseball no-no.

For the most part, the pack of New York writers scoffed that the Pirates were somehow hanging in and looked for one more Yankee blowout to end this nonsense once and for all. "At one time, it was thought Pittsburgh strategy consisted of permitting the enemy to tire himself running the bases and swinging his heavy bats," Powers wrote. Of writers on the major New York dailies, most of whom hadn't watched the National League for two years, only Dick Young of the *Daily News* had conceded at the start of the Series that the Pirates had a shot. "Excessive nervousness is the one thing that could beat the Bucs," Young wrote, predicting a Pittsburgh Series triumph in six games. "If they play their game, they should win. But if their legs grow light and tingly . . . then they will lose, not to the Yankees of 1960 but to Yankee tradition."

Milwaukee manager Chuck Dressen knew better, having seen the Pirates pull out too many close games during the season. "The Pirates should make believe they're playing the Phillies," Dressen said. Elroy Face believes all the doubters were off-base. "I remember facing my first batter in the World Series and having a few butterflies, but after that, it was just another game," he says now. "The 1960 Pirates were just a loose ball club." Apparently, Pirate officials agreed: so confident were they of victory and the prospect of a big postgame bash, they had two truckloads of champagne, beer, and cheesecakes unloaded on the morning of Game 7 at their clubhouse door.

* * *

Across the hallway in the cramped, steamy visitors' locker room after Game 6, Bobby Richardson pondered his fate as the unlikely slugger of the 1960 World Series. The Yankee sescond baseman had batted .252 with one solitary home run during the regular season and couldn't remember ever having such a prodigious power surge, except possibly in American Legion ball back home in Sumter, South Carolina. After his triple in the third inning of Game 6, Richardson tripled again and scored, giving him Series stats that were downright Ruthian: nine Series hits, twelve RBIs, and a hefty .360 batting average. That last triple was the Yankees' seventy-fifth of the Series and set another record that dated all the way back to the 1912 World Series when the Giants tallied seventy-four in an eight-game Series.

Even more unusual was the feat of tripling twice in a single game, a World Series record, and something else Richardson couldn't remember doing in the past. Nearly a half century later, Richardson says that batting eighth in the lineup, as Stengel had him do in the two games when Ford pitched, helped him immeasurably. "To set those records, you have to have a lot of men on base," he says. "They were there throughout the series."

Seated at his locker and peering into a forest of notepad-wielding writers, Whitey Ford, who had also pitched the 10-0 shutout three days before in Game 3, was too drained to offer much in the way of his usual swagger. Ford had started his day at the ballpark by warming up for an inordinately long time: some twenty minutes instead of the customary fifteen. Facing the Pirates, he began slowly—giving up sharp singles in the first to Virdon and Clemente—before settling down with a steady stream of breaking balls that kept Pittsburgh batters off-stride the rest of the way. "I seemed to tire a bit in the 3rd, 4th, and 5th innings, but I finished good," he said. "I wasn't as fast and my curve wasn't as sharp as in the first game I pitched last Saturday in New York, but my slider worked well."

Normally, the slender thirty-one-year-old, 5'10" blond left-hander would be kidding around with reporters. But after Game 6, he was tuckered, having just thrown 114 pitches for his seventh lifetime World Series win, done on guile and smarts—and without either an effective fastball or his usual breaking curve with a little snap. That the Pirates were dispatched on seventeen ground outs and three double plays validated Ford's reputation as the Yankees' money pitcher who shared a nickname with Frank Sinatra: "The Chairman of the Board."

But there was a gnawing uncertainty that Stengel had blundered at the start of the Series in deciding to bypass Ford for journeyman and fifteen-game winner Art Ditmar as his Game 1 pitcher. Baseball custom gives the staff ace the nod in the opening game—and the chance to go twice more in the event of a seven-game Series. That's what the Pirates were doing with Law, but Stengel had played a hunch and gone with the thirty-one-year-old Ditmar, whom the Pirates promptly nailed for three runs, all in the first one-third of an inning. Critics whispered that the move showed that the best years of the seventy-year-old Yankee manager were past, adding that Ford had been the Yankees' Game 1 pitcher in four previous Series. Though former Yankees say for the record that Stengel was very much on top of his game in the 1960 World Series, they remain baffled about how he used, or misused, Ford. "The only thing I didn't understand then, and still don't to this day, is why Whitey Ford wasn't the starting pitcher in Game 1," says Richardson. "He was the Chairman of the Board, the pitcher you always called on in a tough situation. Whitey had been our big pitcher for years."

Nor had Stengel's incessant bench jockeying of the Pirates done much good. Intending to rattle the procession of Pittsburgh relief pitchers in the three Yankee blowouts, Stengel's profanity had drawn some angry stares from third baseman Hoak, but little else. Stengel would "just look at me," Hoak said later, "throw his hands in the air, and shrug, as if to say, 'What's going on? Why the dirty look?'"

But for now, all of that was forgotten in the steamy, postgame glow of another dominating Yankee win. In his own peculiar way, Stengel paid Ford the ultimate compliment by nominating him as "a big professional." Reporters accustomed to soliloquies and shorthand from the Yankee manager recognized that as high praise. In Stengel's book, there were only categories of ballplayers: "big professionals" followed by "professionals" and, lowest of all, "ribbon clerks."

Stengel was his garbled best in explaining why he had selected Ford on three days of rest in Game 6 instead of Bob Turley, with five days off. "In a few innings, I can tell if Ford's good," he intoned. "There's his age with three days' rest and Turley has always won the sixth game, which you can look up."

Actually, you could. Turley had pitched well for the Yankees in

Game 6 of the '56, '57, and '58 Series, but he was no Ford. Meantime, Casey prattled on: "There are two things when you start Ford,"
he said. "How many men will steal?" Sifting through the tea leaves,
reporters figured he was referring to Ford's skill in keeping base runners close to the bag. Why Stengel didn't remove his ace pitcher after
six or seven innings of the Game 6 rout in the event he needed him
today was another question for the writers to ponder. But the Yankee
manager didn't expand on that issue, careening through a blizzard of
related baseball blather, including a broad hint that he'd be gone after
the Series, win or lose.

Stengel's retirement had been rumored for months. By 1960,
Yankee co-owner Dan Topping was convinced that Stengel had lost his
touch and had even offered the Yankee managerial post to White Sox
manager Al Lopez who, in loyalty to his old friend Stengel, had turned
it down. Though the Yankees were year-in and year-out baseball's best,
they had become so by wheeling and dealing more often than other
teams—habitually shipping out popular veterans, usually to Kansas
City—and by "platooning" or alternating players at the same position,
which won games but inspired little loyalty among the players, many of
whom couldn't compile the kinds of statistics of which they were
capable. Ford, for one, had been the Yankee big man for years but had
never won twenty games in a single season. Stengel didn't care whose
egos he bruised as long as the Yankees won. A typical situation had
come back in the second inning of Game 1, when he pinch hit for
third baseman Clete Boyer, who was about to step in for his first World
Series at-bat. Stengel explained his move in trying to play for a big
inning, but it backfired when pinch-hitter Dale Long flied out and the
Yankees failed to score. Distraught and embarrassed, Boyer left the
dugout for the clubhouse, where he wept for a half hour.

Some suggested the Yankee owners were ready to dump Stengel,
having still not forgiven him for bringing the team in at a distant third
the year before. Conjecture that Stengel would soon be gone had at

last become so strong that prior to Game 6 the thirty-five members of the New York chapter of the Baseball Writers' Association of America had prepared a petition asking him to remain for as long as his health permitted. Stengel was touched, as if the decision would be his alone. "It was wonderful of them writers," he said, "but I've been here for twelve years and when a feller stays so long in one place he gets a lot of people mad at him and he gets mad at a lot of people when they blame him for blowing the tight games."

But the Yankee manager had caught a break in Game 6. Noted for frequently beating a path to the mound, Stengel had visited Ford only once, during the fifth inning. "I told him to take his time—that he was trying to pitch too sharp (fast)," Stengel said. "I wasn't going to take him out unless the blister (which Ford had developed on the middle finger of his pitching hand) was bothering him. I told him . . . 'I'm warming up two men (Turley and Bobby Shantz) and I want them to get heated up good. So slow up and give them time. You're going to stay in, but I got to have them ready.' "

So halfway through Game 6, Stengel was already thinking ahead to Game 7. Who would be his starting pitcher? Turley, the Game 2 winner who was well rested after six days, was a possibility. So was the veteran left-hander Shantz, one of those wily veteran pickups who always seemed to shine in the big games and to keep the Yankees dominant. Stengel had other choices as well: the twenty-one-year-old rookie Stafford, who had pitched well in relief in Game 5, and the 6'3" sport starter, Ralph Terry, who in Game 4 had gone six-plus innings in the Yankees' tight 3-2 loss.

A man with a lot on his mind, Stengel delayed his decision, choosing not to name a starter until batting practice the following afternoon. The odds seemed to favor Turley or Shantz, for whom big games were no big deal. Not even the Yankees knew until batting practice when Turley arrived at his locker at noon, an hour before game time, and found a brand-new baseball stuffed into one of his spiked shoes—old-time baseball code tapping the starter. It was another Stengel psych job that was intended to steady his team on the eve of Game 7, but it came with a catch: The Yankee skipper would start Turley but get his bullpen up and loosening *before* the game even started. "Sure, I had an idea it would be me," Bullet Bob would say later, "but you can never tell with Casey."

You *could* tell with Murtaugh. Down the hallway in the Pirate locker room, the manager was absorbed in yet another explanation for his team's shellacking in Game 6, and downplaying it all. "The last time I checked the rule book, they were still settling the World Series on games won and lost, not on total runs," he said. "The standings show the Yankees have been beaten three times, too."

"To win, we have to get good pitching," the Pirate manager continued in another universal baseball truism. Indeed, Murtaugh had his man for Game 7: He would go with the team's ace, Vernon Law, the thirty-year-old right-hander who had already won Games 1 and 4 in the Series and would be headed to the mound on four days of rest. Throughout the Series, Law had pitched on a painful right ankle, so Murtaugh was hoping his ace could give him five strong innings. "If he can give me that," the Pirate manager added, "I'll have Face and Friend ready."

Law seldom went by "Vernon." As an ordained minister in the Mormon Church, he was known as the "Deacon," a man who didn't drink or smoke and who donated 10 percent of his paycheck to his church. Nerves had kept Law awake most of the previous evening. "I had to go out there and give my team a chance," he would say later. "I didn't want to be remembered as the guy blowing the World Series."

That tender ankle had very nearly kept Law from even making it to the postseason. It was said that he had twisted it during horseplay after clinching the National League pennant in Milwaukee. Given that Law didn't even take a nip of the postgame champagne, it seemed improbable that he'd done anything of the sort. In fact, Law had dressed quickly after the pennant clincher and was heading to the team bus when the revelry came to him in the form of several teammates led by Gino Cimoli, who had grabbed at his shoe. When Law resisted, he'd locked his foot and slipped on the beer-stained floor, twisting his ankle.

* * *

Striding to the mound to begin Game 7, Law knew what was at stake. Murtaugh may have wanted his ace to go at least five innings, but Law intended to go longer—maybe six or seven—to make Elroy Face's relief job a little easier. Even with a sore ankle, Law had been effective to date—pitching seven innings in the Pirates' 6-4 win in Game 1, and another 6 $\frac{1}{3}$ in Game 4, with Face saving both games. Face, on the strength of his virtually unhittable forkball, had earned another save in Game 5 and was used to pitching every day; he would be ready when needed.

After all the pomp of previous games—Pittsburgh native Billy Eckstine, the great "Mr. B," had belted out the national anthem before Game 1—all anyone wanted to do now was play the game. In the cramped NBC Radio booth that hung directly under the second-deck back of home plate, announcer Chuck Thompson prepared some brief remarks on "the big one . . . on behalf of your hosts, the General Motors Corporation and the Gillette Safety Razor Company."

"The song that all the ballplayers were singing around the batting cage today was 'There's No Tomorrow,' " Thompson told listeners in the brief pregame show. After all, "all that has gone before is meaningless so far as this seventh game is concerned," he said. "And it matters not that the Yankees have scored 46 runs, have 78 base hits in six games to date. They must win today or it's all in vain. And should the Yankees lose, people who look back on this Series would forever ask themselves: 'How can the Yankees score all of those runs and still not win?' "

The smooth-talking Thompson, the radio voice of the Washington Senators and coanchor of the broadcast with Jack Quinlin of the Cubs, had summed things up in a jiffy. Not so next door in the NBC Television, where Mel Allen, the incomparable voice of the Yankees, was matched with Pirates announcer Bob Prince to describe the action to millions of TV viewers—nearly as many as were expected to tune in to the evening's third presidential debate.

Adjusting his mike at two minutes to the broadcast, Prince, in his first World Series, heard an NBC technician say into his earplug, "All right, let's get 'em. We've got twenty million people watching.' Prince thought about that and suddenly went white, overcome with nerves. Hard to believe that this longtime Pirates chatterbox, arguably the most entertaining and original baseball voice of his time, was experiencing stage fright, an old-fashioned meltdown. The man known as the "Gunner" for his rapid-style delivery, unable to talk? That was about as likely as the J&L steel mill going dark.

Nobody knew what to say. Precious seconds until airtime evaporated. Seeing Prince in distress, Allen figured humor was the best tonic.

"Bob," he said, with twenty seconds to airtime, "do you know who in our broadcasting team here is the most nervous of all right now?" Prince just shrugged, still unable to utter a word.

Allen pointed to the familiar NBC-TV logo of the peacock and quickly adopted an effeminate voice. "Can you imagine how long that dad-gum peacock has been waiting to spread his lovely feathers?"

"That did it," Prince would tell writer Curt Smith. "I nearly fell off my chair laughing." The tension was gone. "From then on," Prince would say, "it was the Old Gunner at work."

* * *

Pittsburghers were hoping history would be with them on October 13, 1960. Twice in the team's history, the Pirates had gone to a deciding Game 7—with Honus Wagner in 1909 against Ty Cobb's Detroit Tigers, and again in 1925 against the Washington Senators—and both times, they had won. There were still a lot of people in Pittsburgh in 1960 who remembered how the great Pirate team from '25, led by Pie Traynor had climbed back from a two-game deficit to best the great Walter Johnson, thanks to a seventh-inning rally in Game 7, triggered by Kiki Cuyler's base-clearing double amidst the mist, gloom, and driving rain of Forbes Field.

At the time, it seemed likely that Traynor and the fabulous Waner brothers, Paul and Lloyd, who joined the Pirates in '26 and '27 would be leading the Pirates to many more championships. Pittsburgh made it back to the Series in '27 against a Yankee team that many consider the greatest team of all time. Aware that the Pirates players were intent on watching the Yankees take batting practice at Forbes Field the day before the Series opener, Yankee manager Miller Huggins shrewdly instructed Waite Hoyt to groove a few to Babe Ruth and Lou Gehrig. Each of the left-handed hitting sluggers took full advantage of the ballpark's 300-foot right-field fence and blasted homer after homer in a prodigious display of power. The writers claimed the Pirates were instantly intimidated, a charge that infuriated Traynor, who denied the story until his deathbed. Either way, the Yankees buried the Pirates in four games—and Pittsburgh would have to wait thirty-three years to make it back to a World Series.

At least this Game 7 was assured of being a beautiful early-fall afternoon—with sunny, somewhat hazy skies and the temperature reaching 78 degrees, this was "shortsleeves" weather. Looking back, participants still marvel about the weather as classic, just as it had been throughout most of the Series, except for a brief shower that fell before Game 2. And at least Game 7 would be the season's finale, so everyone could go back to work or school, finally get to those dirty dishes in the sink, and resume their lives. Day after day of pressure-packed baseball had been draining, especially in Pittsburgh, where big crowds had been descending on Forbes Field all season. More than seven hundred press passes were distributed for Games 1 and 2 at Forbes Field; only five hundred went in Game 7.

From the platform of a truck outside Gate 6 on the far side of Sennott Street, Benny Benack and his Iron City Six tried in vain to stir up some excitement, but most spectators just streamed by, uttering the occasional "Beat 'Em Bucs." All four games at the 36,000-seat Forbes Field were sellouts, though the final attendance at Games 6 and 7 had varied by more than 1,900, with the largest (38,683) squeezing into the park the day before for Game 6 and the smallest (36,676) at Game 1. Attendance on this day was a tad over the opener—36,683, which was capacity but without the standing-room crowd in full force, a victim of Series burnout. "Everybody is in a daze," said Police Inspector Vincent Dixon, watching the crowd stream in the ballpark for the last time in 1960, win or lose. "These people are so quiet I think they're afraid to get excited," added Benny's vocalist, Marcy Lynn. "But we'll be here after the game, and I think they'll be excited then."

Adding to the pregame sense of gravity were the game's surplus of umpires—five of them, two more than worked regular-season games—as they popped out of the Pirate dugout. Dressed formally in conservative black suits, thin black ties, white shirts, and little black caps, they resembled a group of doormen or funeral directors. Then and now, umpires received World Series assignments as year-end bonuses, merit pay for a good job well done. Indeed, this crew was suitably experienced, having served in seventeen previous World Series and All-Star Games, with all but left-field umpire Stan Landes having worked a previous postseason. Behind the plate for Game 7 was a National Leaguer, Bill Jackowski, a forty-six-year-old New Hampshire native. A big-league ump since 1952, Jackowski was an Army veteran of World War II and had earned a reputation as a nononsense disciplinarian despite his nickname, "Bouncing Billy."

Advantage Pirates? Probably not, considering Jackowski had tossed the Pirates' Smoky Burgess in July after an ugly argument.

Up in the press box, Thompson summed up his pregame remarks on "what had to be one of the wackiest, most entertaining of the fifty-five World Series played to date," before pausing for the national anthem. Then it was time to squeeze in one last ad—this one for Papermate's Capri Mark III pen, "the pen that positively won't skip, regularly $2.49 (and) now priced at $1.95"—before everyone got down to business. First, the lineups for Game 7:

For the Yankees, it would be:

1.	Bobby Richardson	2B
2.	Tony Kubek	SS
3.	Roger Maris	RF
4.	Mickey Mantle	CF
5.	Yogi Berra	LF
6.	Bill Skowron	1B
7.	Johnny Blanchard	C
8.	Clete Boyer	3B
9.	Bob Turley	P

And for the Pirates:

1.	Bill Virdon	CF
2.	Dick Groat	SS
3.	Bob Skinner	LF
4.	Rocky Nelson	1B
5.	Roberto Clemente	RF
6.	Smoky Burgess	C
7.	Don Hoak	3B
8.	Bill Mazeroski	2B
9.	Vernon Law	P

Law peered toward the plate for the sign as Richardson, back at leadoff after batting eighth in Game 6, stepped to the plate. Working quickly, he fired a curve outside for ball one—and Game 7 was on. Richardson then lashed at the next pitch and hit it on the nose, just as he had been doing throughout the Series, but directly to Groat at short. There was one gone, quickly.

Top pitchers will say that with a good hitting team, it is imperative to work quickly to make them press. Wasting little time, Law bore down on the next batter, Tony Kubek, who already had ten base hits in the Series. Mixing his fastballs with off-speed pitches, Law got the Yankee shortstop to swing early on a 1-1 changeup and lift a harmless pop-up to Mazeroski, who gobbled the ball in on the lip of the outfield grass for the second out.

Law did the same with Roger Maris, who took three balls and a strike in his cat-and-mouse effort to go deep in the count to see what was being offered. The count moved all the way to 3-2 before Maris, himself hitting "only" .320 with two home runs in the Series, got caught off guard on a changeup and lifted a high foul ball back of third base near the stands, where Don Hoak made an easy catch. Law appeared to be on his game. Three up, three down; the Pirates had started well.

* * *

Casey Stengel was playing both the percentages and history in finally going with thirty-year-old Bob Turley to face the Pirates in Game 7. For starters, there was Turley's success as a big-game starter—those Game 6 performances in '56 and '57, and a Game 7 win for good measure, as well as six-plus innings in relief of Don Larsen to beat the Braves in '58. Bullet Bob joined the Yankees in 1955 in a blockbuster deal with Baltimore, where he'd won fourteen games. Like Larsen, another pitcher the Yankees acquired in the big eighteen-player deal,

Turley didn't use much of a windup, which was different from most pitchers, who pumped their arms up and down in preparing to deliver a pitch. He threw hard. And he won—at least twenty in two of his first three Yankee seasons, while racking up a lot of strikeouts and innings. But then, as with so many power pitchers, Bullet Bob fell off in a hurry; he won eight in '59 and followed up in '60 with a respectable but hardly overwhelming 9-3, dropping him to more of a strong number-three starter than an ace. He tried—oh, how he tried—keeping to a strict training regimen, but he was unable to blow batters away as he once did. "Look at him," Stengel said, gesturing to Turley. "He don't smoke, he don't drink, he don't chase women, and he don't win."

Working to Turley's considerable advantage in Game 7 was the Pirates' Series-long miseries at bat, which through six games stood at a collective average of .241. Never mind that the 1960 Pirates had compiled an NL-leading .276 average during the regular season and hadn't dropped more than four games in a row, or that twenty-three times they had won games in their last at-bat. Or that Groat had batted .325, the best in the majors, or that that their platooning first basemen Dick Stuart and Rocky Nelson had pounded 30 home runs and 118 RBIs. Or that Roberto Clemente, the team's electrifying twenty-six-year-old right fielder had batted .314 in his sixth big-league season—driving in eighty-nine runs and throwing out nineteen base runners, a league high. Though the Pirates had eked out three wins, there was some question whether Game 7 would be another blowout, as in Game 2 when Turley had cruised for eight-plus innings in the 16-3 Yankee win.

Bill Virdon, the Pirates' graceful leadoff hitter, and a .264 hitter during the regular season, was only hitting .200 in the Series. Virdon took ball one and then laced the 1-0 delivery with some authority but on a fly to Yogi Berra, playing to him perfectly in left field. One down.

Stepping in next was Dick Groat, whose .208 Series batting average was far below his capabilities, but explainable. After the Pirates captain's wrist was fractured, team physician Dr. Finegold told him that he planned to remove the cast on October 3—just two days before the Series, and hardly time enough to regain his sense of timing.

Desperate to swing a bat before the Series, Groat pestered his doctors to move up the date when the cast would be removed. As an All-American at Duke in basketball as well as in baseball, Groat said he had always had the capacity to heal quickly. Only a week later, he brokered a deal: Just remove the cast and see if the wrist was still broken. So on September 14—eight days after being hit—doctors x-rayed Groat's wrist and found that it was indeed healing faster than expected. Off went the cast, but with Groat's wrist still discolored, swollen, and painful, he continued to sit out.

Groat resumed batting practice but still wasn't close to resuming play. On September 30 against Milwaukee at Forbes Field in the final series of the season—twenty-four days after being injured—Groat, with his wrist still discolored and swollen, pinch-hit. This time, people urged him to stay on the bench not because of his injury but to preserve his batting average, which by then was the NL's best. After Groat grounded out in his first at-bat back in the lineup, his average dropped, ever so slightly, to .3244—but still .004 ahead of Norm Larker.

Groat could have preserved his leading batting average and won the title by *not* playing. But there he was in the starting lineup the next day, going 2-5 off Warren Spahn, and again on Sunday in the season finale when he was 1-4 off Burdette. "It was important to get my rhythm back, and mentally, to convince myself that I could play," Groat says. "I grew up in Pittsburgh, and playing in a World Series is something you dream about as a kid. I wanted to be ready."

By going 3-10 the rest of the way, Groat raised his batting average just enough to finish at .325, edging out Larkin out by .002 to win the batting title. So Groat would be ready, more or less, after all—maintaining what had become a lethal hit-and-run combination with

Virdon at the top of the lineup. Groat's batting title would also help him sew up the National League MVP award.

"What Groat did in the final three games is just a sample of what has made the Pirates tick," Hoak said. "Nobody thinks of himself. We think as a team and play together. When they speak of togetherness, this is it."

What Groat wasn't admitting to Danny Murtaugh, or anyone else at the time, was how much pain his still-tender wrist was causing him. Fielding was especially difficult when the ball would roll off his glove hand and the pain would shoot up his entire arm. "Fielding wasn't fun, not knowing when you'd go into the hole for a ground ball if it's going to come off your hand," he says. "I couldn't turn my hand, which hurt more than the wrist." He was better off at the plate: "I told myself, 'Don't swing at a bad ball,' " he cursed himself, "because the pain was excruciating (when I lunged), but it worked out fine."

Facing Turley, Groat let a hard one sail high for ball one. Then he swung—perhaps a tad overanxious—and sent a towering pop fly behind short, where Kubek made the catch. Two down. But just when it appeared the Pirates were sunk, things began to jell—just the way they had started so many rallies during the regular season.

This time, the Pittsburgh rally started with Bob Skinner. Back after missing those five games, big Bob and his steady bat received a warm ovation from the crowd. Known as a clutch player, the left-handed hitter delivered—working a full-count walk. He was the game's first base runner.

As if on cue, Stengel shot up to the top step of the dugout, staring out at Turley and, with Ralph Terry and Shantz already throwing in the bullpen, making it clear that he was taking nothing for granted. To the plate stepped another left-handed hitter, Rocky Nelson, who usually faced righties. At thirty-five years old, Nelson was among the seasoned crop of Pirate veterans who seldom flinched at pressure and had a knack of delivering a big hit, particularly in the late innings. Nelson had showed promise in the minors—winning two International League batting titles—but only recently found his true calling in the big leagues as a platooning first baseman. For most of his career, Nelson was a baseball vagabond—wandering from St. Louis to Brooklyn, Pittsburgh, Cleveland, the Chicago White Sox, and a lot of minor-league stops—before landing for the second time in Pittsburgh. Some baseball bigwigs scoffed at the 1958 postseason meetings of general managers when Pirate GM Joe L. Brown stood up and selected Nelson—"You mean Ricky Nelson?" joked Chub Feeney of the Giants, in reference to the popular singer. But Brown had the man he wanted, saying, "I simply could not believe that a guy would have *his* minor-league record and not have ability."

"Don't knock the Rock!" Bob Prince would yelp when Nelson was at bat. No one did—and Pittsburgh took to Nelson. He could hit, he could field, and his nickname was traditional baseball slang for "Rockhead," an affectionate reference to Nelson's tendency to pull occasional bone-headed maneuvers in the field. Nelson, whose real name was Glenn, could even chew tobacco for a full hour without spitting. And he looked like a ballplayer—peering from his baseball card with a plug in his cheek and his cap firmly on his head, perhaps because he was bald and looked aged enough for teammates to grant him another nickname, "Old Dad." At the plate, he coiled in a memorable stance that old-timers still remember—hunching his body and keeping his head low with his front foot forward, comparable to Pete Rose a few years later. In '59 with the Bucs, Nelson had compiled his best year to date, batting .291, and in '60 he did even better—hitting an even .300 with seven home runs and thirty-five RBIs.

The Yankee scouts had advised jamming Nelson with fastballs, high and tight. Having gone 2-6 to date in the Series, Nelson took Turley's curve inside, and another low for ball two. Turley stepped off the rubber to catch himself and peruse his situation, considering this

Skinner, a fast man, was at first. Composing himself, he set and fired for a strike on the inside corner at the knees for a 2-1 count. Registering his disagreement, Nelson jerked his head back and stared at home plate umpire Ed Jackowski, as if to say, "You're kidding." Like Burgess, Nelson and Bouncing Billy had engaged in some verbal sparring in the past. They had a history.

In the radio booth, NBC's Jack Quinlin, described what happened next: "Turley's 2-1, and (there's) a swing and a long drive deep to right field! Way back! . . . Oh, it's a home run!" With the crowd erupting in a sudden frenzy and the ball safely lost in the thick sea of spectators, Nelson, who had put his whole body into the swing, had jump-started the Pirates to a 2-0 lead. The man who always chewed had beaten the pitcher who neither chewed nor smoked.

Hours later, well after the dramatic game was history, Nelson's wife, Alberta, was leaving Forbes Field when her sleeve was tugged by eighteen-year-old John Olah of Oakland, who produced what he said was the home-run ball, and asked her to sign it. "It's not very often I'm asked to sign a souvenir," she said, clutching the ball in her hand for a moment and holding it up for everyone to see. Then she signed and returned it, not thinking for a moment in those prememorabilia days to ask for the ball herself. "This represents Rocky's greatest achievement. Take good care of it, son."

What a start! Sitting in a third-base field box next to the Yankee dugout, Yankee co-owner Dan Topping nervously worked a stick of gum—before the day was finished, he'd wade through three packs of gum and almost three packs of cigarettes, as well as ice cream and several hot dogs. Instinctively craning his neck toward the Yankee bullpen, he bellowed in a voice loud enough for Stengel to hear, "Who's he got warming up down there?"

The message was clear: The Yankees were expected to win. At the plate, Clemente took a curveball on the outside corner for a strike, as the crowd continued to buzz—"going wacky," said Quinlin, "jabbing each other in the ribs, talking to each other." Could the Pirates' right fielder, batting .320 and one of the few Pittsburghers to deliver at the plate in the Series, inflict more damage? He tried, popping a foul ball down the left-field line for another strike before popping an 0-2 fastball up behind second base, where Richardson caught it for the third out. Then came another roar from the crowd, who were giddy at their sudden fortune: *The Pirates were winning Game 7.*

SECOND INNING

2

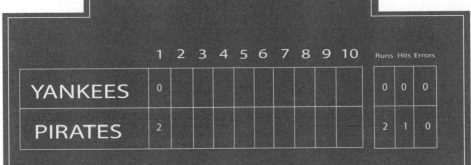

	1	2	3	4	5	6	7	8	9	10	Runs	Hits	Errors
YANKEES	0										0	0	0
PIRATES	2										2	1	0

FOR ALL HIS celebrated gems of twisted logic and, oh yes, his seven Yankee "World Championships," Casey Stengel had always faced an uphill battle in New York. The notoriously cynical New York press corps—"my writers," Stengel called them—loved him. "If you didn't like Stengel, you didn't like anybody," said John Drebinger of the *Times*. Casey's most vexing issue was the team's front office, which from the day he was hired just didn't seem to like his style.

Stengel's quick mind and garbled syntax landed him in hot water from the get-go with his waspy, button-down bosses. Introduced as the new manager after the 1948 season during a press conference at the swanky 21 Club, Stengel called Yankee co-owner Dan Topping "Bob," the name of Topping's playboy brother. Asked about his plans for Joe DiMaggio, Stengel, having previously managed in the National League, said he wasn't that familiar with the Yankee Clipper. Not familiar with the great DiMaggio? It was an awkward moment.

Critics complained that Stengel had gotten the job because he was a friend of George Weiss, the Yankees' general manager. "This is a $5 million business," the new fifty-eight-year-old manager said. "They don't hand out jobs like this because you're a friend." In Boston, Dave Egan of the *Record* wrote snidely that the Yankees "eliminated themselves when they engaged Perfesser Casey Stengel to mismanage them."

Stengel's main shortcoming was that he hadn't won while at the helm of inferior teams. In three years as the Dodgers' manager in the '30s—and then six with the Braves—he had never fielded a team that had risen above .500 or fifth place. Nor did he fit the Yankee mold, appearing more like "the court jester (against) the old Yankee tradition of austere and businesslike efficiency," as Red Smith put it. To Stengel's biographer Robert Creamer, joining the Yankees was as if he "had spent almost 40 years in baseball, and . . . had nothing to show for it."

Stengel persevered, blending his theatrical combination of pantomime, monologues, and storytelling laced with the liberal use of adjectives like "terrific" and "amazing." With the Yankees, he won from the start—overcoming a series of devastating injuries in '49 to dispatch the Dodgers in the World Series in five games. Then he kept on winning, with mind-numbing consistency—five in a row, for starters. By 1960, Stengel's twelfth season as New York manager, his team had claimed ten AL pennants.

The clowning obscured a first-rate baseball mind. Stengel became a big leaguer in 1914. Baseball was his whole life and passion. He never stopped learning and tinkering, and he took nothing for granted. Delivering Series triumphs in each of his first two years with the Yankees earned Stengel a dose of grudging respect from the Yankee brass, along with some leverage. So in 1951, Stengel badgered Yankee management to establish an innovative early-spring instructional school for young players. The "instructual school" as Stengel called it, was a rousing success and helped train many future Yankee mainstays, including Mantle, Bill Skowron, Gil McDougald, and Bob Cerv.

"Everybody thought old Casey was a joke when the Yankees brought me in, and everybody thought it was a joke when old Case set up the instructual schools," said Stengel in the mid-'50s. "Now everybody else is copying the schools. And we're only three years ahead of them."

Stengel's gift for innovation stemmed in part from the great Giants manager John McGraw, for whom he played in the '20s. Stengel had long admired McGraw for his gift in guiding young players. The two were peas of a pod—happily married but childless, and willing to spend long hours in mentoring prospects who showed promise.

Mickey Mantle's prodigious talents were apparent from the get-go. Recognizing that this young country boy from the coal fields near the Ozarks in northeastern Oklahoma could use a dose of self-confidence, Stengel became his surrogate dad, accepting him as the son he'd never had. The prize of Stengel's instructual school, Mantle was the complete package—a switch-hitter with astounding power from both sides of the plate, a powerful arm, and explosive speed. So Stengel lavished praise on his protégé: "My God," he said, "that boy runs faster than Cobb." And he made the Mick his project—advising, adjusting, and lecturing him. Most notably, Stengel moved Mantle from shortstop, where he wasn't gifted, to the outfield so he could focus on his hitting.

In 1951, nineteen-year-old Mantle joined the Yankees. He was still green, with all of two years of low-level minor-league ball under his belt. But Stengel insisted he stay with the big club to watch and learn. The Yankee skipper remembered that was what McGraw had done with Mel Ott, who joined the Giants at the age of seventeen. McGraw kept Ott close, fearful in part that some minor-league manager might want to correct his prize pupil's quirky batting motion, in which Ott prepared to swing by lifting his front foot well off the ground, like stepping across a puddle. The effort paid off; Ott never spent a day in the minors, and three years later, he was the NL home-run king ticketed for Cooperstown. Of Mantle, Stengel mused to a friend, "Can you imagine what McGraw would say if he saw this kid?"

Stengel was serious about his "kids"—the young players he mentored—and wasn't shy about using them to replace veterans, something else he learned from McGraw. He sent Mantle to center field, allowing DiMaggio to bow out gracefully. To third base headed Gil McDougald, who beat out Mantle for the AL's '51 Rookie of the Year honors, and who personified Stengel's favorite kind of player: a solid hitter with power, speedy and able to play any infield position.

In 1960, Stengel was anxious to save some wear and tear on the thirty-five-year-old Yogi Berra—"my man" in Stengelese—and so directed the thirty-year-old Elston Howard to catch more than half the schedule. The steady Howard, who was the Yankees' first African-American player, was ready; finally with a position of his own after spending most of six big-league seasons filling in for others, he had little trouble handling the pitchers.

Success gave Stengel a degree of vindication—all the platooning and quick pitching changes worked. It looked improvisational but wasn't. "People said in 1949 what terrible luck we were having, all those injuries, but that was one of the luckiest breaks I ever got, because I had to use the men," Stengel said. "Every time one of my front players got hurt, I noticed the fella I stuck in his place would bust out with hits."

Though the Yankees won most of the time under Stengel, their success was hardly routine. For much of the 1950s, they relied on veteran pitchers like Ford, Allie Reynolds, Early Wynn, Vic Raschi, and Eddie Lopat, who weren't flashy but could usually grind out a win. Meantime, a parade of players came and went, often shuttling back and forth between New York and Kansas City, with Yankee general manager George Weiss seeming to land some late-season veteran or new slugger or slick-fielding infielder nearly every year.

McDougald was a perennial Yankee all-star in the mid-'50s but found his playing time eroded in 1960 by Bobby Richardson at second and the cannon-armed Clete Boyer at third. The sudden changes and substitutions were a reminder that baseball could be a cold-hearted meritocracy. It could upset the egos, but come World Series time, the Yankees were usually there. Playing no favorites, Stengel and Yankee general manager George Weiss ran their club with an iron fist. Players were shipped out, often suddenly and for the slightest infractions. In early 1954, Vic Raschi was sold for holding out for a new contract after the Yankees intended to give him a paycut. Two years later, Phil Rizzuto was released on Old-Timers'

Day. Playing for the Yankees in the '50s meant the opportunity to pad a salary from the annual World Series shares, but it came with a price, which usually involved platooning with little or no chance to start.

Stengel didn't give a hoot about bruised egos. "The secret of managing is to keep the guys who hate you away from the guys who are undecided," he said. Few understood that concept better than long-time *New York Post* baseball writer Maury Allen, who covered the 1960 World Series as a twenty-eight-year-old reporter with *Sports Illustrated*. "Casey cared about one thing—winning baseball games," says Allen, "and if he hurt or embarrassed a player by taking them out or talking sarcastically about them to the press, he didn't care."

That attitude filtered through the ranks. Traded to the Yankees from the A's prior to the 1960 season, backup shortstop Joe DeMaestri had his "Welcome to the Yankees Moment" when Skowron and McDougald warned him in no uncertain terms, "Don't forget now, you're playing with our money (so) don't screw it up." Their missive was a variation of what former no-nonsense Yankee Hank Bauer had said to Mantle—when, as a rookie, the Mick had bunted at the expense of hitting for power—and more recently to Whitey Ford after a few too many late nights. This was the first time Skowron and McDougald had ever spoken to him, DeMaestri says.

McDougald refers to Stengel's incessant platooning as "Casey shuffling cards, his form of motivation." McDougald says that Stengel rode him hard for in his first five years in New York, until one day on a 1955 exhibition trip to Japan, the Yankee infielder got fed up and told him to stop.

"It doesn't matter if you yell at me," McDougald told him. "You're going to get the same out of me. So do me a favor; trade me or get rid of me."

Stengel listened and from then on, eased up—not wanting to offend his all-star infielder. "After that," McDougald says, "my last five years were great. I'm glad I had that conversation."

Few ballplayers personified the yin and yang of membership in Stengel's Yankees more than outfielder Bob Cerv. Joining the Yankees in '51, Cerv played sporadically until one day in 1957, when Stengel informed, "Nobody knows this, but one of us has just been traded to Kansas City." Banished to the A's, Cerv missed the World Series checks but thrived in Kansas City by belting sixty-nine home runs over three seasons. Traded back to the Yanks in May of '60, he resumed his earlier pinch-hitting and filling in but at least earned another Series check. Then Cerv was shipped to the expansion Angels, rejoining the Yanks in '61 before he was unloaded again, this time to Houston, where his career ended. Cerv's career stats are solid—106 lifetime home runs, including one in the '55 Series against the Dodgers—but the platooning kept him from compiling what might have been many more. Today, he is remembered chiefly as the roommate of Mantle and Maris in Billy Crystal's film, 61*.

Stengel's take on Cerv and all the others? He once divulged to Allen his philosophy of how to run a twenty-five-man, big-league roster. "The first fifteen players, you don't have to worry about," he said. "The next five, you've got to butter them up and be nice to them because you're going to use them a lot more than the last five, who you'll hardly ever use. The trick is to keep the two groups of five apart, because if they get together, then you've got ten players and a revolution."

* * *

The Yankees of the 1950s may have played for Stengel, but they belonged to Mickey Mantle. Blond, blue-eyed, and movie-star handsome, the Mick was the shining star of the best team on the planet. His tape-measure blasts were the marvel of the age, written up, talked about, and admired. He blasted one ball to the roof of Yankee Stadium and another at the Griffith Stadium in Washington that traveled well over 500 feet. He hit not only for power, but for average and in the clutch, despite a progression of devastating leg and knee injuries. Compounding his difficulties was a periodic lack of focus and a late-night lifestyle in which he, Ford, and Billy Martin, the Yankee version of the "Brat Pack," were known to close quite a few New York nightspots. Late one evening, a sportswriter ran into Mantle, who was passed out on a bathroom floor of a midtown New York nightclub. The sportswriter told himself, "I'd better call my bookie quickly and bet the house on the Senators," the Yankees' doubleheader opponents the next day. No way would Mantle be in any condition to play. A slam-dunk, can't-miss bet, right? You can guess the rest: The next afternoon, Mick smashed three home runs, as the Yanks ruled the roost.

Coddled by Stengel, Mantle was neither likable nor particularly articulate; that would come later, long after he had retired. Not that anyone much cared at the time—a generation of schoolyard boys imitated his batting stance, his manner, and the way he walked. "I used to limp around my neighborhood imitating him," the actor and comedian Billy Crystal once said. "I did my Bar Mitzvah with an Oklahoma drawl." Told Mantle was a rube, Jackie Robinson could care less: "We got plenty of guys that dumb," he said, "but we don't have anybody that good." Most writers ignored the reality and focused on Mantle the Idol—the courage with which Mantle played the game, and how, before each game, he'd spend an hour bandaging his damaged legs. It was all true, and it fed the legend and the passion of New York City baseball fandom in the 1950s. That meant siding with the Yanks, the Brooklyn Dodgers, or the New York Giants—and consequently, with whichever of the teams' superlative center fielders, Mantle, Duke Snider of the Dodgers, or Willie Mays of the Giants, was tops. In the end, the Yankees, fueled by their button-down, corporate image, usually ruled the baseball landscape. How true, people said, when during the 1953 World Series, Los Angeles sportswriter Jim

Murray wrote in the *Sporting News*, "Rooting against the Yankees is like rooting against U.S. Steel."

But 1960 was anything but automatic for the Yankees. The team was coming off a disappointing third-place finish in '59—when they finished only four games above .500 and a distant fifteen games back of the pennant-winning White Sox—and then looked aged and vulnerable at the start of '60, especially after enduring a horrid, injury-plagued spring. "Just what manner of team will grace or disgrace those proud Yankee pinstripes this year?" asked Joe Trimble of the *Daily News*. "Can the ball club pick itself off the floor after the worst spring training in 40 years and last year's dismal finish? The answer is YES—a simple answer but made hesitantly because the picture is so complex. The Yankees will have to play their very best ball and the main contenders, Chicago and Cleveland, will have to sluff off a bit."

But these Yankees were hardly the intimidating team of Babe Ruth and Lou Gehrig. "That is the trouble with Casey Stengel's ball club; they have not been the old Yankees since the middle of the 1958 season," opined Roy Terrell of *Sports Illustrated*. "In 1960, they will still be a good ball club—because they have not slipped that far—but they no longer terrorize the league and they are going to have a heck of a time winning a pennant." The once formidable Yankee farm system was thin. Injuries to Bill "Moose" Skowron and Andy Carey had ravaged the Yanks in '59, while Mantle and Turley had had subpar seasons, tapping the Yankees' usual physical and psychological edge. "No one," wrote Terrell, "is in awe of the magical pin-striped uniform any more."

Stengel's immediate concern was a pitching staff with little depth. There was Ford, of course, but it was imperative that Turley bounce back after a disappointing 8-11 regular season, and that thirteen-game winner Ditmar assume the slack. Expectations were minimal— only three of ten *Daily News* sportswriters and one of six writers polled at the *Herald-Tribune* chose the Yanks to take the AL flag, with most opting for Chicago to repeat, or for Cleveland. The Yankees elicited major questions up and down the lineup: Could Mantle recover from his latest injury, an arthritic knee? He'd hit *only* thirty-one home runs in '59, but a far cry from his magical fifty-two homers in '56. Could the team's new acquisition, Roger Maris, star in New York? Could the hard-throwing, hard-living master of the bullpen Ryne Duren continue to develop? "There are just too many 'if's' on the club," wrote the *Daily News*'s Jimmy Powers, who picked the White Sox to take the American League. "It is downright disturbing."

Stengel's health was another pressing issue. Stengel was said to be drinking more than ever during spring training, and his wife, Edna, was urging him to retire. In April, he suffered chest pains, and many thought he was having a heart attack, though it turned out to be a viral infection. When Stengel went to the hospital, the team turned to Ralph Houk, a former Yankee catcher who had turned down an offer to manage the team's top farm club in Denver, to coach the big club. But then Stengel got better and left the hospital with an extra bounce in his step, anxious to get back to work. "They examined all my organs," he said. "Some of them are quite remarkable and others are not so good. A lot of museums are bidding for them."

Stengel's return reenergized the Yankees. Riding the Yankees hard all year—"Driving, driving all the time," reliever Ryne Duren said of Stengel—Casey held the team together with what seemed like Band-Aids and Scotch tape. In June, New York surged with twenty-three wins in twenty-eight games. Ford and Turley were in form, and several of the untested pitchers, such as Terry, Stafford, and Jim Coates, contributed big wins in both spot starts and relief. But the real trigger to the team's success was an off-season acquisition from where else but Kansas City: Roger Maris, an unassuming twenty-five-year-old slugger whose powerful left-handed swing was built for the 314-foot right-field porch at Yankee Stadium. Batting cleanup behind Mantle, Maris gave the team a devastating one-two punch in the lineup.

On the field, Maris and Mantle complemented one another. But the soft-spoken Maris wasn't keen on big-city life, taking a Queens apartment with Cerv—Mantle would join them in '61—while pining for his family back in Kansas City. Nor did he like the intrusive questions asked by the rugby-scrum pack of reporters who followed the Yankees.

Born in Minnesota, Maris had moved as a boy to Fargo, North Dakota, where his father worked on the Great Northern Railroad. In high school, he starred in football and set a national high school record by scoring four touchdowns on kickoff returns in a single game. Because of the long winters in North Dakota, Maris's high school had no baseball team, so he played American Legion ball and led his team to the state championship.

Recruited by the legendary Bud Wilkinson to play football at the University of Oklahoma, Maris signed instead with the Cleveland Indians for a $5,000 bonus, with another $10,000 due if he reached the majors. In 1954 at Keokuk, Wisconsin, Maris's manager Jo Jo White taught him to pull the ball, and the young slugger hit thirty-two home runs. After four years in the minors, Maris broke into the majors on opening day 1957 with a flair—going 3-5 for the Indians against the White Sox—and the next day slugged his first big-league home run. Maris hit fourteen homers that rookie season, and twenty-eight in 1958, prompting the moniker, "Cleveland's future Mickey Mantle." That riled the ego of the Indians' incumbent slugger, Rocky Colavito, who complained that Cleveland wasn't big enough for the two of them. So Maris was shipped off to Kansas City for a season and a half, and then to the Yankees in December of '59, along with Kent Hadley and DeMaestri.

Maris got to work quickly with the Yankees. He socked two homers on opening day 1960 against the Red Sox at Fenway Park in the Yankees' 8-4 win. Stengel was thrilled. "When we got this young man from Kansas City, I figured he was good," Casey said. "But I am ready to admit that Maris has been far more spectacular than I dared hope he would be." In early July, Maris earned most of the votes from his fellow American Leaguers for the all-star team and socked home runs at such a pace that writers told him he could threaten Babe Ruth's sixty homer record. But Maris, who would finish with thirty-nine home runs for the season—one less than Mantle—didn't give a hoot for stats. "I'm not thinking about the record," he said. "What I want most is for the Yankees to win the pennant."

On July 30 of that year, Stengel turned seventy years old. "Most people my age are dead at the present time," he said. There were whispers about Stengel looking particularly haggard and there were jokes about the bent-over way he walked to and from the mound. Well aware that he and Connie Mack were the only men to ever manage at seventy in the big leagues, Stengel got testy when he was reminded about it. Asked for his plans by a Detroit reporter, Stengel snapped, "You can go catch your plane or your train because I con-sider this my personal business."

Midway through the season, the Yankees were in a three-way race for the AL lead, kept close by Maris's lethal bat. Mantle himself remained in a funk, one that started even before the season when he held out for two weeks and eventually signed a contract for $65,000—a $7,000 pay cut after his subpar season in '59. Holding out had consequences, prompting Mantle to step up his training reg-imen, which backfired when he aggravated his old knee injury. Unable to plant his foot properly when swinging a bat or throwing, Mantle dogged it, a fog lifted briefly on July 4 when he socked his three-hun-dredth career home run off Hal Woodeshick in Washington. On August 14, the Mick hit bottom when batting against the Senators. With Maris on first, he hit a routine infield grounder and didn't even leave the batter's box, resulting in an ugly inning-ending double play. Running the bases hard, Maris chugged into the knees of Washington second baseman Billy Gardner, bruising his chest so badly that he would miss the next seventeen games.

The contrast between the hard-running Maris and the diffident

Mantle wasn't lost on Stengel. As Mantle waited near the first-base line for a teammate to deliver his mitt, Stengel replaced him on the spot—sending Bob Cerv to center instead. The Yankee skipper was making a statement—benching the great Mick in front of the home folks, many of whom cascaded him with boos as he headed to the dugout. "It don't look very good, us trying to win when the man hits the ball to 2nd or 3rd and doesn't run it out." Stengel said. "That's not the first time he's done that. If he can't run, he should tell me."

With Maris out, the booing directed at Mantle intensified. In a sense, the Yankee fans were venting their anger at the fact that Mantle wasn't able to repeat the heroics of his 1956 triple-crown season, when everything he hit seemed to be a tape-measure shot. Radio announcer Red Barber said that Mantle was paying the price for all those years of Stengel's coddling him as the fair-haired boy, as the next DiMaggio. Nor was Mantle's surliness toward reporters helping his popularity. "He's booed because he's not a colorful player like Babe Ruth," Barber said. "Ruth was a freewheeling guy on and off the field. He had magic, but Mantle isn't a showman."

No, he wasn't. But the benching was a jolt, a sudden ignition of the Mick's competitive fire. The next day, Mantle hit two home runs at Yankee Stadium against the Orioles, including a two-run game winner off Hoyt Wilhelm, which he deposited in the right-field seats. Trotting back to the dugout, Mantle tipped his cap to the fans—something players rarely did in those days because it was considered disrespectful to the pitcher. "I wanted to be good tonight more than I ever wanted to be good in my life," he said after the game. "I don't know what I would have done if I had had another bad day like yesterday."

Mantle kept hitting, and the boos quickly turned to cheers. He had again become the Golden Boy, first in the hearts of the mercurial Yankee fans—for the moment anyhow. Mantle's performance was infectious, and even without the ailing Maris, the Yankees were winning, thanks not just to hitting, but to fielding and pitching as well. Berra replaced Maris in right, and the reliable Elston Howard took over behind the plate. Bullpen stability arrived when, from the International League, the Yankees acquired the well-traveled thirty-three-year-old right-hander Luis Arroyo from nearby Jersey City. Using a nifty screwball and pinpoint control, Arroyo had become a go-to man, not scored on in all but three of his seventeen appearances. His stellar pitching had capped a topsy-turvy season for the Jerseys, which had relocated in mid-July to Jersey City after being driven out of Havana by Fidel Castro. The long-range ramifications of the move were enormous—it essentially ended the rich pipeline of Cuban players to the big leagues, particularly after the Eisenhower administration broke off diplomatic ties with Cuba in January 1961. But New York baseball scribes stuck to the short view: "(Arroyo) would never have been discovered," mused Arthur Daley of the *Times*, "if Castro hadn't chased him to Jersey City."

Then the Yanks topped off their late-season run, as they often did in the '50s, with a valuable late-season veteran pickup—in this case, Dale Long, a thirty-four-year-old slugger acquired from the Giants on waivers. Pirate fans had fond memories of Long, the man who had belted eight home runs in eight consecutive games for the 1956 Pirates. It was Pittsburgh's greatest baseball feat of a mostly dismal decade, and it resulted in the sport's first curtain call. A solid lefty bat off the bench and still a deep-ball threat, Long had batted .366 in twenty-six games with the '60 Yanks.

Oddly, the team's turnaround didn't spike public interest in the Yankees, who for all their success never drew anywhere near the crowds they deserved. Such was the curious state of New York City baseball in 1960: After the Dodgers and Giants abandoned New York for the West Coast, the Yankees had licked their chops, expected to benefit from a boost in attendance afforded by their newfound monopoly. Who were they kidding? Dodger and Giant fans, conditioned to loathe their ancient crosstown American League rivals who had dashed the hopes of their teams so often, could never become Yankee fans. They were not about to trade their longing for their dearly departed just for seats at Yankee Stadium. In the World Championship year of '58, Yankee home attendance actually fell to its lowest mark in fourteen years. All that winning had become so routine that many fans took to rooting against the Yankees, just for something different. For A. J. Liebling, author of *The Sweet Science*, the Yankees were the most hated of ball clubs "because they win, which leaves nothing to 'if' about."

New York's new baseball landscape created a particular challenge for the city's newspaper sportswriters. Suddenly, New York had one moderately supported baseball team and not three, creating a need to fill the pages of the sports section. Reporters didn't have to stray far to find a new media darling to capture the hearts of demanding New York sports fans. That new team was the Giants—not the city's late, great baseballers but the New York "Football Giants," as they were commonly known. Led by dashing, telegenic stars like Frank Gifford and Sam Huff, the Giants by 1960 were among the NFL's elite, playing to sold-out crowds at Yankee Stadium. Television helped—the contours of football seemed perfect for watching at home—and the sponsors flocked accordingly, creating stiff new competition for baseball. "The NFL Giants and pro football, in general, filled the void that had so suddenly opened in the city's sporting affections," writes Henry Fetter in *Taking on the Yankees*, his compelling study of the business of baseball. In November 1959, Huff earned a cover profile in *Time* magazine, a telling sign that football players had reached the elite of the celebrity athlete. Green Bay glamour boy Paul Hornung had "greater appeal in a more sophisticated culture than any baseball players (who) remained trapped in the personas of 'aw shucks' overaged Little Leaguers," Fetter writes. "Hornung was endorsing Scotch; (Mickey) Mantle, Wheaties."

In September, the Yankees turned a close race with the stubborn Orioles into a rout. Tied for the league lead as the teams entered a mid-September four-game series at Yankee Stadium, the Yankees swept the Orioles and never looked back. On hand for the series was

Ty Cobb, just back from the summer Olympic Games in Rome and anxious to catch up with Stengel, his old friend and rival. The Yankees kept winning—taking their final fifteen games in a row and nineteen of twenty-one. Success came so readily that coach Jim Hegan, ever mindful of baseball superstition, claimed to "almost wish we'd lost one" as the teams entered the World Series. The pennant, the team's twenty-fifth, was theirs. Mantle took the AL home-run title with 40, edging out Maris right behind at 39. Throw in Skowron's 26 homers and Berra's 15, and the Yankees pounded an AL-record 193 home runs. Even the pitching held up—despite the fact that nobody was even close to twenty wins—thanks to the performances of Ford at 12-9 and of youngsters such as Ditmar, who finished at 15-9, and Coates, at 13-3. The pitching staff tied the Orioles with a league-leading 3.52 ERA. Cobb hailed the pennant as Stengel's masterpiece, saying, "He has already done more with less than any of the other years that I can recall that the Yankees won under his guidance."

* * *

So what could the heart of the Yankee order do against the Pirates' Law in the second inning of Game 7? First up was Mantle, back to his old slugging self with a hefty .375 to date in the Series and three home runs—including a jaw-dropping right-handed shot off left-hander Joe Gibbon in Game 2 that sailed over Forbes Field's old 15-foot-high iron gate in *right-center,* a feat accomplished only by lefty sluggers Duke Snider, Stan Musial, and Dale Long. Afterward, a policeman had fished the ball from the vines of Schenley Park, some 478 feet from home plate. But here, against the right-handed Law, Mantle was batting from the left side.

Taking a fastball inside for ball one, Mantle was at bat to hack, hoping to jump-start another Yankee rally to finish off these Pirates once and for all. He fouled another fastball, this one off the mask of umpire Bill Jackowski, and thought of hitting the next pitch, a curve, before jerking the bat out of the way to let it go for ball two. Then Law went with a changeup, which fooled Mantle, who swung a spilt second too soon and popped the ball to right-center field. Virdon caught it for the first out.

To the plate stepped the righty-swinging Berra. A squat 5'7½", he always looked a tad overmatched when swinging a bat, especially in the on-deck circle when he swung two. But his other numbers stood out: Now in his eleventh World Series, Yogi was looking for his eleventh Series home run and, if possible, the all-time Series RBI lead, giving him a well-deserved reputation as the Yankees' biggest big-game player of all. Pitching carefully, Law started Berra with a breaking-ball strike at the knees and surprised him by coming back with a fastball that the Yankee batter smacked foul down the third-base line. After another ball, this one low and away, Berra let loose and smashed the next pitch sharply—but perhaps 10 feet off the third-base bag, where Hoak moved slightly to his left, and fell in a heap to keep the ball in front of him. Then Hoak got unsteadily to his feet, fired the ball across the infield to first to nail Berra, and fell again. The Pirates third baseman had made a highlight stop—stealing a zinger of a drive destined to be a single or even a double for Berra. "A dazzling play!" Prince cried on television. There were two down. The Pirates had dodged another bullet.

Next up: Bill Skowron, who at .370 for the Series was another in a seemingly never-ending hit parade for the Yankees. The man called "Moose" was hacking, too—swinging and missing on the first pitch, a breaking ball, for strike one. Then Skowron let a fastball tail away for ball one before swinging and sending a chopper to Groat, who threw to first for the third out. And just like that, the Yanks were gone in the second, with the Pirates headed to bat.

* * *

Was the Pittsburghers' two-run first a sign that they were emerging from a Series-long batting slump? Stepping in to face Turley, the squat Pirates catcher Smoky Burgess aimed to find out and took a curve high and outside for ball one. Still undecided about Turley's effectiveness, Stengel kept tinkering with his bullpen—Stafford directing to keep throwing, so the more-experienced Shantz could rest in the event the Yanks could use him later. All the strategy was a little dizzying so early in the game.

The Yankee manager soon got his answer. Jumping on a fastball, Burgess rifled a decisive shot down the right-field line between Skowron and the first-base bag. Maris fielded quickly and delivered the ball to Richardson at second, though Burgess's notable lack of speed held him to a long single. With a base runner and nobody gone, the Pirates appeared to be mounting another rally.

That was enough for Stengel. Bolting from the steps of the dugout, he chugged toward the mound—"like a man whose vest is buttoned to his trousers," someone said—to get Turley. Then he peered into the Yankee bullpen in the left-field corner and summoned Stafford. Quite a spot to be in for a twenty-one-year-old rookie up since midseason, but it seemed right. The hard-throwing right-hander had added considerable depth to the Yankee pen, displaying excellent control and uncommon poise to win three of four decisions. And he had been the Yankees' unsung hero of Game 5, replacing an ineffective Luis Arroyo and pitching five shutout innings in the 5-2 loss.

Facing Don Hoak would require every scrap of Stafford's moxie. Hoak was a hard man and a hard out—the Pirates' seventh batter, who provided depth up and down the lineup. A .282 regular-season hitter, batting .250 in the Series, Hoak was patient at the plate and would just as soon reach base with a walk or by letting the pitch strike him. New Yorkers knew Hoak and reserved a special affection for him as the third baseman for the 1955 Dodgers, the only Brooklyn team to ever take a World Series—and against these Yanks no less. In the stands, Pirate fans, used to rallies, looked for another, which would come in handy against the homer-happy New Yorkers.

Stafford threw, sending a fastball way high for ball one. He followed with a curve, which sailed up in the vicinity of Hoak's head and nowhere near the strike zone. The count was 2-0. From behind the plate popped Yankee catcher Johnny Blanchard, who, sensing his young pitcher was nervous, tried to slow the pace. Walking 20 feet toward the mound, Blanchard called for a new baseball and fired it to Stafford. That helped, but not enough. Sending the 2-0 pitch lower, Stafford was outside, to make it 3-0. Then he fired low again. Hoak had barely lifted the bat from his shoulder and walked on four pitches. There were two on, and still no outs, for Bill Mazeroski.

Pittsburgh's second baseman was a .286 Series hitter through six games. Celebrated more for his glove, Mazeroski was a compact hitter with pop in his bat, a man who had remade himself in 1960—batting .273 to raise his average .32 points and atone for a dismal '59. Sensing Stafford's discomfort, Yankee third baseman Clete Boyer called time and walked to the mound to chat with the young pitcher. Down the left-field line, the Yankee bullpen kept busy as Terry continued to warm and Shantz got up again.

Some figured the Yankees were right to approach Mazeroski with caution. The World Series can be a showcase for the unexpected batter to shine—someone overlooked in a lineup of stars. Wasn't Richardson the last Yankee you would expect to be hitting grand slams? And don't forget Billy Martin, the former Yankee with a .257 lifetime batting average who somehow managed to bat .500 in the 1953 World Series. Before Game 1, the former Pirate pitcher Nellie King, now a radio broadcaster with WSHH in nearby Latrobe, had asked several Pirates to predict who would emerge as Pittsburgh's Series star. Some said Groat, others Skinner. But not Harvey Haddix, who told King that the star would be Mazeroski. Why? "Because they'll pitch to him," Haddix said.

Looking for the double play, the Yankee infield moved in a few steps, willing to give up another run for two outs. With that, the Pirates third-base coach Frank Oceak signaled for something intended to outsmart the Yankees: On Stafford's delivery, Maz pulled his bat in and *bunted* down the third-base line. Springing from the mound, Stafford gathered in the baseball, reared and fired a strike down to Richardson covering at first base. Safe! The bases were loaded—"F-O-B," or "full of Bucs," as the team's former radio announcer Rosey Rosewell would often say. And there were still no outs.

The crowd at Forbes Field erupted—"shook to the rafters," as Chuck Thompson intoned on NBC Radio. Could the Pirates do what the Yankees had done to them in their three lopsided wins? From the shadows of the dugout popped Stengel—again—as he ambled to the mound to discuss strategy with Stafford. "Ignore the distractions," the Yankee manager told him, "and just throw strikes like you're back in Little League." And up to the plate stepped the other pitcher, Vernon Law, who had a .181 regular-season average and could handle a bat—the epitome of the "good-hitting pitcher." After all, it was Law who had keyed the Pirates' big three-run rally back in Game 4 at Yankee Stadium with a run-scoring double—a pitcher who had "helped his cause," as the cliché went. So Law gave it a shot, taking a slider outside and then swinging and missing. Then he missed again—and on a 1-2 pitch, swung and tapped the ball back to Stafford, who fired home to easily nail the slow-footed Burgess. Catcher Blanchard then winged the ball down to first to nail Law for a double play.

It was nifty fielding, the kind the Yankees seemed to come up with when they needed it most. Just like that, there were two gone, but Stafford was still in a pickle with Hoak standing on third and Mazeroski on second. "That's fine pitching by Stafford, but he still is not out of it," said Thompson. "(Now comes) the toughest spot he could possibly be in."

For one thing, Bill Virdon, the top of the order, was at bat. The left-handed batter's goal: to drive the ball toward right field, away from the base runners, which would score them both—making it 4-0 Pirates, a tough spot for even the Yankees to stage a rally. Out on the mound, Stafford tried taking Stengel's counsel to heart—though it was hard to blot out distractions like pesky batters, two men in scoring position, and, oh yes, forty million viewers eying your every gesture. He gave it a shot anyway—firing a curve that the left-handed hitting Virdon fouled down the right-field line. Then Stafford threw another curve, a surprise to Virdon, who was behind on the ball and sent it foul down the left-field line. Ahead 0-2, Stafford could afford to waste a pitch and delivered a fastball, high and tight—meant to intimidate Virdon and back him away from the plate. But those tactics didn't work on the veteran twenty-nine-year-old center fielder, and he got right back in the box, not conceding an inch. So in came the 1-2 pitch, and out went a solid base hit, rifled into right, exactly where he had intended. Hoak trotted home, followed by Mazeroski. In right field, Maris bobbled the ball for an error, allowing Virdon to take second. Two more runs were in, and Forbes Field was rocking again.

Then Groat bounced out to third, and mercifully for the Yanks and their battered pitching staff, the inning was done. The Pirates were up 4-0, but Game 7 had a long way to go.

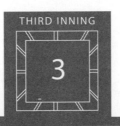

THIRD INNING

3

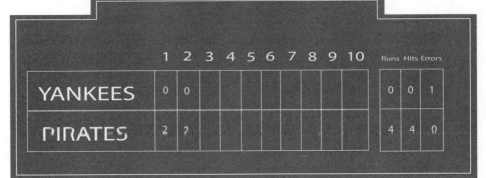

	1	2	3	4	5	6	7	8	9	10	Runs	Hits	Errors
YANKEES	0	0									0	0	1
PIRATES	2	2									4	4	0

GAME 7 WASN'T even one-third of the way finished, and already Stengel had seemingly sprouted up just about everywhere at Forbes Field. From the dugout, he popped up like a groundhog from its hole in the ground to beat a path to the mound. Back in the dugout, he didn't sit but paced nervously, phoned the bullpen to keep track of his pitchers, and spent a lot of time staring hard toward the diamond from the top step. Stengel was playing a game within the larger game, strategizing like it was the late innings to shut the Pirates down and give his team the chance for a comeback.

But you had to look hard to find Danny Murtaugh, who had only left his perch at the end of the Pirate dugout to congratulate the four Pirates who had scored runs. The Pirate manager was rarely demonstrative—and his quiet, steady leadership was just the tonic his team needed to stay focused. They were in good shape for now, with batting depth up and down the lineup and their ace on the mound. Besides, Skinner was back, and there was a lights-out closer in the pen.

Unlike Stengel, Murtaugh had made no moves to this point. No need. This was the team he wanted. "There are a lot of great managers around, but I've never seen a manager in the same category as Danny Murtaugh," Smoky Burgess once told writer Jim O'Brien. "He studied everything and got the most talent out of his players. You had to treat a Dick Stuart or a Dick Groat or myself differently. Danny did."

A native of the shipbuilding town of Chester, Pennsylvania, near Philadelphia, Murtaugh was a product of the Depression and grew up poor. Life was hard, and as a boy Murtaugh would walk the railroad tracks, scooping up errant pieces of coal to take home to heat his family's home. Murtaugh followed his father into the shipyards, where he worked for 34 cents an hour in a rivet gang, before participating in a tryout camp in 1937 at nineteen and signing with the Cardinals.

At 5'9", Murtaugh was squat but surprisingly agile, with steady hands and speed. So he became a second baseman and reached the majors in 1941 with the Phillies, though his career was checkered, thanks to the war years, which carved out a significant portion from the heart of his career. In 1944, Murtaugh joined the U.S. Army infantry and served in Europe and the Pacific. Back in baseball, Murtaugh made the most of it—batting a credible .254 in his nine-year career with the Phillies, Braves, and Pirates. His best year: 1948, when he hit .290 with Pittsburgh and formed a snappy double-play combination with Stan Rojek, which helped the Bucs take fourth, twelve games above .500.

In 1952, Murtaugh signed on as manager of the Pirates' farm team in New Orleans, where he started a long relationship with the Pelicans' young general manager, Joe L. Brown. Danny's team took fifth, then fifth again the next year, and Brown admitted his skipper had potential, but faced a steep learning curve. "At the time, I thought Danny was too soft on the players," Brown said. "We had nineteen players and he was always concerned about how the ten guys who weren't playing felt."

Murtaugh learned. His great advantage was a way with people and solid baseball knowledge. He dealt with everyone on the level, drilled his players on fundamentals, and played the game by the book. Murtaugh's teams excelled at bunting and were superb fielders. They sacrificed without complaint and could hit-and-run. Anchored by a self-deprecating sense of humor, Murtaugh was never flashy and put

his players at ease. He even asked after the families of sportswriters—
so different from most hard-edged baseball men. Brown developed a
deep admiration for Murtaugh, particularly in New Orleans after he
grew harder on his players and led the team to a second-place finish
in '54, before getting fired in '55 in a payroll move.

"I should have been fired," Murtaugh deadpanned later. "I spent
money recklessly. One night, I let my players foul off two $3.25 base-
balls. They could have used that $6.50 to buy a player."

Murtaugh joined the Phillies as third-base coach in '56, but Brown,
by then the general manager in Pittsburgh, had his an eye on him for
the Pirates' top spot. On August 3, 1957, in the middle of a dismal
season, Brown figured it was time to replace Bobby Bragan as manager. Following protocol, he offered the job to general manager Branch
Rickey's top scout Clyde Sukeforth, knowing full well he would decline
the offer. After Sukeforth did as expected, Brown tapped Murtaugh—
his only mistake was leaking the scoop to the press before he actually
informed Bragan, who heard the news on the radio.

Whereas Bragan criticized and often belittled his players with
profanity-laced tirades, Murtaugh was a straight shooter and seldom
cursed. It was just the tonic the Pirates needed. Facing his players in
the year's first and only team meeting—a "pep talk," he called it—
Murtaugh got to the point: "I don't want you to respect me just
because I'm manager," he told them. "I want to earn your respect."
He did so quickly, and the Pirates rallied—for them, anyway—and
went 26-25 the rest of the way. Murtaugh's formula was simple—
treat his players like adults, make moves only when forced, and quell
dissent discreetly and usually in private.

Murtaugh had a few prohibitions: He levied small fines for bad language, saying only, "That will cost you." Anyone missing a team bus
was automatically fined $25, except for the time Vernon Law missed
the bus after his name was posted late to the spring-training travel list.
Law, the ordained Mormon lay minister, paid anyway, but Murtaugh

refused to take it. Law still paid, insisting that if the Pirate manager had any qualms about accepting the money, he could turn it over to the building fund of the local Mormon church. That sounded good to Murtaugh, a devout Roman Catholic, who not only abided by Law's wishes, but contributed $25 of his own to his pitcher's church.

In dispensing justice with a touch of whimsy, Murtaugh's role model had been Billy Southworth, his manager in Boston. With the Braves at spring training in 1947, Murtaugh and his roommates once played poker all night and into the midmorning—so long that they all left their roadside motel directly for the ballpark without a wink of sleep.

"Did you sleep well last night?" Southworth inquired gently as he greeted his unshaven and hungover players that morning.

"Like babies," they dutifully answered in chorus.

"That's good," Southworth countered. "I was afraid you might have been disturbed by that truck that crashed through your room in the middle of the night."

Murtaugh's poker days were long finished when he took over the Pirates. Never a carouser, Murtaugh dutifully went home every night to Kate, his wife, and their three teenage children. He didn't drink, preferring milk to calm an ulcer and to humorously toast Pirate wins. At his Forbes Field office, he'd relax by sitting in a rocking chair for hours before and after the game and would chew tobacco, spin tales, play some cards, and nap. "This is my office, this is where I work," he said of the chair. "I can relax here and think."

"So with all that clean living, why do you look so old?" a writer kidded him.

"Have you ever looked up my batting average?" countered Murtaugh.

But Murtaugh had done some thinking. "Psychology?" he once mused. "I didn't go far enough in school to use that." But he studied other baseball men and absorbed their knowledge. From Bucky Harris, his manager in Philadelphia, he learned to treat his players as grown-ups. "It was Bucky's belief," said Murtaugh, "that the more responsibility you gave players, the better they reacted." While playing in the Texas League, Murtaugh took the advice of a future AL umpire named Art Passarella, who advised him that he'd better not throw anything when arguing a call. "Ever since, I've been very careful of how I handle my equipment," Murtaugh deadpanned.

* * *

Little rattled him. Murtaugh was patient, stern when he had to be, and practical. On the road, he didn't care much for bed checks, saying, "They're all big boys and they should know what they're doing." Asked by Hoak where to play the future Hall of Famer Richie Ashburn, Murtaugh just shrugged. "I was looking in this little record book the other day and it shows that Ashburn has been getting 170, maybe 200 hits a year for ten years," he said. "Just play him anyway you want him." Even so, Hoak worshipped his manager. "As long as you're doing okay, he doesn't touch you," he told writer Bill Surface. "If you're messing up, he's just over your shoulder showing the right way."

Murtaugh used his wry wit to considerable advantage. On a rainy day in 1957, while waiting for the weather to clear at Forbes Field, Murtaugh noticed Mazeroski eying the attractive young assistant to scout Rex Bowen. But the Pirate second baseman was too shy to do anything further until Murtaugh directed him to call her "right now" for a date. Mazeroski blushed, staring at his manager in bewilderment. "Look," Murtaugh said. "They send guys back to the minors if they can't take orders. That's an order." So Maz telephoned Milene Nicholson to ask for a date. In 1958, they married.

Murtaugh helped Mazeroski in other ways. Bobby Bragan was an inveterate tinkerer of a manager, who in 1957 experimented by dropping Maz to ninth in the order, behind the pitcher. Bat behind a pitcher? Mazeroski's teammates worried that the move would erode the young infielder's confidence. Murtaugh quickly restored Maz to seventh in the order and announced that he was the team's second baseman no matter what. "I used to be scared to death during games," Mazeroski said. "I feel like an elephant has jumped off my back. . . . There's no pressure."

At the time Murtaugh arrived, Bob Skinner was a man without a position—jumping from first to third to the outfield, which the Pirate manager figured inhibited the young slugger from relaxing and reaching his potential. The gangly Skinner "looks as if he could be pushed around," the *Times*' Arthur Daley wrote, "but once he steps into a batter's box, he's whipcord and dynamite." Murtaugh called Skinner to his office and told him that he was in the team's left field position "until you play yourself out of it."

Skinner relaxed. He focused. Working tirelessly at his new position, Skinner learned how to play caroms off the Forbes Field's big left-field scoreboard and to uncork his throws quickly to compensate for his average arm. As the team's designated left fielder, Skinner improved other aspects of his game: Running on his toes, he picked up speed on the base paths, while at bat, he developed into an accomplished gap hitter, capable of spraying line drives into all parts of Forbes' substantial outfield.

Murtaugh breathed new life into the Pirates. In 1958, his first full season, the team improved a whopping twenty-two games to take second place, fourteen games above .500 and only eight back of Milwaukee. Playing with confidence, Bob Friend—with his big leg-kick—won twenty-two games, and Vernon Law, fourteen. Meantime, Skinner batted .321; Groat hit an even .300; and third baseman Frank Thomas, another Pittsburgh native, belted thirty-five home runs. These Pirates won for their victory-starved fans, and all year long, the fans streamed into Forbes Field—some 461,000 more than the previous season. Murtaugh took NL manager-of-the-year honors, hands down.

Many predicted a Pirates pennant in 1959. To fortify the team's prospects, Brown engineered a blockbuster seven-player trade before the season that dispatched Thomas and three others to the Reds for

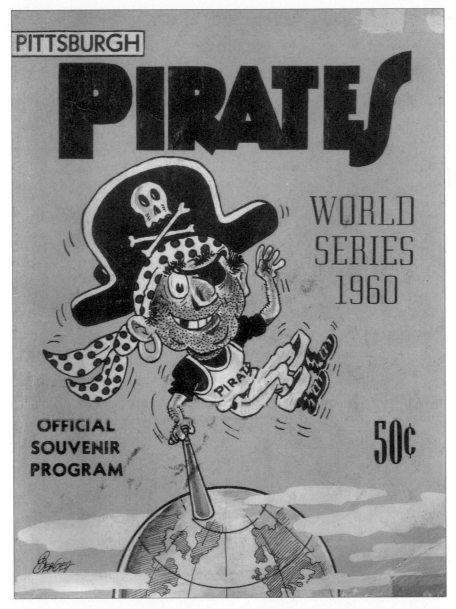

Pennsylvania heirloom: a weathered program from the 1960 World Series. (Collection of the author)

Imagine paying $2.20 a ticket to sit in the bleachers at baseball's best game ever? (Courtesy of Dr. Jean Oertel)

Find your seats, please! Forbes Field is just about set for the 1960 World Series. (National Baseball Hall of Fame Library, Cooperstown, NY)

The one and only Gunner, Bob Prince. (National Baseball Hall of Fame Library, Cooperstown, NY)

Too old at seventy-three to manage in the World Series? Some said the best years of Yankee manager Casey Stengel's life were behind him. But not his players. (National Baseball Hall of Fame Library, Cooperstown, NY)

NEW YORK YANKEES
1960 AMERICAN LEAGUE CHAMPIONS

First Row, Left to Right: GIL McDOUGALD, BILL SKOWRON, BOBBY RICHARDSON, JIM HEGAN, EDDIE LOPAT, FRANK CROSETTI, CASEY STENGEL, RALPH HOUK, JOHNNY BLANCHARD, ELSTON HOWARD, YOGI BERRA.
Second Row, Left to Right: JOE SOARES, CLETIS BOYER, JOE DEMAESTRI, TONY KUBEK, DALE LONG, HECTOR LOPEZ, BOB CERV, MICKEY MANTLE, ROGER MARIS, GUS MAUCH.
Third Row, Left to Right: LUIS ARROYO, DUKE MAAS, ELI GRBA, RYNE DUREN, BILL STAFFORD, JIM COATES, RALPH TERRY, BOB TURLEY, ART DITMAR, WHITEY FORD, BOBBY SHANTZ.
Seated on Ground in Front: Batboys FRANK PRUDENTI, FRED BENGIS.

(National Baseball Hall of Fame Library, Cooperstown, NY)

Calm, reassuring, and usually with a plug in his cheek: That was Pirate manager Danny Murtaugh. (National Baseball Hall of Fame Library, Cooperstown, NY)

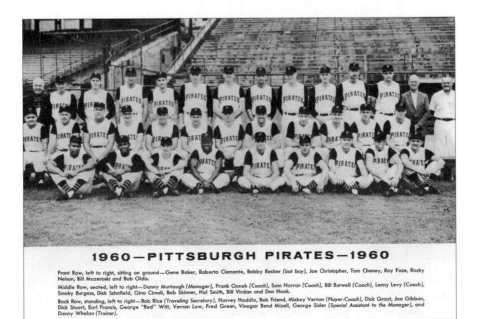

1960—PITTSBURGH PIRATES—1960

Front Row, left to right, sitting on ground—Gene Baker, Roberto Clemente, Bobby Recker (bat boy), Joe Christopher, Tom Cheney, Roy Face, Rocky Nelson, Bill Mazeroski and Bob Oldis.

Middle Row, seated, left to right—Danny Murtaugh (Manager), Frank Oceak (Coach), Sam Narron (Coach), Bill Burwell (Coach), Lenny Levy (Coach), Smoky Burgess, Dick Schofield, Gino Cimoli, Bob Skinner, Hal Smith, Bill Virdon and Don Hoak.

Back Row, standing, left to right—Bob Rice (Traveling Secretary), Harvey Haddix, Bob Friend, Mickey Vernon (Player-Coach), Dick Groat, Joe Gibbon, Dick Stuart, Earl Francis, George "Red" Witt, Vernon Law, Fred Green, Vinegar Bend Mizell, George Sisler (Special Assistant to the Manager), and Danny Whelan (Trainer).

(National Baseball Hall of Fame Library, Cooperstown, NY)

Two-thirds of a potent Yankee outfield in 1960: Mickey Mantle (left) and Roger Maris. (National Baseball Hall of Fame Library, Cooperstown, NY)

Roberto Clemente. His infield single in inning 8 of Game 7 gave him a base hit in every game of the 1960 Series, a feat he would duplicate in '71. (National Baseball Hall of Fame Library, Cooperstown, NY)

"Man, do we love to hit here," Yogi Berra said of Forbes Field. Overhearing his catcher's words, Casey Stengel added a few of his own: *"Berra could last five more years hitting in this park."* (National Baseball Hall of Fame Library, Cooperstown, NY)

October 13, 1960, was a day to remember for Bill Virdon: two base hits, two RBIs, and a run scored. (National Baseball Hall of Fame Library, Cooperstown, NY)

A pennant and a parade: after clinching the team's first NL pennant in thirty-three years, the Pirates were welcomed home from Milwaukee with a torch-lit parade that snaked through the streets of downtown Pittsburgh. Here, Jean Oertel (l) of Penn Hills in Pittsburgh and her friend, Sandy Waibel Laurie, display their loyalties.

Welcome home, National League champs: Roberto Clemente.

Another parade scene from September 25, 1960: Danny Murtaugh and his wife, Kate. (All photos by Byron F. Oertel, courtesy of Dr. Jean Oertel)

Don Hoak, Smoky Burgess, and pitcher Harvey Haddix. Pirate fans were mortified that Brown had the nerve to deal Thomas, the local favorite, and peppered him at home with angry phone calls. "Has your husband gone crazy?" asked one caller of Brown's wife, Din. Actually, Brown hadn't: The three new Pirates would all play pivotal roles. And Thomas? He'd slump to twelve home runs with the Reds.

Keyed up at the team's prospects, Pittsburghers by the thousands streamed to the airport in April of 1959 to greet the Pirates on their arrival home from spring training, then gave them a torchlight parade through the downtown streets. But the Bucs got off to a rocky start and never got on track, taking a distant fourth, only two games above .500. Overconfidence was a major reason—both Mazeroski and Friend had reported to spring training overweight and became the team's major scapegoats and targets of the Forbes Field boo-birds. Early in the season, Mazeroski pulled a thigh muscle so badly that he missed twenty games and never regained his range, while at the plate, his batting average plummeted 34 points to .241. Friend's season was even worse; 22-14 in '58, the durable right-hander could muster only eight wins in '59 and led the league in losses, with nineteen.

Others faced troubles as well. In the season's second week, Skinner ran into a fence in Milwaukee, never regained his patented level swing, and paid the price: a 39-point drop in his batting average. Groat's average tumbled 25 points, and though Clemente played with his usual flair, he injured his elbow and missed nearly sixty games. Though the Pirates caught steam after the All-Star break and moved within three and a half games of the league-leading Giants in late August, that's as far as they got.

The Pirates' unlikely high spot of 1959: the improbable evening of May 26 at County Stadium in Milwaukee, when the 5'9" lefthander Harvey Haddix pitched the greatest game in baseball history. Though he had a cold, the thirty-three-year-old Haddix took his turn anyway against Lew Burdette and the Braves. Then Haddix retired thirty-six batters in a row, taking his perfect game into the twelfth, a game that lasted so long only because the Pirate hadn't scored any runs either.

Haddix mixed his fastball, slider, and changeup to keep the Braves off-base. Sparkling plays by shortstop Dick Schofield twice robbed Braves shortstop Johnny Logan of a base hit, to preserve the pitching masterpiece. Though Milwaukee manager Fred Haney had loaded his powerful lineup with seven right-handed bats, Haddix shut down everyone, including Hank Aaron, Eddie Mathews, and Joe Adcock. Realizing they were seeing history, the County Stadium crowd of 19,194 gave Haddix several warm ovations as he stepped to bat in the late innings.

The game sailed to the eighth, then the ninth, and into extra innings, still scoreless with both starters matching zeros. Finally, while leading off the Milwaukee thirteenth, the Braves' Felix Mantilla reached first on Hoak's throwing error and was sacrificed to second. The tiring Haddix intentionally walked Hank Aaron, and Joe Adcock followed with a home run. Adcock passed Aaron on the base path (making the final score 1-0), but the no-hitter and the game were both lost. Haddix's twelve and one-third innings of perfection are the big leagues' longest ever.

Perhaps the most remarkable aspect of the evening, if Milwaukee's Bob Buhl is to be believed, is that catcher Burgess was tipping off the Braves hitters on what Haddix was about to throw. "We'd yell from the bench what he was calling," Buhl told historian Danny Peary. "But Harvey was doing such a good job of putting on and taking off speed that the hitters couldn't time him."

But in the end the Braves, behind Burdette, who went the whole way and scattered eight hits, won the game—leaving Haddix with just another loss, which gnawed at him for years. "Harvey didn't even go to bed that night," recalled Elroy Face. "He just walked the streets until sometime in the morning." Added Marcia Haddix, Harvey's widow: "He felt that game was a loss for his team, and he didn't play to lose."

Looking at the Pirates in 1960, sportswriters weren't expecting much. Kansas City offered Roger Maris to the Pirates for Groat—a fact that still makes the former Pirate captain smile in a kind of "Imagine that?" manner—but dealt the A's slugger to the Yanks instead. Murtaugh had been the one to nix the deal, telling Joe L. Brown, "I don't want to trade him." Instead, Pittsburgh acquired another outfielder, Gino Cimoli from the Cardinals, and otherwise entered the new season with few changes.

Murtaugh figured that by running on all cylinders, the Pirates could challenge for the pennant. Their lack of power was an issue; only Dick Stuart, with his twenty-seven home runs in '59, could be called a legitimate long-ball threat. "We couldn't get the power hitter we needed—it seems they're hard to come by," said Murtaugh, stating the obvious. "(But) we don't expect guys like Friend, Skinner, Mazeroski, and Groat to have two bad years in a row. What a lot of people forget is that with all our injuries and off years, we made a hell of a run at the leaders there in late August."

But once the Pirates appeared headed for the 1960 pennant, a steady stream of writers beat a path to Murtaugh's Forbes Field office in search of inside dope and pearls of wisdom. Sitting in his customary rocking chair and usually chewing tobacco or puffing on a cigar, Murtaugh didn't concede much. Even with his wit, he never pretended to be someone he wasn't. "I just ain't good at answering fancy questions," Murtaugh said. "It's the players, not the manager, you know." Asked by Arthur Daily about his secret to success, Murtaugh paused in contemplation before responding: "(The key was) brilliant managerial thinking," he finally said, "and dumb Irish luck."

* * *

Looking to jump-start the Yankee third inning, catcher Johnny Blanchard wasn't being terribly selective. Coming off a World Series game for the ages—Blanchard had collected three hits in Game 6—the twenty-seven-year-old right-handed batter was hacking. Swinging at Law's first pitch, he sent a high pop-foul back of the Yankee dugout. He swung at pitch number two as well and chopped a ball right back to Law, which the Pirate pitcher stabbed using his backhand and threw to first. One down quickly—and seven in a row.

But then the next batter, Clete Boyer, slowed things down, though not intentionally. Standing at the plate and taking his practice swings, he realized his bat was cracked and quickly called time to retrieve another. Up in the radio booth, Thompson smiled at the small oversight, something that happens perhaps a half-dozen times a season. But in this case, it broke the tension of a big game that was heating up by the minute.

Back in the batter's box with his new bat, Boyer was in a swinging mood, looking to nail Law early in the count. That seemed to be the Yankee strategy so far: Get him before he got you, which, given Law's bad ankle, may not have been the best move. Why not wait him out, get him to throw lots of pitches and make a mistake? It was one of the subplots of the early going of Game 7 that would be quickly forgotten with all the later dramatics. So on the first pitch, Boyer swung and sent a harmless fly into short center field. Backing up, Mazeroski took it. Two down, and eight in a row for Law.

Reaching the bottom of the order, Stengel continued maneuvering. Needing quality at-bats to overcome the four-run deficit, the Yankee manager decided to pinch-hit for the pitcher, Stafford. Batting would be Hector Lopez, the Yankees' fine utility man and still another former Kansas City A to end up playing in the Bronx. Lopez, 2-6 to date in the Series, was hacking as well: Letting a curve go for ball one, he sent the next pitch on a long drive toward right that hooked foul. Next, he sent another foul, this one into the upper deck in right, where a fan made an impressive leaping two-handed catch of the ball. "Sign him up," a voice rang out from the stands. Everyone laughed. The count was 1-2.

Then Lopez drilled a single into the hole between short and third. Finally, the Yankees had their first base runner, vindicating Stengel, and sending Richardson, at the top of the order, to bat. Could this be the start of a rally? Pitching carefully, Law fired a curve, high, for ball one. Richardson met Law's next delivery solidly—when hadn't he done so in this World Series?—but on a line to Bob Skinner in left, who moved up a step and made the catch. Law had disposed of the Yankees in the third, throwing only nine pitches—to make thirty-two total thus far—not that anyone was keeping tabs in those days. But they were still up 4-0.

* * *

Ambling in from the bullpen to pitch the third, Bobby Shantz served as a reminder of why some jokingly called the Kansas City A's a Yankee farm club. At thirty-five years old, Shantz was the veteran stability that Stengel craved to stop the Pirates from further scoring. A lot was riding on the sore left arm of this pint-sized 5'6" hurler from Pottstown, Pennsylvania, who was just one short of one hundred career wins.

Shantz had pitched with the A's of Kansas City *and* of Philadelphia. A big leaguer for eleven years, he'd been with some of Connie Mack's dismal teams in Philadelphia, where he had somehow managed to win eighteen games in '51 and go 24-7 in '52—earning both the AL MVP award and the unfortunate baseball honorarium as "a great player on a lousy team." His arm went sore in 1953, but the Yankees, realizing his durability, coveted him. "Imagine what he'd do as a Yankee?" pondered General Manager George Weiss. So Shantz, like seemingly everybody else who succeeded as an A became a Yank. Nobody thought much of it when Shantz moved; it was only after the Mack family sold the A's to Chicago real-estate man Arnold Johnson, who moved the franchise to Kansas City in time for the 1955 season, that the unseemly relationship of the two teams became apparent.

Anxious to move his new team to Kansas City, Johnson had turned to his friendship with Dan Topping and George Weiss of the Yankees. In 1953, Topping and Weiss had leased Yankee Stadium to Johnson and his brother and then leased it back. Flush with cash, Johnson moved the A's to Kansas City, but only after Topping graciously sold him the rights to Kansas City, where the Yankees' top farm club, the Blues, had enjoyed a long and fruitful history. So the Yankees' triple-A team moved to Denver, and Arnold Johnson owed the New Yorkers a big debt of thanks—something he would end up paying for again and again.

For a time at least, the move to Kansas City was profitable for the A's. Playing at the renovated and renamed Municipal Stadium, the 1955 A's drew nearly 1.4 million, more than four times the number of their final year in Philadelphia. But the team's lineup of aging stars and untested young players was dreadful, and the team that finished sixth in '55, then slid the following year to the familiar territory of last place and a nearly empty grandstand.

Looking for a spark, any spark, Johnson discovered the Yankees were a steady source of income and players with star appeal. Like a surrogate farm club, the A's began steadily peddling their best young talent to New York in exchange for cash and aging veterans who no longer fit the Yankee plans. Every year, it seemed, the Yankee roster featured a talented former Athletic; Shantz, Hector Lopez, Clete Boyer, and Art Ditmar, all of them A's in '55, became New Yorkers. Of the Yankees' twenty-five-man roster for the '60 Series, ten were former Athletics. Even Shantz's younger brother, Billy, a catcher, was part of the pipeline—he was another member of the '55 A's who ended up in the Bronx, though his career was little more than the proverbial cup of coffee. Billy batted once with the '60 Yanks and never again played in the big leagues.

Johnson was banking that the appeal of one-time Yankee big names like Don Larsen, Hank Bauer, and Billy Martin would improve the gate in Kansas City. It didn't. Nor did the infusion of ex-Yanks improve the team's performance, as the A's continually hovered at the bottom of the standings. For the most part, the Yankees exchanged quantity for quality—three-for-ones or five-for-twos were common. The New Yorkers even sent a few players to Kansas City for more seasoning and actually reacquired those players when they were deemed ready; Ralph Terry was banished to the A's midway through '57 as part of the Martin deal, but brought back two years later. Enos Slaughter went from New York to Kansas City and back to New York. "We've got too many big leaguers and had to cut down," Weiss's assistant Lee MacPhail explained self-righteously. "And we were not going to let them go for the $10,000 waiver price."

Old-timers recognized the trend as something the deep-pocketed Yanks had practiced effectively back in the '20s with the Red Sox—handsomely paying their AL rival for bright new stars like Babe Ruth, Herb Pennock, and Waite Hoyt, who then became cogs in the team's dynasty. Critics called the A's little more than a Yankee pawn, a "triple-A farm team masquerading as the Kansas City Athletics of the American League," according to Glenn Stout in his book, *Yankees Century*. AL president Will Harridge finally but half-heartedly responded to the complaints when, in June 1958, the Indians sent Roger Maris to the A's—a move widely seen as a prelude to another trade to New York. Harridge prohibited the A's from sending the young outfielder to New York for at least eighteen months. But days after the deadline was up, the Kansas City owner did the inevitable, swapping the slugger to New York. And the A's? Same old, same old: They got Bauer and Larsen, whose best years were past.

* * *

Sore arm or not, Shantz was just the veteran presence Stengel needed to stem any further damage by the Pirates in the bottom of the third inning. A starter early in his career, Shantz had lost velocity in recent years but relied on a curve that Ted Williams called the best in the American League, and on an ability to change speeds and keep batters off-balance. For good measure, he threw an occasional screwball and even a knuckleball, a pitch his former manager Connie Mack, the old catcher, had prohibited him from using early in his career. Though Shantz hadn't started a game all season for the Yanks, he had overcome a persistently sore arm to go 5-4 in forty-two games—tied with Ryne Duren for most appearances by a pitcher on the team. It didn't hurt that he was the league's premier fielding pitcher—a Gold Glove winner in each of the award's first three years (and he would win another in '60).

Shantz was rested—having gone only parts of single innings in Games 2 and 4. And what a treat it was to enter Game 7 with the bases empty and not have to pitch from the stretch. Shantz took full advantage and worked quickly—throwing a ball, high and outside, to Skinner, the first Pirate batter, before getting him to bounce a soft come-backer to the mound. There was one down.

Nelson, fourth in the order, was next. Standing in at the plate to another rollicking Forbes Field ovation, an acknowledgment of his laserlike first-inning home run, Nelson wasn't getting much to hit. Better to pitch around the hot hitter, Stengel had figured, and go after the next batter—the free-swinging Clemente. So Shantz threw a fat curve that was high for ball one and followed with an even slower curve that Nelson, his timing thrown off, committed to an instant early and sent in a long loping foul down the right-field line. That was a break for the Yanks, confirmation that Shantz should stay cautious against the hot-hitting Nelson. He threw three more balls and walked the Pirate first baseman.

In hindsight, it is hard to fathom that the Yanks were being so careful with a thirty-five-year-old journeyman to reach Clemente. In most ways, 1960 was a breakthrough season for the twenty-six-year-old right fielder, already in his sixth big-league campaign: He had batted .314, fourth-best in the NL, while serving notice that he had a magnificent right arm. Like Willie Mays, Clemente was an electrifying defender, already noted for tearing across the outfield to make basket catches, usually losing his hat in the process. He almost dared base runners to take the extra base—and had thrown out a league-leading nineteen runners. But Roberto Clemente in 1960 wasn't yet a superstar, but a player still developing at the plate and bedeviled by a nasty habit of chasing bad pitches.

The Dodgers were the first big-league team to recognize Clemente's gifts. In 1954, they secured this son of Puerto Rican sugarcane workers after two seasons with the exquisitely named Santuce Crabbers, a Puerto Rican winter league team that featured a mix of Latin Americans and big leaguers, including Mays. Brooklyn signed Clemente for $10,000 and a $5,000 bonus, after which baseball's bonus rule kicked in, which specified that the Dodgers place him on the major league roster, or potentially lose him in a special postseason draft. The Dodgers sent Clemente to their triple-A minor league affiliate in Montreal, where several biographers have claimed the team tried to hide him by ordering the team's manager Max Macon to play his nineteen-year-old budding star sparingly.

Clemente played only eighty-seven games for Montreal, batting a modest .257. But the tale of why a player of such promise didn't play regularly is more complicated than a team intent on "hiding" him: The 1954 Montreal Royals were loaded with outfielders, several of whom had been transferred in mid-May from St. Paul, the Dodgers' other Brooklyn triple-A team, and were well ahead of Clemente on the depth chart. Homesick and speaking little English and no French, Clemente started slowly and chased bad pitches and, by early June, was batting barely above .200. When he finally started to jell, all that continued competition made it hard for the right-handed hitting Clemente to even crack the lineup, so much so that Macon platooned him, mostly against lefties.

Little of that mattered to Rickey's assistant Clyde Sukeforth. Journeying to Montreal to track the young pitcher Joe Black, Sukeforth saw Clemente uncork a couple of 300-foot bullets from right field in pregame warm-ups and took note of the young outfielder from Puerto Rico. In the seventh inning, when Clemente bounced a pinch-hit grounder to shortstop and hustled down the line so fast that he nearly beat the tag, Sukeforth was smitten. Convinced that the last-place Pirates could use a prospect with such speed and a powerful arm, Sukeforth returned to Pittsburgh determined to draft Roberto Clemente.

Fortunately for Pittsburgh, the Dodgers weren't focused on Clemente and saw no need to protect him. They had Carl Furillo, the incumbent right fielder, who at thirty-two was in his prime. So the Pirates, due to pick first in the November draft, paid Clemente's $4,000 purchase price and had a new right fielder. Hearing the news back home in Puerto Rico, Clemente admitted, "I didn't even know where Pittsburgh was." The Pirates had picked well: "If we didn't (choose him)," said the Pirates' Latin American scout Howie Haak, "any of fourteen other clubs would have."

Bob Friend vividly recalls his first impression of Clemente, at spring training in 1955. "He was by far the best athlete in camp," he said. "You could see it in his physique, his speed, and the greatest arm I ever saw. And it didn't take long to realize he was going to be a great hitter. It took him a little time to really feel good about everything, but you knew he was going to be a great ballplayer."

Others came to recognize Clemente's gifts. "There aren't many bright spots on the last-place Pirates," *Pittsburgh Press* beat writer Les Biederman wrote in '55, "but one of the brightest is Roberto Clemente." Pirate fans quickly took to their new outfielder and his all-out approach to chasing a fly ball and running out even the most routine ground ball. Those things were appreciated in a town that valued hard work. Clemente himself returned the affection, saying that "people are wonderful (in Pittsburgh), . . . I wouldn't play for nobody else."

But the same writers who praised Clemente also called him selfish and a hot dog, while ridiculing his pidgin English. Clemente's supreme self-confidence was mistaken for arrogance; his pride, for selfishness. "The more I stay away from the writers, the better I am," Clemente once told Pittsburgh writer Phil Musick. "They are trying to create a bad image for me. You know what they have against me? Because I am black and Puerto Rican."

That was partly true. In a game still dominated by white men with crew cuts, Clemente didn't fit the mold. As baseball's first great Latin American player, Clemente was different from anyone the writers of the mid-1950s had seen. Some thought him black, others Hispanic; Clemente himself said the confusion made him feel like a "double nigger" living in a city with a microscopic Latino population. In a way, it was a reminder of how long ago this era really was: Clemente followed Jackie Robinson's big-league debut by less than a decade. For his first half-dozen years at spring training in Florida, Clemente and other non-white members of the Pirates roomed in segregated hotels, crosstown from other white teammates. His experience in the Jim Crow South of the 1950s appalled the young Puerto Rican, who had never experienced such blatant racism and hostile atmosphere—and would never forget it. That Clemente was still learning English sent him even further into retreat; always a fan of jazz music, the unmarried ballplayer lost himself in his extensive record collection and often went to hear live music at the Crawford Grill in Pittsburgh's Hill District.

Only twenty years old and a long way from home, Clemente was a fish out of water in the United States of the mid-1950s. Those same reporters who recognized Clemente's potential—he had the first of his fourteen .300-or-better seasons in '56—would mock his accent by quoting him directly. "I feel better when I am sick," Clemente once said. This treatment was galling to Clemente, an immensely proud man who was made to feel stupid. He would never overcome his animosity toward the press.

By 1960, Clemente had yet to put together his many formidable skills and still showed a tendency to chase bad pitches and lose himself in temper tantrums when things went sour. Plaguing him, too, were chronic neck and back pain from a 1954 auto accident—a condition which, more than anything, kept him from developing into a power hitter. Many who saw him play remember the way he would step up to the plate slowly and crick his neck and grimace as if he were in pain, before rifling another line-drive double into the gap. Clemente was also a light sleeper and constantly grumbled how he could really use a good's night's rest. "If I could sleep," he once said, "I would hit .400."

Years later, Clemente would admit to Pirate broadcaster Nellie King how nervous he had been in his first World Series. "Things change when you get to the World Series, (with) all the publicity and all the different people who you've never seen before," he told King. "It's a different atmosphere than any other game you will ever play, and you have to get accustomed to that. I wasn't accustomed to that in 1960, afraid I was going to make a mistake. I don't think I played that well."

Clemente compared the 1960 Series experience to his first year in the majors. "I wasn't a very good player (in 1955)," he told King. "I was so anxious. Playing right field, I had tunnel vision and could see the batter, but not the infielders. Then I started to relax and could see everything. I was in the picture, not outside looking on, but inside."

Clemente would put the memory of his anxiety during the 1960 World Series to good use the next time he got there, in 1971. According to King, Clemente called Pirate teammate Willie Stargell to his hotel room on the eve of Game 1 in Baltimore for a tutorial on the importance of focusing amid all the distractions.

In hindsight, the intensely proud Clemente was probably too hard on himself about his performance in the 1960 World Series. Through the first six games, he was quietly having a sensational Series: the only Pirate to hit safely in every game, he was batting .320, and had given America a clinic of how to play the outfield. With the Pirates clinging to a two-run lead in the seventh inning of Game 4, Clemente had served notice—fielding Gil McDougald's single and firing a low, no-bounce strike to Burgess at home plate to keep Moose Skowron at third. Though Skowron scored on the next play, the Pirate lead held up.

Following Clemente's every move was a sizable Latin American press corps and a national television audience back home in Puerto Rico. But few in the mainstream U.S. press were paying much attention— although taking note of the postgame locker room scene, where Clemente sat alone in front of his locker as most writers surrounded pitchers Elroy Face and Harvey Haddix, was a new admirer, Ted Meir of the Associated Press: "The unsung hero of the World Series?" Meir wrote. "That phrase could well apply to Roberto Clemente, the Pittsburgh right fielder with the rifle arm." Also noticing was Stengel, impressed by a play in Game 5 when Clemente had nearly doubled Berra off second base. "We discovered then," Casey said, "that they have a good right fielder."

Facing Shantz in Game 7 with Nelson on first, Clemente had an opportunity to put the game further out of reach. Playing the percentages, Clemente squared to bunt but pushed a foul off third base. He took a curve, low, evening the count at 1-1. Then, on the next pitch, Clemente swung and sent a routine chopper down to second, where Richardson fielded, threw to Kubek, who took the force and threw to first for a double play—"lightning-like," as Thompson put it. Shantz had stopped the bleeding in a hurry. For the first time in Game 7, the Yankees had shut down the Pirates.

FOURTH INNING

4

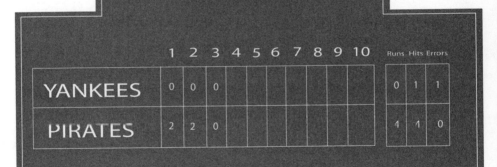

	1	2	3	4	5	6	7	8	9	10	Runs	Hits	Errors
YANKEES	0	0	0								0	1	1
PIRATES	2	2	0								4	1	0

OVERLOOKED AMIDST THE early Yankee pitching traumas was another
gritty performance from Vernon Law. Through three innings, the
thirty-year-old Pirate ace had retired eight of nine batters—working
rapidly in mowing down the Yankees like a buzz saw, despite an inability
to put full weight on his injured ankle. Seated behind home plate,
Mary Gray of suburban Penn Hills Township, a neighbor of Elroy and
Jean Face, echoed the sentiments of many in the crowd. "Bring it to
Pittsburgh, Vernon," said Mrs. Gray, sixty-five, again and again, as if
out on the mound, Law could hear her. "That's our boy, Vernon."

All Murtaugh wanted of Law was for him to stay sharp and throw
strikes for five innings—about two turns through the batting order—
so the Pirates could get to Face. With the heart of the Yankee batting
order due up in the fourth, the game was moving into its middle
innings and growing more tense with every minute. In the first two
Series games, Forbes Field concessionaires had already sold a whopping forty-eight thousand of the 50-cent souvenir program, with its
cover shot of the bearded Pirate mascot spinning about on a globe.
But for now, concession sales had tapered off, with most spectators,
consumed by the drama, glued to their seats.

In Section 23 of the bleachers overlooking the Yankee bullpen sat
sixteen-year-old Jean Oertel and her father, Byron, also from Penn
Hills Township. The Oertels had received two tickets to Game 7

through the Pirate ticket lottery, which Jean, then a sophomore at Penn Hills High School, says greatly disappointed her because she figured the Yankees would dispose of the Pirates long before then. But on the morning of Game 7, Jean's mother, Isabel, wrote a note to her teacher to excuse her from school. "Mom figured it was more important that I go to the World Series than to school for another day," Jean says. "God bless her and my dad." So that morning, Jean put on a dress and heels, and her father, a suit, tie, and hat, and together they took the bus to Forbes Field. "You dressed like that in those days, especially for a World Series game," recalls Jean, now a psychologist in Massachusetts. "People dressed up for special occasions."

In the press box, not far from the Oertels, sat the ballgame's Odd Couple—sportswriter Dick Schaap and his newest pal, the comedian Lenny Bruce. The unlikely pairing of *Newsweek*'s sports editor and the raunchy nightclub performer had come about the evening before Game 1, when Schaap encouraged a gaggle of New York newspapermen to catch Bruce's show at a suitably named nightclub, the Fallen Angel, on Washington Boulevard. An equal-opportunity insulter, Bruce played it up in front of the mostly New York crowd. The writers roared, while the few locals there sat stone-faced. When an unappreciative Pittsburgher heckled Bruce, the iconoclastic comedian responded with a stream of unprintable barbs that *Newsday* writer Stan Isaacs, who was there that night, vividly remembers.

"The man, whose name was Kalish, made the mistake of trying to one-up Bruce and the results were brilliant," Isaacs recalls. "It was Lenny Bruce at his iconoclastic best, which, sadly, didn't last as his drug addiction took over. But that night, Bruce was brilliant. We loved it. It was one of my most memorable memories of covering the World Series that year."

Bruce's sharp brand of humor captivated Schaap. The two men had grown up in the same town on Long Island, and they hit it off. So the evening before Game 7, Schaap invited Bruce to accompany him to the last game of the Series, which fell on Bruce's thirty-fifth birthday.

Though Bruce had never been to a big-league game, he took to the "theatricality of the game," Schaap wrote in his memoirs, particularly to the part when the two men wedged their way afterward into the winning locker room and were doused with champagne. But Bruce left soon thereafter to prepare for his performance that evening, the next-to-last of his stay in Pittsburgh. He never attended another game. Less than six years later, Bruce was dead at forty of a drug overdose.

Presenting a more sober portrait of Forbes Field Game 7 fandom was Mayor Joe Barr of Pittsburgh, seated in his field box with his friend, Assistant Police Superintendent Lawrence Maloney. The two men had also shared the box during Game 1, with Maloney wearing his full-dress uniform for the Pirates' victory. But when they switched to Governor Lawrence's box for Games 2 and 6, for which Maloney wore civilian clothes, the Pirates were manhandled. This time, the mayor and the superintendent, back in full regalia, had returned to their Game 1 seats. Anything to help.

So if rooting for the Yankees was like rooting for U.S. Steel—ironic given that that very steel company was based in Pittsburgh—what was it like cheering for the 1960 Pirates? Let us count the bad analogies: cheering for a plumbing and heating company? A hardware store? An all-night diner? Unlike the Yankees, the Pirates had no national following—none of the romance of the cuddlesome Cubs, the lovable losers of the National League, nor of the Red Sox, for whom losing was branded as noble and deeply meaningful by Boston highbrows. In a blue-collar town that was proud of it, the Pirates were a scrappy, no-nonsense team that was as much a part of the landscape as skyscrapers downtown (where the tallest was the thirty-eight-story Gulf Building, with its observation deck and funky wraparound neon beacon that blinked orange for fair skies and blue for foul), the coal barges that floated up the Monongahela, and the blast furnaces that lit up the night sky, along not just the Mon (pronounced "Mawn") but the Allegheny and Ohio rivers, too.

If the Yankees presented a button-down, corporate image, the Pirates were anything but—a blend of what *Time* magazine called "the shy and the brash, the pure and the profane . . . (men who) ridicule their differences with some of the sharpest locker-room needling in the majors." Well, why not? "The kidding relaxes the whole team," Don Hoak said. "That's good because baseball is a very simple game unless you make it tough. Just hit the damn ball and run to 1st. Just pick it up and throw to 1st."

What wasn't to like? In 1960, Elroy Face was the highest-paid Pirate player, earning $35,000. That was a stack of dough, but no more than a top executive at one of those big buildings downtown earned. There just wasn't the great divide that there is today in ballplayer salaries; people of all ranks could identify with Groat or Hoak, whose autographs were easily available after a game by standing outside the clubhouse door that emptied into the first-base concourse. And whereas many ballplayers today leave for their winter homes when the season ends, most of the established Pirate players in 1960 had settled in Pittsburgh year-round, thanks to local off-season jobs: Groat was a sales representative at Jessop Steel Company; Friend, a broker with Federated Investors, handled mutual funds; and Face was a union carpenter. As a Pittsburgher, you would want Elroy Face to redo your den, and maybe show your son how to grip a forkball. Imagine getting a sales call from Dick Groat? Yup, you'd take the call and probably brag about it for months afterward. Smart move, Jessop Steel.

In the age before *ESPN SportsCenter* began blasting highlights of every major-league game far and wide, and national broadcasts started to homogenize baseball, playing in small-market Pittsburgh could be a surprisingly intimate experience. The city was slightly off the radar— explaining to some degree why it took Bill Mazeroski so long to reach the Hall of Fame. "I just never saw him play," many writers said of Maz. If only they had.

In his lovely book *A Day in the Bleachers,* about Game 1 of the 1954 World Series, the day Willie Mays made his famous catch at the Polo Grounds, Arnold Hano gets one thing wrong. With a decidedly New York bias, Hano criticizes fans of several National League teams, including Pittsburghers, whom he labels as ignorant for harmlessly booing opposing pitchers who throw to first to keep a runner close. What he doesn't take into account is that many fans, and a much larger percentage of the crowd at the Polo Grounds that day, were children. What he fails to mention as well is that the small-market Pirates were by the late '50s drawing the league's third or fourth best annual attendance—and actually outdrew the Yankees in 1960 by more than 178,000 people. Ignorant? Maybe by New York standards. Passionate? You bet.

Then as now, Pittsburgh was more of a football town, a factory of memorable gridders. The Steelers have owned Pittsburgh since their Super Bowl glory of the '70s, but the city's devotion to baseball's Pirates in 1960 was comparable. That became crystal clear on Sunday, October 9, when thousands of people attend the Steelers-Giants game at Pitt Stadium, but also tuned to the Series radio broadcast, started cheering the three-run Pirate rally in Game 4 in New York. The bellowing started just as the Giants were driving into Steeler territory and created an ongoing wave of sound, which was out of context and confusing to the football players, in particular Giant quarterback George Shaw. A sympathetic referee called time, the crowd calmed down, and the football game resumed.

Bob Friend notes that interest in the Pirates had been building for quite some time—and pinpoints the exact year that the fog lifted for good as 1956. "Ralph Kiner did a lot to popularize the Pirates in the late '40s, establishing a lot of records and some magical moments," says Friend. "Good things were happening to us; I won the ERA title in '55, Dale Long (and his eight homers in as many games) caused a lot of excitement in 1956, and then we put it together in '60. We had great support from the area. You might call it a football town, but it's a great sports town, too. There's a lot of tradition."

Being a baseball fan in Pittsburgh in 1960 usually meant you were somewhere near a radio with Bob Prince talking . . . and talking . . . in the background, whether that somewhere was in a bar, at home, or in the car. Pittsburgh's population in 1960 was six hundred thousand, making it the nation's sixteenth largest city, but the place felt like a big version of a small town—not so much a metropolitan area as a collection of neighborhoods strung together. Leave town and you were from Pittsburgh, but stick close to home and you were from Mt. Lebanon, Aliquippa, or Crafton. Not that people traveled much in those days anyway—a weekend excursion was often to the observation deck at the airport—"Greater Pitt"—to watch the planes come and go. Landlocked and hundreds of miles from an ocean, Pittsburgh doesn't have the water tradition of other towns, where a weekend at the beach or the shore is no big deal.

"Pittsburgh is the town you can't wait to leave, and the town you can't wait to get back to," the city's very own former middleweight champ Billy Conn told Frank Deford in 1985 *Sports Illustrated* profile. Conn, who had once almost beat Joe Louis despite a 25-pound weight disadvantage, was in a position to know; he had traveled widely, practically owned the old Madison Square Garden in New York in the late '40s, and even lived in Las Vegas for a time, working as a greeter at the Stardust. But he always went home to the house on Denniston Avenue in Squirrel Hill that he bought in the summer of 1941 for $17,500.

Populated by practical, blue-collar people, many of whom were from families who had emigrated from Eastern Europe to work in the mills, Pittsburgh was a city where most jobs were grueling but delivered a steady paycheck. For the most part, Pittsburghers stuck with their own—the Irish on the Northside and in East Liberty; Poles and Slavs on the Southside; Germans on Troy Hill; and Italians in Bloomfield or Oakland, particularly in the hollow behind right field at Forbes

Field. Many Jews, originally in the Hill District, had by the 1950s moved to Squirrel Hill, replaced by African-Americans. Sticking close to home gave Pittsburgh the feel of a small town, where it was said that a guy could get sucker-punched on Friday night in East Liberty, and people all over town would know about it by Saturday.

This all gave Pittsburgh its own accent, rich sense of humor, and distinct jargon. It has been suggested that Pittsburghers have a collective inferiority complex to New York that wraps itself in fierce pride for the city's sports teams. That's half right, because Pittsburghers don't generally compare themselves to anyone—except maybe people from Cleveland—while embracing their working-class ethos and trading ethnic barbs about "Polacks" or "Hunkies," but with laughter and the understanding that a night out included the occasional fist-fight, which was always honored and quickly forgotten.

No wonder Mon Valley steelworkers took to worshiping a mythical figure named Joe Magarac. A kind of patron saint of Pennsylvania laborers, big Joe had well established credentials: Legend has it he could twist iron ingots with his bare hands, lived on a pile of ore next to a blast furnace, and once appeared out of nowhere to right a falling 50-ton crucible that would have killed scores of steelworkers. Though the origins of the Magarac legend have been forgotten, the most common story is that it started with a joke played on a reporter igno-rant of the fact that "magarac" is the Hungarian word for "jackass."

On Pittsburgh television stations, blow-dried anchor types were in short supply. The most popular, Bill Burns, looked like a teamster and had a voice to match. So did the backup voice of the 1960 Pirates, Paul Long, who later switched to news, where he became a beloved, longtime anchorman on WTAE. But they both delivered the news with gravity, insight, and occasional humor—and spent a combined seventy-four years in broadcasting.

Every morning, the *Post-Gazette* featured gossip columns by syndi-cated New York writers, but the glitz and glamour of New York seemed far away. Most Pittsburghers in 1960 didn't give a hoot and celebrated their own rich array of characters. Billy Conn was a beloved figure—admired as a local guy who roamed but ultimately stuck around—and remained a vibrant, vital presence around town, occasionally making the papers after taking exception to a remark passed in a bar and popping somebody.

Conn's great pal was a behemoth of an Irishman named Joey Diven. Known as the "White Knight of Oakland" or just "Big Guy," Diven stood 6'5", weighed nearly 300 pounds, and knew everyone worth knowing. A beefy, gruff Pittsburgh version of Zelig, Diven worked variously as a bodyguard, constable, Allegheny County detective, and beer salesman but seemed to have time to kill and a propensity to end up in the center of things—often seated on the banquet dais, at ringside, or loafing with a ballplayer.

Most of the Pirates befriended Diven—Bob Friend just grins and shakes his head when asked about him—and so did Hank Aaron, Art Rooney, and the Catholic Bishop of Pittsburgh, the Most Rev. John Wright. Joey could usually be found at Forbes Field, at an Oakland bar, or at the Carlton House downtown, where he'd sit in the back room and play cards. Damon Runyon would have loved Diven, who looked at life in black and white—show him friendship and you had a lifelong pal, but cross him and you might regret it. "You are who you hang with," Joey counseled kids. "It is better to be alone than in bad company." A man of strong loyalties, Joey once turned a restaurant upside down in Oakland after learning that Don Hoak had been roughed up there. Another time, he took on a half-dozen University of Pittsburgh football players on the eve of a game in defense of a friend he felt the players had slighted. Legend has it he led a Shetland Pony, of all things, into a bar along Forbes Avenue, where it ate the plants and ruined the carpet. The reason why is lost to history, but the story lives on.

Anger a Pittsburgh guy and you were a real "jag off." Pittsburgh guys didn't hang at the corner; they "loafed." Expecting rain? Don't forget your bumbershoot (umbrella). Snowy? Watch it: it could be slippy aut. And the 'Burgh's equivalent of "you" or the plural "you guys" or the southern "y'all"? It is the baffling "yunz" (sometimes spelled "yins"), as in "Yunz wanna go to the movies?"—a key component to the Pittsburgh's distinctive accent, a weird blend of Mid-Atlantic and Appalachian. Vowels don't stand a chance in Western Pennsylvania but are swallowed up as if they don't exist and mixed indiscriminately with consonants. After all, Billy Conn hadn't been the town's only great bawxer; there was Harry Greb, the "Pittsburgh Windmill," the middleweight champ in the '20s; and Fritzie Zivic, the "Croat Comet" from Lawrenceville, the featherweight champ in the early '40s. Need directions to the *Part* (Pirate) game? Head dawn to the *cawledge* (college) campus and look for parking *autside Car-NEG-gie* (outside Carnegie) Library. Be home early *'cause yunz* gotta work the long shift tomorrow *dawn* (down) the *still* (steel) mill. Finish up and there'll be plenty of time to hit the bar for *an Imp and an 'Arn* —Pittsburghese for the favored version of the boilermaker, a shot of Imperial whiskey chased with an Iron City beer.

Then as now, Pittsburghers had an innate ability to laugh at themselves, with nobody proving that point more than the wacky Rege Cordic, KDKA's hugely popular morning drive-time radio show host, whose stable of characters drew on a colorful cast of people he'd known as a boy in Hazelwood. Cordic kept Pittsburgh in stitches while enjoying a massive dominance in the ratings, with a lot of listeners never bothering to change the dial from the previous evening's baseball broadcast. The Pirates fueled the ratings, and Cordic responded by inventing characters like Carmen Monoxide and her lousy puns; Quick n' Easy O'Brien, a pickpocket; and Louie Adamcehvitz, the philosophical Slav garbage man.

At his peak, Cordic drew an astounding 85 percent of the local audience. Helping him achieve those ratings was his wacky sense of humor as he peddled Olde Frothingslosh beer, with "the foam on the bottom instead of the top," and Cordic Cardboard Coffee, "a delicate blend of domestic coffee and imported cardboard that will rival the taste of anything spewed forth from the automatic coffeemaker at the office or factory." Cordic offered no tired "Smoky City" jokes, instead making his listeners, as one critic wrote, "almost believe that Pittsburgh was the hip place to live."

Cordic started his run on KDKA in 1954, but it wasn't until the station picked up the Pirate games the following year that his ratings soared. "People would turn their radios off at night after listening to the ballgame and just turn on the morning," says Nellie King. Cordic's run would go all the way to 1965, when he left for the bright lights of Los Angeles, which he ended up not liking very much. "There's no there there," he said of his new home in Southern California. "It's like 20,000 Monroevilles."

Taking immense pride in their city, Pittsburghers honored not just the jocks but the successes of other locals, such as Dr. Jonas Salk and his staff, who just five years before had conquered polio in a drab, windowless lab at the University of Pittsburgh School of Medicine, just a few blocks from Forbes Field. Though Salk had moved by 1960 to California, his revolutionary inoculation program drew the attention of the world to Pittsburgh in the mid '50s. Dr. Benjamin Spock, whose *Common Sense Book of Baby and Child Care* became the bible of American mothers, had been at Pitt around the same time, as a professor in the early '50s. Fred Rogers and his television show for kids had been on the air locally for three years by 1960, and later became a national institution.

Pittsburgh celebrated its history—even the quirky bits. The tip of downtown known as "the Point," the triangle-shaped land where the city's three rivers come together, was the one-time site of Fort Duquesne: ground zero during the French and Indian War. That was the war that established British domination of North America, and where a young soldier named George Washington made his name. The city was home to the country's first gas station, a Gulf on Bigelow Boulevard. And KDKA, the Pirates' flagship station, became the world's first commercial radio station when it broadcast the Harding-Cox presidential election returns on November 2, 1920, from a shed housing a studio and transmitter atop the K Building of Westinghouse's East Pittsburgh plant. The following August, a young engineer named Harold Arlin scored another breakthrough— converting a phone into a microphone to broadcast the first major-league game on radio, a 9-5 Pirates' drubbing of the Phillies at Forbes Field. Arlin's dabbling into baseball was prescient; a half century later, his grandson Steve pitched for the San Diego Padres.

Pittsburgh always contributed far more than its demographic share to the national show-business talent pool. Locals marveled at the irony of how the little suburb of Canonsburg, 20 miles to the south, had developed not just one great crooner, Perry Como, but another, Bobby Vinton, only twenty-five in 1960 and already gaining a following. They took pride that people as varied as songwriter Stephen Foster and playwright George S. Kaufman came from Pittsburgh, as did artist Mary Cassatt, writer Gertrude Stein, and movie-star dancer Gene Kelly; just getting started at the time was a pasty-skinned kid from Dawson Street in Oakland named Andy Warhola, later Warhol. Natives could comprise a whole wing of the Big Band and Jazz Hall of Fame, from Billy Eckstine to Stanley Turrentine, Artie Blakey, Billy Strayhorn, Mary Lou Williams, Ahmad Jamal, and George Benson. There had even been a hit song about Pittsburgh, back in 1952, the one that started, "There's a pawnshop on a corner in Pittsburgh, Pennsylvania," though neither the writer, Bob Merrill, nor the singer, Guy Mitchell, had any connections to the area.

These were all important ties to a sense of identity in a city often mistreated by history and misunderstood by visitors. Periodic labor troubles clouded most people's perceptions of Pittsburgh, as in the tragic

Homestead strike of 1892, when three hundred Pinkerton detectives battled mill workers, leaving sixteen people dead and scores wounded. Floods were a more constant menace, most recently back in 1936, when on St. Patrick's Day the three rivers rose to more than 30 feet at the Point and even higher in other low-lying areas like the "Bottoms" in McKees Rocks. Just as jarring were the derisive and often-quoted comments from famous visitors, like novelist Anthony Trollope, for whom Pittsburgh was "the blackest place . . . I ever saw." The biographer James Parton did him one better, calling the city, "Hell with the lid taken off," a phrase that unfortunately stuck when the muckraker Lincoln Steffens used it as the title of his exposé of the city's shame.

In a sense, the Pirates' success, as the Steelers would prove a few years ahead, became a symbol of the "new" Pittsburgh, matching a new, more upbeat view that residents had of their city in 1960. For years, the smoke and grime had left the sky thick with smog and darkness, so much so that downtown streetlights in the '40s often blazed through the day. For the most part, the locals put up with the pollution, knowing it was a by-product of a booming economy; "black sugar," it was called. But after World War II, something miraculous happened: Casting aside their traditional differences, the unions, labor leaders, city fathers, and newspapers had formed a working group to clean up the air, control flooding, and rebuild decayed parts of the city.

On one side was Pittsburgh's Democratic mayor and later governor David Lawrence, elected as mayor in 1945 and known to Pittsburghers forever after as "Davy." On the other were the largely Republican, probusiness members of the Allegheny Conference on Community Development, whose primary mover, Richard King Mellon, was a publicity-shy executive who controlled a vast banking empire. Driven by a simple desire to help their hometown, they formed an unlikely but powerful team—the old-fashioned Irish ward leader and the blue blood who would rather be fox hunting.

So the wrecking balls got swinging and down went a lot of old, rotting buildings, and with them Pittsburgh's reputation as a dark, industrial wasteland. City Hall was demolished, and so were the Penn Avenue Warehouse; the Wabash Terminal, vacant since a fire had nearly destroyed it back in 1946; with more than thirty-seven hundred other buildings deemed an eyesore. Even Forbes Field was a target from the mid-1950s onward, with city planners proposing a new municipal ballpark, first in Monument Hill on the Northside before settling on an area by the banks of the Allegheny River facing downtown. Their vision would come true eventually with nearby Three Rivers Stadium. Today, the area is a parking lot serving both Heinz Field and PNC Park.

There were mistakes, to be sure, in transforming the city. Great chunks of older neighborhoods like the Hill District and East Liberty were leveled, and not always for the better. Deflecting challenges from angry property holders, Pittsburgh's urban redevelopment program became a steamroller, uprooting more than fifteen hundred businesses and five thousand families. The program was particularly hard on African-Americans in the Hill District, where hundreds of blocks were cleared from the "Lower" Hill section, just across Center Avenue from downtown, site of the Civic (now Mellon) Arena. The razing forever altered the Hill, where jazz once flourished and where August Wilson would set his memorable plays exploring the African-American urban experience.

Halfway through the 1950s, a new skyline had risen, filled with glittering office buildings and plazas. The rivers were cleaner, thanks to pollution abatement programs. Apartment buildings shot up along Grandview Avenue on Mount Washington, with the bluff offering dramatic vistas of downtown. The Point drew particular attention as buildings were ripped down and replaced by a park and one of America's most striking skylines. Drive toward town from the airport and pass through the Fort Pitt Tunnel where the Monongahela River meets the Ohio, and the city hits you all at once—a sudden and dramatic urban tableau. Even the *New York Times* was impressed, calling Pittsburgh "the only city in America with an entrance."

Visiting Pittsburgh in 1956 on assignment was former *Life* photographer W. Eugene Smith, who had covered wars and traveled the globe, but who was instantly captivated by the city's kaleidoscope of rugged beauty, refreshing working-class ethos, and spirited people. Smith arrived intending to spend three weeks in Pittsburgh but started shooting pictures and instead stayed for years. His stunning collection of nearly seven thousand prints, most of them black-and-white and some collected in a 2001 book, *Dream Street: W. Eugene Smith's Pittsburgh Project,* provide a Hopperesque vision of the city. There, in all its urban glory, is Pittsburgh: the starkness of its open hearths, its steep, spectacular landscape dotted with small houses and the onion domes of orthodox churches, its moody rivers crisscrossed by bridges, its Walnut Street nightlife, and even the scene outside the Home Plate Cafe at a Pirate game.

Mill life and labor were the hot-button issues that dominated Pittsburgh in 1960. A crippling steel strike had shut down local mills for 116 days in 1959, as strikes had many times in the past, often with violent consequences. Big labor's support was the reason so many politicians made Western Pennsylvania a frequent stop when running for national office. Pittsburghers took pride that the two candidates for president that autumn, Vice President Richard M. Nixon and Senator John F. Kennedy of Massachusetts, hadn't just visited Pennsylvania several times during the campaign, but actually had launched their national careers years in 1947 in nearby McKeesport. That spring, the two freshmen members of Congress had debated the Taft-Hartley labor reform bill there, and then by sharing a berth on the sleeper train back to Washington formed a genuine friendship.

Most coal, coke, and steel plants fielded baseball teams, which often played on makeshift diamonds in the shadow of the blast furnace or slag heap. Sports gave immigrants a way to assimilate to their new surroundings and a chance to stand out from the drudgery of a dead-end mill job, or just to enjoy an afternoon out. Immigrants could also join the Homestead Library Athletic Club, the Polish Falcons, or any of the other dozens of clubs, where you could always find a pickup basketball game and a whole philosophy that stressed the importance of exercise on character. The Falcons' motto: "A Sound Mind in a Healthy Body." And it was among these organizations around Western Pennsylvania that sports sowed the seeds of the region's legacy, which, as University of Pittsburgh historian Rob Ruck wrote, "as much as steel, has cast an indelible image of Pittsburgh to the world."

* * *

Nurtured on mill teams and the sandlots, athletes from Western Pennsylvania played baseball and football, boxed and sometimes did all three. One of the best was Art Rooney, a multisport star and the son of a Northside bar owner, who, as a boxer representing the Pittsburgh Athletic Association, once whipped Olympic gold medalist Sammy Mosberg. Turning to football in 1933, Rooney used his racetrack winnings and, taking advantage of a revision in the state's blue laws that allowed pro sports on Sundays, bought a franchise in the fledging National Football League. The tough, hard-hitting team he fielded, which he called first the Pirates, then the Steelers, lost a lot more often than they won.

Organizing a baseball team from a group of skilled black workers at the Homestead Steel Works, Cumberland Posey developed the nucleus of a group that became the greatest Negro League team in history. They were the Homestead Grays, winners of nine Negro National League pennants in a row and home to legends like Josh Gibson, Oscar Charleston, and Smokey Joe Williams. When Hill District gambler Gus Greenlee bought control of another black team, the Crawfords, in 1930 and signed Gibson and Charleston along with Satchel Paige and Cool Papa Bell, Pittsburgh became the capital of black baseball, giving the city, for a time in the late '30s, *three* major-league–caliber teams.

Meantime, the region continued to produce extraordinary athletes in all sports arenas with the efficiency of the J&L rod mill. From nearby Latrobe came the charismatic golfer Arnold Palmer, already the winner of two Masters. Two college football players from the area had won the Heisman Trophy at Notre Dame: Connelsville's Johnny Lujack in '47 and Leon Hart, from Turtle Creek, in '49. Former Pitt All-American linebacker Joe Schmidt, from Brentwood, had helped lead the Detroit Lions to NFL championships in '53 and '57. A sore spot with Pittsburgh fans was how the habitually dismal Steelers— dubbed "S.O.S." for "Same Old Steelers" in the local vernacular— had inexplicably discarded the great Johnny Unitas from Mount Washington. Drafting Unitas out of Louisville in 1955, the Steelers considered him too small and, according to Steeler Coach Walt Kies-ling, too "dumb" to make it in the NFL. Could it have been a case of sour grapes, since he had beaten out Art Rooney's son Dan as the city's top Catholic high school all-star quarterback? (No, not at all.) Released by the Steelers, Unitas worked construction and picked up a few extra dollars playing for the semipro Bloomfield Rams and then signed as a free agent with the Colts. Anyone could recite what hap-pened next: Unitas won titles—two before 1960—and became foot-ball's best quarterback.

"The Steelers are hard to take—like castor oil and taxes," declared the *Sun-Telegraph* in 1959. Indeed, the Steelers' inability to recognize Unitas' gifts fit right into the team's startling inability to recognize young talent, especially among its quarterbacks; others let go included Sid Luckman, Jim Finks, Jack Kemp, and Len Dawson. The '60 team appeared to be the Same Old Steelers—the usual collection of retreads and former stars, like quarterback Bobby Layne, and headed to another sub-.500 season. But the University of Pittsburgh had nabbed a good one—Aliquippa's Mike Ditka, a 6'3" steamroller of a tight end, a preseason All-American who could often be found wearing his letter jacket and loafing at Pirate home games. Other local athletes with promising futures were Beaver Falls High quarterback Joe Namath—described by the *Press* as a "tremendous ball-handler, passer and runner"—and a hard-throwing seventeen-year-old lefty pitcher from Central Catholic named Sam McDowell. That May, the man they'd one day call "Sudden Sam" had drawn a flock of scouts from thirteen big-league clubs to the school's dusty baseball field a half mile or so from Forbes Field.

Ah, Forbes Field. Long the focal point of the city's sporting life, it was a ballpark where most of the thirty-eight thousand or so seats were decent—except if you happened to sit behind a pillar or in the upper left-hand corner of the bleachers, which offered a lovely panorama of the field, except for home plate. Like the city, Forbes was a practical, utilitarian place—not handsome in the conventional sense, but a little quirky and built with thought and foresight.

As the major league's most spacious park—a no-hitter was never thrown there—Forbes had so much room in the outfield that the batting cage was stored *on the field* in deepest center. In 1912, Pirate outfielder Chief Wilson belted an unworldly thirty-six triples, all but twelve of them at Forbes Field—a big-league record that will almost certainly never be broken. Sit up high and you could see all the way to Flagstaff Hill in Schenley Park, another burst of green. Sit close to the field and you could hear the infield chatter. There was no canned music, organ, or exploding scoreboard at Forbes Field, meaning fans could focus more on the game, helped only by the friendly voice of public-address announcer Art McKennan as he announced the batting orders and the batters. Nor did any billboards mar the picturesque red brick and ivy of the outfield walls; the only exception had been during World War II, when a sign for war savings bonds rode the left-fence wall. The park's sole ads, for Duquesne Beer ("Four '6-places' to a case, . . . Easy to carry! Easy to cool!"), were understated, relegated to spaces atop the exit ramps.

The field was spacious, but the dugouts and clubhouses were

anything but. Visiting teams occupied the third-base dugout but reached their clubhouse through the Pirates' dugout, which often created a postgame logjam of baseball humanity. The clubhouses were not the kind of places you'd want to pass the time: "The Forbes Field clubhouses were awful, just awful—cramped, crowded and steamy," recalls writer Maury Allen. That goes for pitchers who, on leaving the game, couldn't watch the rest of the game on the clubhouse TV because there wasn't one. At least the radio worked.

Visiting players complained about the ballpark's rocky, pebble-strewn infield. "That infield was like concrete," says Yankee shortstop Joe DeMaestri. "There was a crust on it and when you ran, you broke the crust and a runner's footprints practically left holes in the ground. You had to keep smoothing it out." But the Forbes Field infield "was perfect for us," claims Pirate shortstop Dick Groat, a groundball hitter, who said that the hard surface and low cut of the grass made ground balls come off the bat more quickly. "If we'd had high grass and a slow infield, we'd have never won in '60," Groat says.

Most got to Forbes Field on streetcars or buses. Parking was limited, except at gas stations and private lots around Oakland. The Carnegie Library lot was meter parking and almost always full, but one option was to park in the front yards of the small row houses facing the park on Boquet Street, where for $1, residents would direct you with a blizzard of hand signals to a spot on their lawn, pocket your bill, and then go back to their front porches to listen to the rest of the pregame show on KDKA. At least you could count on knowing the time while at Forbes Field, thanks to the enormous Longines clock with the speaker horns on its top that rode the top of the giant scoreboard in left field. Nor was going to a Pirate game in 1960 likely to drain your bank account at $3 for a box, $2.50 for reserved, and $1.50 for general admission. For $1, the bleachers down the third-base line that overlooked the visitor's bullpen were a bargain, and spacious enough to fit most every Cub Scout pack or VFW outing.

Forbes Field was already the NL's oldest park in 1960, but its bandbox size was typical of most league parks of the era. Former *Sports Illustrated* photographer Neil Leifer recalls not just Forbes but other cramped, quirky parks like Crosley Field in Cincinnati, Connie Mack in Philadelphia, Chicago's Wrigley Field, and Sportsman's Park in St. Louis, where the seating capacities didn't stretch beyond thirty-nine thousand. Built without field photo boxes, these old parks left photographers to do their best by crouching in the aisles, provided they found a willing usher and didn't block anyone's view, or by claiming a spot in front of a pillar, of which there were many, to get a clear view of the action. What a contrast this was to the bigger AL parks in New York, Detroit, Cleveland, and Baltimore.

Duquesne wasn't the only beer to sponsor the Pirates. Iron City, which had a big plant in Bloomfield and had just come out with pop-top cans, and Rolling Rock ("brewed with pure mountain spring water") out in Latrobe ("LAY-trobe"), about 50 miles east of Pittsburgh, were the others. Pirate fans knew the sponsors and most of the jingles by heart, from beer to Sealtest Ice Cream (with gallons given away for home runs) to Atlantic Gasoline, which "keeps your car on the go, go go!"

If the ballpark remained relatively free of advertising, the scorecard didn't. A blizzard of local sponsors plastered ads in the 15-cent program, all of which gave a good sense of where Pittsburghers in 1960 could head after the game. Oakland itself was full of bars and eateries, the most notable of which was just two blocks up Forbes Avenue at Frankie Gustine's, owned and operated by the Pirate third sacker of the '40s, a three-time all-star known for his blazing starts and cold finishes at the plate. Opened in '52, Gustine's was nothing like Toots Shor's in New York, which bristled with big names and big-town sophistication: Here was a nice, authentic sports bar offering "major league meals at minor league prices," sports photos on the wall, a handsome bar, and a lot of opinions. Gustine's became a favored hangout for fans and players alike, a joint where you could always place a bet and get the latest scuttlebutt.

Half a block from Gustine's was the spanking new, elegantly named "Original Hot Dog Shop," aka the "Dirty O"—the Nathan's Famous of Pittsburgh. A stone's throw away was the new Ascot Room of the Webster Hall ("No End of Pleasure"); while back downtown was the Flame Steakhouse at 5th and Liberty, where an 11-ounce sirloin with a baked potato, salad, and a "piping hot" French roll was yours for $1.19.

Forbes Field was central to Oakland, in large part because so many of the men who lived in its small row houses supplemented their incomes as ushers. Sadly, the neighborhood had recently lost its other arena, the old car barn–turned–skating rink called Duquesne Gardens at Craig and 5th. The "Gardens," as it was fondly known, was torn down in 1956, but not before a generation of roller derbies, dance marathons, fights, circuses, and minor-league hockey games rolled through. Squeezing in about five thousand at capacity, the arena had been home to many a Billy Conn tussle and, from '36 to its demise, to the American Hockey League Hornets. The Hornets perished with the arena but would make a comeback in '61 with the construction of the Civic Arena and play until the NHL Penguins arrived in 1967. In 1998, the part of Craig Street that once housed the Gardens was renamed Billy Conn Boulevard.

Adding a small-town, folksy air to Pirate baseball was the team's radio broadcaster: the one and only "Gunner," Bob Prince. It's almost unfair to label Prince as simply the broadcaster, for he was far more: the Pirates' unofficial ambassador, a one-man PR brigade, a cultural icon, and the team's most visible symbol. The Gunner's mantra was to mix the action on the field with a stream of irreverent stories, rants, and schmaltzy birthday and anniversary wishes to just about everyone from Jeannette to Johnstown. Prince was your crazy uncle, a motormouth who rambled endlessly about everything from the flowers that bloomed in Schenley Park to the perils of driving in fog. You'd learn about his friends—who was getting married, who was celebrating an anniversary—and his thoughts on college football, all of it punctured by his decisive Pirate home-run call: "You can kiss it good-bye!"

Rambling was in Prince's blood. An Army brat whose father, Frederick, had been a West Point football star, the Gunner, by his own count, had attended fourteen or fifteen schools before graduating from Schenley High in Oakland. A superb athlete, Prince lettered in swimming at Pitt, dropped out, enrolled at Stanford, then wound up at the University of Oklahoma, where he swam again and finally earned a degree in business. Thinking he'd be a lawyer, he went to Harvard Law School but dropped out and went back to Pittsburgh to be a radio host.

Chances are Prince wouldn't have made a good lawyer; he'd have gotten sidetracked. Joining the Pirate WWSW broadcast team in 1947, Prince became an understudy to the beloved Rosey Rosewell, the team's longtime radio voice. An earlier, softer incantation of Prince as the face of the team, Rosewell was noted for his own distinctive homer call: "Open the window, Aunt Minnie," Rosey would yell in describing a Pirate blast, "here it comes!" This was in the days when road games were "re-created" by broadcasting the action—sound effects included—from a studio while reading game information on the Western Union ticker, all of which gave Prince the freedom to fill the dead periods by focusing on his strength: telling stories.

Albert Kennedy "Rosey" Rosewell had earned his moniker. A cheerful, gregarious man, he wrote a book of poetry (naturally) called *Rosey Reflections,* was hokey to the core, and never pretended to be anything but a shameless Pirates fan. He was discreet on only one question: never revealing the identity of Aunt Minnie, who was probably fictitious. Rosey loved everyone except one person: Prince, whose growing popularity he resented. But the Gunner bided his time, absorbing what he could (which included using just the barest of statistics) and adhering to Rosey's cardinal rule: Make it as fun as possible, because first and foremost, baseball was entertainment. Seldom did Prince carry anything into the press box but a scorecard, a pencil, and a rich repository of stories. "Rosey taught me an important lesson," the Gunner once said. "If you're losing 14-2 in the 2nd inning, you've got to keep the people interested with funny stories, names and reminiscences. You can't be interested about who hit .280 in 1943."

Branch Rickey, the Pirates' general manager in the early '50s, didn't like Prince either. Stiff and humorless, Rickey couldn't understand the young man's appeal, didn't see the need of spinning anecdotes in a broadcast at the expense of dry analysis. But when Rosewell died in 1955—the same year that KDKA outbid WWSW for the Pirate broadcasting rights—the Gunner got the Pirates' top job and laid on the schmaltz. A Pirate nipped at first was out "by a gnat's eyelash." A sharp single through the heavy Forbes field infield was "an alabaster blast." A slumping Pirate was in need of some "hidden vigorish." And perhaps the Gunner's signature call: his late-inning, on-air pleading for "a bloop and a blast," which the Pirates of 1960, with their knack for winning late, seemed to provide. Most fans loved it, and so did the players, for whom Prince was a "homer," or devoted local fan, and an eccentric sidekick—especially after his celebrated, and evidently sober, late-night 1957 dive from the third floor into the pool at the Chase Hotel in St. Louis, to settle a bet.

The Gunner pegged ballplayers with goofy nicknames that stuck—Skinner was "Doggie" for his long face, a name actually left over from his Marine Corps days, while Virdon was the "Quail" and Harvey Haddix, the "Kitten," so named for his resemblance to Harry "The Cat" Brecheen, who had been his pitching coach in his Cardinal days. Okay, it was a stretch, but it worked, as did the splendid moniker for the May pitching pickup, Wilmer "Vinegar Bend" Mizell, named for the Alabama hamlet, population thirty-seven, where he was raised. In

return, Prince schooled many of the younger players in how to talk to
the media and got them involved in his favorite charity, the Allegheny
Valley School for Exceptional Children, for which he raised more than
$4 million in his lifetime. Fluent in Spanish, Prince was particularly
giving to black and Hispanic players; Clemente in particular became a
close friend.

Some preferred Prince's more standard sidekicks—Jim Woods,
nicknamed "Possum," and Paul Long, the future newscaster. No,
the Gunner wasn't for everybody—"Shut up, Prince!" more than
one person was heard to scream at the KDKA booth in a voice loud
enough to be heard by listeners. He *could* be exasperating—as
during one spring evening when he got caught up in describing the
flora and fauna of Schenley Park. Turning to public-address
announcer Art McKennan, Prince wanted to know what kind of
trees were in the park. So McKennan called the city's director of
parks and found they were in fact honey locusts, which prompted
the Gunner to ramble on another few minutes. Then the phone
rang, with the irate general manager, Joe L. Brown, on the line:
"For God's sake, Bob, give the score once in awhile!" he cried. "To
hell with those honey locusts!"

Pittsburgh adored Prince, honey locusts and all. Walk past the row
houses of the Southside on a soft summer evening in 1960, and his
voice boomed from a hundred radios on stoops, on front porches,
and in living rooms. "You could walk down the streets anywhere in
Western Pennsylvania and listen to the game coming from radios of
fans sitting on their front porches and following a Pirates game
without missing a beat," recalls Nellie King, who became Prince's
broadcasting partner in 1967. The fact that KDKA, the world's first
radio station, was the region's most powerful radio station on the AM
dial embellished his popularity, as did the lack of air-conditioning, of
all things. "People had to sit on their porches because it was cool out
there and too hot to sit inside," King says. "You either listened to

Pirates baseball with Bob Prince and Jim Woods or you didn't listen at all. And believe me, they listened."

The Gunner called Forbes Field the "House of Thrills"—turning it into the equivalent of the courthouse square, the community block party where everyone gathered and had a good time. Forbes was a destination, even for the collection of well-dressed retirees who would *not* attend the game, content merely to line the row of park benches in Schenley Plaza at night and soak in the buzz of the crowd. Visit Forbes Field and you'd see a true cross-section of the city, everybody from the dressed-up business elite in the rows of boxes to those on bowling league outings and mill socials, many of whom would take off their shirts on hot, sunny days to soak up the rays in the bleachers. Leaving the ballpark after the game, many would choose to walk out onto the edge of the field, traipse along the warning track, and depart through the big "Iron Gate" in right-center field. During the dismal years of the '50s, the Pirates remained a vital community asset, thanks in part to Prince. "Come out to the ballpark; there's plenty of seats available," he would plead as late as the third inning—and by golly, a few more *would* turn up.

More than anything, Prince was an unabashed homer, calling the team "Our Bucs" and croaking after each win, in his voice made raspy from too many cigarettes, "We had 'em alllll the way!" Out-of-town critics panned his work—the *Sporting News* once called him "glaringly biased." The Gunner could care less. "Who do I broadcast for, the Pennsylvania Turnpike?" he asked. "If I did, I'd tell you about the charm of the tollbooths. I broadcast for the Pittsburgh Pirates. They belong to every fan in Pittsburgh."

* * *

Although there were no statistics in 1960 on the rate at which base hits by the heart of a team's order increased over the course of a game—especially on their second and third at-bats. Experienced hitters, after seeing what a pitcher was throwing and where the umpire had established the strike zone, could change the course of a game in a hurry.

The Yankees were down by four runs, but their deep repository of firepower meant there was no cause for panic. Here in the top of the fourth, no Yankee had yet struck out. And the New Yorkers were certainly getting their hacks, like the one back in the first when Berra could easily have sent a ringing double down the left-field line into the corner had it not been for Hoak's smothering play. Richardson's fly to left in the third was drilled but hadn't dropped. The hits would come and so would the breaks.

For the Yankees, the immediate challenge was an opposing pitcher who, sore ankle or not, appeared to be at the top of his game. Through three innings, Law had deftly changed speeds, setting the Yankees up with fastballs and getting them to commit and lunge at changeups, most of which they popped up early in the count. Law was also getting his first pitch to batters over the plate for strikes—a sure sign that he was in command—and causing some Yankees to swing early in the count.

But here were Kubek, Maris, and Mantle leading off, so Law would have to stay sharp to preserve the four-run Pirate lead. These were the Yankees, after all, and not the Indians or the Orioles or the Tigers. Finding a way to win was part of the team's mystique—what Maury Allen calls a version of "New York arrogance"—an attitude, mirrored by many in the press, that these were the Yankees, with whom no other team could compete. "The Yankees always went into the World Series with the feeling that this is routine," Allen says, "and that 'we'll make our $4,000 share because we'll win it.' "

Law started Kubek off with a letter-high fastball for strike one. Then he changed speeds, getting the Yankee shortstop to break his bat in sending a weak pop-up toward shortstop, where Groat backed up a step, moved slightly to his right, and squeezed his mitt on the ball for the first out.

Now came the real challenge. Jumping on Law's first pitch, a fastball, Maris sent a line shot—"a clothes liner," as Thompson called it—but it headed directly at Clemente in right field. Three pitches in the fourth had netted two outs. The crowd roared, but as giddy as they felt being four runs up, these *were* the Yankees, a team against which no lead was safe.

No New York batter emphasized that point like Mantle. Perhaps more than anyone in baseball, he feasted on pitchers in his second and third at-bats in a game, in large part because he was one of the game's handful of 1960-era switch-hitters and the first great power hitter to hit from both sides of the plate. It all fed the legend of Mickey Mantle: Taught by his father to switch-hit, the Yankee superstar considered himself a better right-handed batter but actually hit more home runs from the left side. His astounding abilities at the plate single-handedly transformed the art of switch-hitting, from slaps and singles by a few specialized batters to shots of pure power.

Never one to analyze pitchers, Mantle relied instead on instinct and a prodigious blend of speed and skill to wear them down. In retirement, Mantle recalled his conversation at the 1956 All-Star Game with Ted Williams, who used his encyclopedic memory to analyze what he did at the plate on virtually every pitch, depending on the pitcher, the count, and even the wind conditions.

"Ted liked to talk to other hitters and ask them their theories, things that he might be able to apply and use himself," Mantle said. "He was always asking questions, looking for new theories on hitting, telling his own theories, anything to learn more about hitting and maybe improve. He started asking me which was my power hand, which hand did I use to guide the bat. And when I left him, I started thinking about all the things he told me, and I didn't get a hit for about twenty-five at-bats."

But Mantle understood his strengths. Wielding his 34^1/$_4$ -inch long Louisville Slugger 125 Pro Model, which weighed 31.4 ounces—the bat company sent two bats to each Series player in those days—he seemed to anticipate what Law was about to offer: It was a big, roundhouse curve that the Mick met squarely and torched between first and second for a single, his ninth base hit of the Series.

Headed to the plate was Berra, always swinging two bats, which made him look smaller as he tossed one aside just prior to stepping to bat. Berra was swinging early as well, hoping to jump-start his team back into the game. He swung hard at Law's first pitch, a curve, but only caught a piece and fouled it straight back at the screen. Strike one. Then he took a fastball outside for ball one. Law was giving him heat, as if to dare him, saying, "Here's what I have, so let's see what you have."

Yogi took the bait, swung hard again at the 1-1, and sent another laser down the right-field line, which Clemente charged and caught with one hand near the corner for the third out. Twice, Berra had scorched the ball hard but come up short. The Pirates had survived the Yankee fourth.

* * *

The teams changed quickly in what was a brisk game to that point. On NBC Radio, Thompson read an ad for Gillette Super Blue Blades "Words can't do justice to the comfort you get. . . . It's almost like wiping your beard away"—which could be yours at 69 cents for a dispenser of ten and $1 for fifteen. In contrast to today's postseason games, with their seemingly endless ads between innings, these teams were ready to go within ninety seconds—about a third of the time it takes today. Judging by current standards, sports marketing in 1960 was prehistoric.

Could Shantz continue to stop the Pirates in the fourth, as he had the previous inning? He didn't have to wait long to find out, with the top batter, Burgess, sending Shantz's first pitch on the ground to second, where Richardson took his time to throw out the lead-footed Pirate catcher by four steps.

Due up were Hoak and Mazeroski, the Pirates' seventh and eighth hitters, who gave unusual depth to the bottom of the Pittsburgh batting order. Greeting the feisty Hoak with more noise than usual was the Forbes Field crowd, appreciative of the third baseman's substantial contribution thus far: his great fielding play in the first inning and his walk that scored the Pirates' second run in the next. Nicknamed "Tiger" by Bob Prince for his competitive disposition on the field, the thirty-two-year-old red-headed third baseman had a thin face that gave him the appearance of a hawk. Filled with "pugnacious drive," as Roy Terrell of *Sports Illustrated* put it, Hoak was the team's spiritual center, its spark plug, and a fitting bookend to quiet team leaders like Groat and Law.

Hoak's qualities appealed to Pennsylvanians, who appreciated grit; at the time, their state still produced the most big leaguers and would until the late 1980s when it was finally passed by California. While Groat was a born-and-bred Pittsburgher, Hoak grew up in the northern Pennsylvania hamlet of Roulette, population fifteen hundred. Raised only four hours from Pittsburgh meant Hoak was practically a native—a point drilled home repeatedly by Prince, who took these things seriously. Hoak had even taken up with a local woman—not just anyone, but the popular singer and movie star Jill Corey, the former Norma Jean Speranza from the nearby coal-mining town of Avonmore, whom *Life* magazine had heralded back in '53 in a cover story on her "Cinderella life" and appeal.

They had met that summer at Forbes Field, where Corey was publicizing her upcoming gig at the Vogue Terrace, and quickly became Pittsburgh's golden couple. "He knew me, knew where I was playing and told me that he was going to come and see me perform," Corey remembers of their first meeting. "And I asked, 'What do *you* do?' Don told me he plays third base, so I made him point to the bag as a joke. 'So *that's* your position,' I told him."

But Hoak knew Corey. A confirmed fan, he had once hired a bus while playing with the Reds to take his teammates to the drive-in to see Corey in the film *Senior Prom*. Separated from his wife, Hoak stuck to his word and was in the audience that night at the Vogue Terrace, seated next to her family with full knowledge that Corey would be out at the intermission to see them.

At intermission, there were introductions all around. Then Hoak got Corey on the dance floor, where he quickly spun her around and whispered in her ear that he was going to marry her. "That's a little complicated," Corey remembers telling her dance partner, "since I'm engaged to a Brazilian diplomat."

Hoak persisted, asking for her telephone number. Corey refused. He invited Corey to a game, which she attended in the company of her sister and brother-in-law. Then several weeks later, while performing a show in Covington, Kentucky, near Cincinnati, Corey was dressed in a bright, full-length orange feather boa and was headed into a spotlight on stage when she heard snickers and giggles coming from the audience.

"Something was wrong; I thought my coat might be ripped or that I might be wearing one black shoe and one white shoe," Corey thought to herself. With the club bathed in darkness, she asked that the lights be turned up, so she could get to the root of the problem. That became quickly apparent: Don Hoak was seated stage left at a table adorned with a white tablecloth, a bottle of champagne on ice, and two dozen red roses.

"What are *you* doing here?" Corey asked.

" 'Well, you never gave me your number,' " said the ballplayer, in town to play the Reds.

"People in the audience were roaring," Corey says. "Because he had played with Cincinnati, he knew the club owner and could set something like that up. Nobody else could have arranged it."

Some weeks later, Corey was performing at a club in Hot Springs, Arkansas, and heard some off-key notes emanating from the trumpet section of the band. Turning to the band with puzzlement and concern, she found the trumpet-playing culprit: Hoak. How bad was he? "He was a much better ballplayer than a trumpet player, I'll tell you that," says Corey.

But despite how poorly Hoak played the trumpet, his persistence and sense of humor had paid off. "Okay, okay," Corey told him. "I give up. I'll give you my number." And with that, Jill Corey, the star of the NBC TV show *Your Hit Parade,* broke up with the Brazilian diplomat in favor of Pittsburgh's favorite third baseman.

Hoak played every game hard. "If I'm not tired when I leave the ballpark, then I haven't played a good game," he said. Competitive and belligerent, he had arrived in Pittsburgh in the big '59 deal with the Reds, the one that that also brought Burgess and Harvey Haddix. Though the Pirates dropped their first five games in '59, an ominous start to a shaky season, Hoak was a force from the get-go and still hadn't missed a game in more than two seasons. Hoak had an inner drive to be on the field, a point driven home on the evening of Saturday, August 13, when he went for a swim at a friend's party and gashed his right foot between his second and third toes while climbing the ladder from the pool.

Hoak had suffered a major injury. One of the guests at the party was a doctor who volunteered to accompany Hoak to the hospital to get stitched up. But the Pirate third baseman wouldn't hear of it, demanding that the physician stitch him up right there, without anesthesia. So the doctor did, sewing up his foot with eight stitches.

Knowing he'd be shelved if Danny Murtaugh and the team training staff knew about the injury, Hoak fired off another request, this one to everyone at the party, which included Bill Virdon, Bob

Friend, and Gino Cimoli. "I don't want a word of this to get out," he insisted. No one crossed him—and the next afternoon, Hoak played all twenty innings of a marathon extra-inning doubleheader-sweep of the Cardinals, and even drove in the winning run in the eleven-inning nightcap. Wearing an old pair of spikes because his regular shoe wouldn't fit over his swollen, discolored right toe, Hoak winced through the pain. Several stitches became undone; by the end of the day, his right sock was soaked in blood.

The Pirate beat writers could have blathered about Hoak's injury. But they didn't, taking refuge in an unwritten code with the players to keep their reports to what happened on the field. In New York, a mob of reporters, driven by competition, would gather in a scrum around the stars and quote their every utterance. That wasn't the case in small-market Pittsburgh, where writers from the city's three daily papers—down to two after the *Post-Gazette* had purchased the *Sun-Telegraph* that spring—were the only ones to travel with the team.

Les Biederman of the *Press* and Jack Hernon of the *Post-Gazette* were homers who, like Bob Prince, gave Pirate ballplayers the benefit of the doubt. Experienced baseball men—Biederman, an Ohio State graduate, had been on the Pirate beat since 1938—they stuck to the script. That meant adhering to that unwritten code of baseball's small-market beat reporting, and writing about what players and managers did on the field, leaving out the occasional naughty bits, like drinking or women-chasing. Falling mostly in line were the two papers' sports editors, Chet Smith of the *Press* and Al Abrams of the *Post-Gazette*, who filed long analytical columns about every aspect of the pennant race and would jump on the front office, but rarely took the players to task.

Most responsible for the code was the long shadow of one Charles J. "Chilly" Doyle, the longtime *Sun-Telegraph* baseball scribe and bon vivant who had died in late 1959. For more than four decades, Doyle was a Pittsburgh institution, a man who won the *Sun-Telegraph* baseball beat in 1915 on the strength of a poem ("Listen my fans, the sports ed raves / Of the daylight ride of the Boston Braves / On the 14th of April, they started their car / But the darn thing was rusty and couldn't run far") and charmed most everyone he met with his endless repository of stories and Irish songs. Doyle's great gift was friendship—he and Honus Wagner were close from the get-go, and it was Chilly himself who was master of ceremonies on the memorable day in 1939 in Cooperstown when Honus was part of the Hall of Fame's inaugural class. Ballplayers could confide in Doyle, and he returned the favor and seldom wrote of their foibles. His only demands were that the Pirates give him full access to anyone in the locker room and that the players consider attending the Pittsburgh baseball writers' winter "dinner" show, where Chilly was usually the star. Accepting his offer in the winter of 1955 was ex-Pirate catcher Joe Garagiola, who served as master of ceremonies. The event launched his career in broadcasting—with Joe always sure to make himself the butt of jokes for his servitude on the 1952 Pirates.

On occasion, the writers crossed the line. In mid-August 1960, when Dick Groat jumped into politics by declaring himself firmly behind Republican Richard Nixon for the presidency, it became a national story—reported by *Time* Magazine. Groat was a one-time roommate of Nixon's younger brother, Ed, at Nixon's law-school alma mater, Duke. He reportedly received a few boos when he stepped to bat at Forbes Field in the first game of an August 16 doubleheader against the Phillies. But any discontent was quickly forgotten when Groat slammed six base hits in eight at-bats, helping the Pirates sweep. Groat himself seldom had any problems with the writers, whom he considered his friends. "They could see you falling down drunk and they'd never write anything about it," he says. "They weren't looking for something dirty. They were very factual, and if we screwed up, they wrote it straight."

Did the code make reporting better than today? Groat thinks so. "I think Les and Jack would admit that it was a lot more fun traveling with people and rooting for them," he says. "I get the feeling that the modern-day writer likes writing something negative." A broadcaster of University of Pittsburgh men's basketball for nearly thirty years, Groat has the perspective of both sides: "Pitt fans don't want to hear us root for somebody else," he says. "You can't go to the practices, know the coaches, and travel with these kids like I do without living and dying with the team."

The relationship of writers to ballplayers in 1960 personified an antiquated media landscape. But times were about to change, as advancing electronic media gained power and captured the attention of the players—sending newspaper reporters off in search of fresh material beyond the game. Early in 1960, a journeyman relief pitcher named Jim Brosnan showed that baseball writing was ripe for a new era with the publication of his book *The Long Season,* an intelligent diary of the '59 season, which he started with the Cardinals and ended with the Reds. Without the profanity of a lot of typical baseball talk, Brosnan and *The Long Season* took readers inside the game as no sportswriter could. In doing so, Brosnan, who was on hand at Forbes Field covering the Series for *Life,* raised the bar of sportswriting—suddenly, it wasn't so fawning anymore. Nicknamed "The Professor" by teammates to acknowledge his budding literary career and the glasses he wore, Brosnan would follow up in 1962 with another superb book, *Pennant Race.* Meanwhile, the sportswriters, particularly the gaggle from New York and especially the hard-charging Dick Young of the *Daily News,* responded as best they could—by asking harder questions, not always about baseball, and growing ever more critical.

The line in the sand was crossed forever at the 1962 World Series with two simple questions from Stan Isaacs of *Newsday* to Yankee pitcher Ralph Terry: Had his wife been at the game to see him pitch?

"Actually no," replied Terry. She was at home nursing their new baby.

"Breast or bottle?" asked Isaacs, serving notice that press coverage had changed forever.

* * *

Only during the World Series, when Friend finally revealed the extent of Hoak's foot injury to Milton Gross of the *New York Post,* did the story of the stitches become news. By then, Hoak had picked up a painful groin injury as well, but even that didn't stop him from playing in the World Series. "That's the way Don is," Pirates trainer Danny Whelan said. "I've never seen a guy with more guts."

There was an edge to Hoak. At Roulette High School, he played baseball, football, and the trumpet—picking up a few extra dollars as a member of a dance band. At seventeen years old, Hoak joined the Marines and fought in the Pacific. Then he became a boxer—fighting professionally in thirty-nine fights, winning twenty-seven. But losing four of his last six bouts by knockout—"I got a little tired of being flattened," he said—was a sign that perhaps there were less hazardous ways to make a living. So Hoak became a ballplayer.

Paying his way to the Brooklyn Dodgers minor-league camp in 1947, Hoak played well enough for the club to sign him and assign him to its Class D franchise at Valdosta, Georgia. From there he worked his way toward the big leagues—through Nashua, New Hampshire; Greenville, Mississippi; Fort Worth, Texas, where he was married one August night in 1950 at home plate; and then to Montreal and St. Paul. Playing winter ball one steamy evening in Havana, he was stepping into the batter's box when a bearded, chunky, twenty-something man in glasses and green fatigues bolted from the stands and pranced to the mound like a big shot. So Hoak stepped in and took three pitches—"a pretty fair curve and a good fastball, but no control," he recalled. Hoak never even swung, but after police had removed the man to the third-base stands, he realized he had just faced Fidel Castro.

In 1954, Hoak reached Brooklyn, and though he never hit .300 for the Dodgers, he stuck around by virtue of his glove, speed, and guile. Though Hoak was at third when Johnny Podres shut down the Yanks in Game 7 of the '55 Series for the team's only world title, the Dodgers were loaded at the position with Billy Cox and Jackie Robinson. So off Hoak was sent to Chicago, shipped to the Cubs, where his lowly .215 batting average got him traded again, this time to the Reds.

It was in Cincinnati that Hoak's competitive spirits got the better of him. Standing on second base against the Braves, he instinctively broke up a double-play ball hit by teammate Wally Post by fielding the ball bare-handed to keep the Milwaukee infielders at bay. Subsequently, Rule 7.09(g) was adopted, giving the umpire authority to call the batter and runner out when a base runner intentionally interferes to break up a double play.

Playing with the Reds, Hoak focused on his troublesome batting average—and saved his career. With the Cubs, Hoak had been plagued by an unusual health problem: sharp, recurring headaches that sapped his strength and often made sleep impossible. Thinking he had a pinched nerve, Hoak went to the doctor and discovered that he had been suffering from a badly damaged nose—residue from boxing days. In the ensuing operation, surgeons extracted twenty-six pieces of bone splinter and cartilage from his nose, eye, and sinus areas, and the headaches cleared up.

On the advice of Reds manager Birdie Tebbetts at spring training, Hoak adjusted his batting stance. His career was in the balance, Tebbetts told him, because big-league rosters didn't have room for .215 hitters. "Nobody knew it better than I did," Hoak said. Tebbetts instructed Hoak to stop swinging for the fences, a bad habit honed while playing with the Dodgers at cozy Ebbets Field. With big bashers like Post and Ted Kluszewski, the Reds had more than enough power anyway.

Tebbetts gave Hoak an old-fashioned hitting tutorial: encouraging him to move his feet closer together, straighten his stance, extend his elbows, and meet the ball squarely. Hoak worked hard and his efforts paid off: At spring training in 1957 he batted .416, and on opening day stroked two doubles. Hoak was soon hitting the pitchers who used to retire him routinely, in particular top fastballers like Don Newcombe, Johnny Antonelli, and Robin Roberts. This was no fluke—Hoak made the NL all-star team in '57 and raised his batting average a whopping 78 percentage points to finish at .293. But when Hoak slumped in 1958 to .261, Tebbetts grew impatient, so it was off to the Pirates, where he rebounded in '59 with a career best average of .294.

But here in the fourth inning of Game 7, Hoak was pressing against Shantz's big slow curveballs. Swinging at the first pitch, he lunged and tapped the ball on the ground just to the right of second, where Richardson, perfectly positioned, gobbled it up, whirled, and threw to first for the second out.

Shantz had thrown two pitches and secured two outs in the Pirates' fourth. Wanting the Yankee reliever at least to break a sweat, Maze-roski took a couple of pitches—a ball outside and then a curve inside—before swinging on another curve and popping up to Kubek at short. Make that five pitches and three outs, proving that excellence in big games can look deceptively easy. The Pirates were gone in the fourth, but still up by four.

FIFTH INNING

5

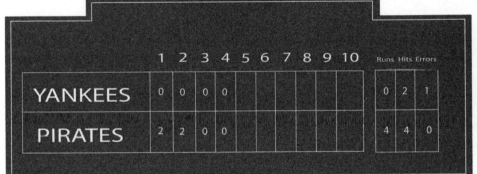

	1	2	3	4	5	6	7	8	9	10		Runs	Hits	Errors
YANKEES	0	0	0	0								0	2	1
PIRATES	2	2	0	0								4	4	0

HIS EYES GLUED on Vernon Law as the Pirate ace tossed warm-up pitches in the fifth, Danny Murtaugh wondered how long his ace could last on his tender right ankle. All season long, Law had been the go-to Pirate starter, the man who had gotten the team's first win of the season against the Phillies back on a chilly April 20 at Forbes Field and had not let up until he had taken his twentieth, a complete-game 5-3 victory over the Reds. The major leagues' first twenty-game winner in 1960, Law would finish 20-9 with a 3.08 ERA. Only two others, Warren Spahn and Ernie Broglio of the Cardinals, would join him as twenty-game winners; each had twenty-one wins.

Whenever the Pirates hit a rut in 1960, Law had gotten them back on track, just as he had today, when he had thrown all of thirty-nine pitches in mowing down the Yankees through the first four innings. As Law went, so did the Pirates; the Deacon was the team's rock, its rudder. At 6'2" and 195 pounds, Law wasn't a power pitcher in the conventional sense, relying instead on pinpoint control and his unwavering ability to start batters off with a strike to get ahead in the count. But no big-league pitcher, with the possible exception of a knuckleballer, can survive for long without the ability to push hard off his ankle; just ask Curt Schilling, whose bloody sock and flimsy-ankle woes became a famously big story in the 2004 World Series.

Law was rarely ever out of control, either on or off the field. The

Meridian, Idaho, farm boy was one of ten children, a church deacon at twelve years old who was ordained at seventeen. Quiet and never demonstrative, he had been thumbed from a game only once in his nine-year career with the Pirates—and that was just because umpire Stan Landes, after being subjected to a rather colorful tantrum from the Pirate bench, sidled to the dugout and advised him, "You don't belong around here listening to all that nasty stuff." Prayer was a constant in Law's life. Every morning he prayed, along with his family, all of whom had "V" names—his wife, Vanita, and their four sons Velvon, Veryl, future big leaguer Vance, and Vaughn. He had led his entire family in prayer prior to beating the Yankees 3-2 in Game 4, and on the mound he often bowed his head while silently beckoning to the Lord.

Law was the longest-serving Pirate of the '60 team, having signed a contract in 1948 at the age of eighteen, thanks in part to some deft maneuvering by the team's scouts, who could have used a dose of prayer themselves. Without a draft system in those days, teams competed head-to-head to sign the top prospects. The Pirates learned about Law from Herman Welker, a U.S. senator from Idaho who recommended the young right-hander to Bing Crosby, a part-owner of the Pirates and a former classmate at Gonzaga University. A real baseball fan, Welker would also help steer another Idahoan to the majors—the future Hall of Famer, Harmon Killebrew.

So with scouts from eight other big-league teams visiting Law's parents in Meridian, Babe Herman and Herman Welker, representing the Pirates, had some friendly advice for their rivals: The best way to earn the respect of Vernon's father, they said, was to take him a box of cigars. So the next morning, scouts from most every team but the Pirates marched to the Law home bearing boxes of cigars.

Advantage Pittsburgh. As members of the Church of Jesus Christ of Latter Day Saints, Mr. and Mrs. Law despised smoking. Later that morning, Herman and Welker strode to the Law home themselves and presented Mrs. Law with a box of chocolates and a dozen roses.

Invited to stay a while, the two men were chatting with the Laws when the telephone rang. A pleasant and oddly familiar voice was on the other end asking to speak with Mrs. Law: Why, it was the great Bing Crosby himself, who had a few words with Mrs. Law, telling her how much his team coveted her son and how the organization would go out of its way to provide a healthy atmosphere for him. That sealed it, and the Pirates signed Law to a contract worth $175 a month plus a $2,000 signing bonus. "She almost fainted on the spot from excitement," Law recalls of his mother. Added Welker: "I felt guilty pulling that trick on the scouts from other teams. . . . *Almost* felt guilty."

Law reached the big leagues in 1950, finishing 7-9 for the last-place Pirates. In '51, he tore his rotator cuff while pitching before and after a prolonged rain delay at Wrigley Field. Not much was known about treating shoulder injuries in those days; he got no ice for his arm, and doctors actually removed his tonsils, thinking it would help relieve the pain. What helped Law was military service in '52 and '53—two years in which he didn't pitch and rested his arm. Back with Pittsburgh in '54, Law and fellow right-hander Bob Friend became the team's workhorses, solid pitchers for a woeful team. Law typically worked more than two hundred innings a season and used good control and the ability to hit spots to his advantage.

Bob Prince nicknamed Law "The Deacon," a reminder of his roots. On the surface, Law's background didn't seem adequate preparation for the rough-and-tumble world of the big leagues, but he generally had no problem in buzzing a batter with a high, tight fastball, or doing whatever it took to win. Ordered by Danny Murtaugh to throw a knockdown pitch at the first batter he faced after a Pirate batter had been nailed, Law refused at first. "Skip," he said, standing in the dugout, ready to take the field, "it's against my religion. The Bible, after all, says, 'Turn the other cheek.' "

Murtaugh wasn't swayed. "It'll cost you $500," he said, "if you don't knock him down."

Needing to make up his mind—and fast—the big pitcher faced a moral dilemma of sorts. "The Bible also says, 'He who lives by the sword shall also die by the sword,' " Law said to himself. He knocked the batter down.

On July 19, 1955, Law faced against Milwaukee at Forbes Field after only three days' rest, forced into action when Ronnie Kline, the scheduled starter, came down with a sore shoulder. Pirates manager Fred Haney promised to relieve Law if he got tired, but the Deacon felt strong and pitched the regulation nine innings, giving up just two runs.

But the Pirates had only managed to score two runs themselves, so Law pitched the tenth and then, as the game remained deadlocked, the eleventh and the twelfth. Still, no one scored, and Law kept at it. When he left the mound *after the eighteenth inning,* the crowd erupted in cheers, acknowledging that they had watched a man pitch two complete games in one day, something no one had accomplished since the early days of baseball.

Haney finally relieved Law with Bob Friend, who gave up a run in the top of the nineteenth. But then the Pirates tallied two runs in their at-bat to win 4-3. Wrote Al Abrams in the next morning's *Post-Gazette,* "Vernon Law turned in a performance the equal of which the great pitching titans of the past would have been proud to call their own."

Law himself remained self-effacing, often discussing the power of prayer. "I ask for strength," he told writer Ray Robinson. "I don't expect my prayers to be answered in a positive way at once. I just want to be able to do my best. Prayer doesn't guarantee anything for anyone; it's just that a person needs to be humbled once in a while." But he never took his philosophy to extremes, always playing Sundays though he didn't like the idea. "A contract is an obligation," he said. "I know the church would want me to fulfill the obligation."

Fulfilling that obligation was instrumental in helping the Pirates break fast from the gate in 1960, and win twelve of their first fifteen.

Nowhere near as talented as the Giants or the defending World Champion Los Angeles Dodgers, the Pirates got on a roll from the get-go and never let up. It was as if the fairy dust from the 1951 movie *Angels in the Outfield,* filmed in Pittsburgh, really had been sprinkled on Forbes Field. In that delightful film, only divine intervention fueled by the attention of a young Janet Leigh secured a Pirate pennant.

As May rolled on, with the Pirates continuing to lead the pack, experts predicted the Giants of Willie Mays, Orlando Cepeda, and Willie McCovey would be "run(ning) off from the rest of the league any day now," as Walter Bingham of *Sports Illustrated* wrote. But the Pirates were proving to be "the bulldog of the league, hanging on to the ankle of the giant, refusing to let it get away," Bingham admitted. "Pittsburgh works miracles; losing 5-0 in the 9th, they score six to win."

Law and Friend were instrumental to Pittsburgh's early success; each had a tremendous start. Before more than thirty-four thousand at the home opener, Law, 18-9 in '59, disposed of the Reds 13-0 in his first start, then won his second and his third as well. Friend, anxious to avenge a disappointing 8-19 record in '59, only a year after winning twenty, had started the season in the best shape of his career, nabbing his first win in start two, a four-hit 5-0 shutout of the Reds in an Easter Sunday doubleheader at Forbes Field. What a difference a year makes: In '59, an overweight Friend had had to wait eleven starts until May 28 before winning his first game, by which time he was 0-7.

"This was a big one for me, and I wanted to win it badly," Friend said after his first win, on April 17. "I don't even want to think about 1959. I knew how long it took me to win my first game last year and this was in the back of my mind when I went out there to pitch this one. Winning it was a great mental lift for me."

That set the tone. In the nightcap of the doubleheader, the Pirates couldn't do a thing against the whiplike right-hander Raul Sanchez, who shut them down for eight innings. Trailing 5-0 with one gone in the bottom of the ninth against ace reliever Bill Henry, Burgess, Virdon, and Mazeroski all drilled singles for one run. Then backup catcher Hal Smith clubbed a three-run homer over the wall in left-center to bring the Pirates within a run at 5-4. To the mound ambled the Reds' rookie reliever Ted Wieand, who got Don Hoak for the second out, before giving up a bouncing single through the box to Groat. Wieand worked the next batter, Bob Skinner, to a 2-1 count, before the Pirate left fielder parked the next pitch into the right-field seats for a stunning 6-5 victory.

The crowd of more than sixteen thousand, most of whom seemed to be age ten and under, went berserk. Dozens of them scooted over the railing and onto the field, where they formed a massive welcome party for Groat and Skinner at home plate. "I put my head down and ran—and when I looked up, all I saw was kids," Skinner said of his home-run trot. "They just about carried Dick Groat and me into the dugout. Or maybe I was just walking on air."

It was only mid-April, but the game made believers of the Pirates. "We can win this thing," said Hoak in the boisterous locker room after the game. "We have to become the kind of team that once we gather momentum, we must keep going. We got up some steam last year, then fell apart. But if one player falters, another must be ready to step in." Looking back, Groat agrees, calling the nightcap win the moment that convinced the Pirates that a special season was possible. "It was then that we thought we had the team to do it," he says.

On April 24, Harvey Haddix beat the Braves, 7-3, to send the Pirates into first place for the first time in the season. Four days later, Bob Friend threw another shutout, this one 3-0 over the Phillies, for the seventh Pirate win in a row. Friend struck out eleven Philadelphians, one short of the Pirate record. Then the team would win two more for its longest winning streak since 1945.

Things went a bit sour in early May, and the Pirates, on their first trip to brand-new Candlestick Park in windy San Francisco, dropped four in a row to the Giants before Law got them back on track with a 3-2 complete-game win in Los Angeles. The team kept finding ways to win, underscoring Hoak's clarion call by doing it with a changing cast of heroes. On May 13, Groat went six for six against the Braves, and five days later, Law pitched them back into the NL lead with another complete game, a 4-2 win against the Cardinals. Then, on May 22, Hal Smith pulled out another game, this time with a bases-loaded pinch-hit single in the eleventh to beat the Giants 8-7.

These Pirates were finding ways to win, often in the final innings. But even if most writers still picked the Giants, it was the Dodgers and their outstanding pitching staff that brought the Pirates back to earth. Sandy Koufax stopped the Pirates on May 23 in a 1-0 one-hitter, with Pittsburgh's sole hit a second-inning single by his mound opponent, Bennie Daniels. Johnny Podres beat Pittsburgh the following night, 4-2, and Don Drysdale did it the night after that, 5-1, helped by a 550-foot home run by Frank Howard, the 6'7" Dodgers' rookie.

Right-handers Law and Friend, and Haddix, a lefty, gave the Pirates three solid veteran starters. Face was the stopper in the bullpen. But the rest of the Pirate pitching staff was streaky at best, prompting GM Joe L. Brown to act quickly. On May 27, Brown obtained the veteran twenty-nine-year-old left-hander Vinegar Bend Mizell, a thirteen-game winner in '59, from the Cardinals for two farmhands. The move seemed solid, but in hindsight it was much more than that—it gave the Pirate starting rotation the depth they needed to contend. Mizell would win four straight in July and August, a streak that included consecutive shutouts, and match his thirteen wins from the previous season.

Every time things got rocky for the Pirates, there was Law to steady the ship; twice, the team lost four games in a row, and both times, there was the Deacon to erase the streak with a win. Playing on Forbes Field's hard, pebble-strewn infield, the defense was solid. On the bench sat a dependable cast of veterans, from Nelson to Hal

Smith, Dick Schofield, Gino Cimoli, and Bob Oldis, who seldom got rattled and could hit for average and deliver timely hits in the late innings. Brown knew what he had, saying, "I don't believe any team ever got more out of its ability than that club."

These Pirates also had chemistry, an intangible blend of professionalism under pressure and, thanks to pranksters like Cimoli and third-string catcher Oldis, an ability to relax. Jill Corey tells the story of how the power of positive thinking used to help Don Hoak when he was in a batting slump: "I'm still helping the team," he would say. How's that? "I hang around the lobby of the hotel and look good." No wonder the 1960 Pirates, as Haddix once said, were "the loosest club I've ever been associated with."

Law pitched Pittsburgh back into first place on May 29 with an 8-5 win over the Phillies. There the team remained through June, taking fifteen of twenty-six games. On June 30, first baseman Dick Stuart broke out of a power slump by swatting three home runs, his ninth, tenth, and eleventh of the season, in an 11-6 win over the Giants at Forbes Field. Big Stu owed his big day to Clemente, from whom he had borrowed a bat several ounces lighter than his own. "Swing it," Clemente had instructed him after seeing his name posted. It was indicative of the way the Pirates were developing the knack of winning late, and often at the expense of the NL's better teams. The next night at Forbes Field, they won again, improbably, beating the Dodgers in the tenth as Joe Christopher dashed home from second on Clemente's infield hit and Roberto scored the winner a minute later, steaming all the way from first on Stuart's pop single.

The twenty-seven-year-old Stuart, platooning at first against left-handers, was the Pirates' only legitimate power hitter *and* the team's biggest liability—a designated hitter before there was such a thing, Stuart struck out a lot and fielded baseballs like a sack of rocks, which, combined with a periodic lack of focus, made him the target of Forbes Field boo-birds. Not that Stuart was without potential: Playing with

Lincoln, Nebraska, in the Class A Western League in 1956, Big Stu had drawn national attention and a report in *Life* magazine by launching sixty-six home runs, which he matched with titanic cockiness. *Life* called him "an irrepressible egotist," but Stuart didn't care; to his mind, he was the second coming of Babe Ruth.

Bob Prince would plead, "Don't boo Stu! He's overdue!" But there were times when Stuart's monstrous ego could test a Pirate fan's patience. Arriving in Pittsburgh in 1958, Big Stu signed autographs by affixing a "66," for his number of home runs in the Western League, next to his name. Striding into Gustine's for the first time, he peered at the picture of Ralph Kiner behind the bar and announced that before he was through, he would make the city forget all about the seven-time NL home-run champion. In 1960, Stuart bounded about town in a brand-new Cadillac, bought with his $6,000 in profits from *Home Run Derby*.

Stuart kept hitting home runs—sixteen in '58 and twenty-seven the next season—while piling up the errors, strikeouts, and his own personal highlight reel. There were plenty of downers, but a lot of ups as well: Stuart hit the game-winning home run in Friend's twentieth win in 1958. Facing Glen Hobbie of the Cubs on June 5, 1959, Stuart launched what many swore was the longest home run ever at Forbes Field. The ball sailed well over the tractor stored in the deepest part of the park and by the base of the 457-foot left-center field wall before coming to rest in Schenley Park, some 525 feet from home plate. Groat described the reaction in the Pirate dugout as "numb." Hobbie called the pitch "a sinker that didn't sink" and thanked Stuart for not hitting the ball lower, since "I might not have been here to talk about it." The only other person thought to have hit a home run at the same spot of the cavernous ballpark was the great Josh Gibson. Stuart's ho-hum reaction: "One of my best shots, but I can't really say if it was my very best."

Batting guru George Sisler worked hard to instill Big Stu with more discipline at the plate, but he continued to rack up the strike-outs. Meantime, Stuart's poor fielding habits were becoming legend, as in the tenth inning of a night game in Los Angeles when Gil Hodges smacked a hard shot that struck Hoak's glove and dribbled toward the hole, where Groat picked the ball up and fired a perfect strike to first base. But Stuart had already figured the ball had gotten through the infield and was turning his head to chat with the umpire when the ball went whizzing by. Stuart just shrugged, chiding Groat in the dugout about the inscription in the scorebook: "E-6; 2-base error." Another story, probably apocryphal but one that Stuart enjoyed telling in retirement, by which time he had become more self-deprecating, came on the night when thirty thousand people at Forbes Field gave him a standing ovation for actually catching something—"a hot dog wrapper on the fly."

By late June, Pittsburgh fans were talking openly of winning the pennant and wondering who their team would be playing in the World Series. *Press* sports editor Chet Smith reminisced at length about the last time the Pirates had won the Series—in 1925—and pined to play Cleveland, long a rival with Pittsburgh in both football and image. The Pirates versus the Indians "would take the country by storm," Smith wrote, quoting, "one old baseball head," and would be "much more exciting than the Giants-Yankees scraps, away out in front of a match between the White Sox and Cubs or the Sox and Braves."

Resilience became a mantra, as did patience at the plate and win-ning in dramatic and unusual ways, as if it were ordained. Nellie King vividly remembers the drama of June 18, as Arnold Palmer followed up his spring victory in the Masters by charging from seven strokes down on the final day to win the U.S. Open in Denver. That night at the Coliseum in Los Angeles, the Pirates staged a memorable come-back of their own, beating the Dodgers—after being three down with the bases empty and then two down in the ninth—thanks largely to Hal Smith, who belted a two-run homer in the ninth and the game-winning single in the tenth. "How can you take two events in one day and expect *that* to happen?" says King. "It was dramatic, just dramatic as hell. And the Pirates came from behind, from the beginning of the season to the end. Their trademark was owning the last three innings."

On July 17, after dropping the first game of a doubleheader against the Reds at Forbes Field, the Pirates faced the hard-throwing Don Newcombe, a former Cy Young Award–winner, in the nightcap. Looking for an edge, Murtaugh resorted to an obscure rule: noticing the big right-hander's left sleeve of his shirt was a different length from the right sleeve, he cited an obscure major-league rule that stipulated the sleeves must be "approximately the same length" and demanded that Newcombe change shirts. That triggered Newcombe's volcanic temper, and he was tossed even before throwing a single pitch. In stepped emergency starter Cal McLish, the same pitcher the Pirates had tattooed back in April. They got to McLish again, and to reliever Bob Grim, while the Pirates' twenty-four-year-old right-handed spot-starter Tom Cheney, just up from minor-league Columbus, tossed a three-hit, 5-0 shutout.

On July 23 at Candlestick Park against the Giants, a high-kicking twenty-two-year-old rookie right-hander from the Dominican Republic named Juan Marichal stopped the Pirates cold in a game a lot of people back in Pennsylvania watched: It was KDKA-TV's first West Coast broadcast. The following night, the Giants' Billy O'Dell beat the Pirates to dump them from the lead for the first time in nearly two months. But on July 25, Bob Friend beat the Cardinals at Sportsman's Park and the Pirates moved back into a lead they would not relinquish. Critics called it luck, but the players knew better: On August 6 at Forbes Field, the Pirates scored three runs in the tenth to win 8-7— the team's ninth straight win against the Giants. Facing San Francisco the next day in the nightcap of a doubleheader, rookie outfielder Joe Christopher made the most of his first big-league home run—a three-run shot off O'Dell to tie the game that the Pirates went on to win.

As the Pirates drove toward the pennant, Pittsburgh city officials tackled a new concern: the expectation, as Louis Rosenberg, Pittsburgh's director of public safety put it, "that excitement will run high and restraint may be lacking." Rosenberg wasn't referring to Benny Benack and his Iron City Six. Nor did he mean the bearded loner who had taken to showing up at Forbes Field and honking the Pirates onward with duck calls. But with record crowds streaming into the ballpark all summer, officials decided to clamp down on what they called an increase in alcohol-inspired rowdyism. And so, on the evening of August 9, Rosenberg directed waves of policemen through the aisles of Forbes Field to confiscate all the alcohol they could find. With beer sales prohibited at the ballpark in those days, people brought their own six-packs and coolers, particularly in the bleachers where there was usually enough room for a picnic. All in all, the officials gathered quite a stash, but the outcry was so long and loud that the rules were relaxed. In the end, the controversy was a tempest in a teapot, one of the few distractions as the Pirates inched closer to the World Series.

On September 6, the Pirates got a double dose of what it meant to be a pennant contender. That day at major-league headquarters in New York, Commissioner Ford Frick announced he'd be meeting the following Tuesday with representatives of six teams, including the Pirates, Cardinals, and Braves, to go over ground rules for the Series. That night, when Dick Groat threw up his left hand to protect himself from Lew Burdette's high, hard one, his wrist was fractured—and a shudder shot richocheted through Western Pennsylvania over whether the pennant was lost. But others picked up the slack, including backup shortstop Schofield, and Clemente, who at George Sisler's prodding was starting to lay off bad pitches, which helped improve his early-September batting average to .323. Maintaining a lead of anywhere from six to eight games, the Pirates continued to plow ahead on all cylinders.

In early September, the Pirates announced a mail-order Series ticket plan, and tens of thousands responded—many more than could ever fill the thirty-six thousand or so seats at Forbes Field. By selling tickets on an individual-game basis and not in strips, the Pirates did what they could to keep the tickets away from speculators and scalpers. Meantime, fans made phone calls to anyone with a remote chance of scoring a seat, scrambled to find anyone who already had tickets, and continued to fill Forbes Field. The Pirates' final record attendance of more than 1.7 million would stand as the team's best for twenty-eight years.

Looking to October, Pirate officials planned accordingly. A World Series would draw a media mob—upward of 750 credential reporters, just a few more than the usual Forbes field crowd of twenty-five media representatives who easily fit into the snug little third-deck press box. Where to seat them all, including the influx of Spanish-language writers and broadcasters drawn by Clemente's presence? How to feed everyone with box lunches? These were big questions, all of which meant a busy September for Jack Berger, the Pirates' PR director. With cool efficiency, Berger directed the building of an additional broadcast box that was suspended from the second deck. He reserved blocks of additional seats for the writers in right field and in the old upper-deck third-base press box that the Pirates had built back in 1938 in anticipation of winning that year's pennant.

With just a fraction of the press corps able to fit into the tiny club-houses, the Pirates rigged up a public address system to pipe the postgame interviews directly into the press boxes. Just as critical was finding space for the sixty-five Western Union operators who would be handling the flood of news, which by Game 7 had reached more than one million words. The place chosen was press headquarters at the Hilton, where the operators retyped the reporters' stories into tele-type machines, a kind of rudimentary fax, which sent the copy to newsrooms around the country. To help photographers quickly develop and transmit their images, the Pirates installed a portable dark room in a tent in the bowels of the grandstand. With the makeshift press box in right field meaning a possible loss in ticket revenue, Berger and his crew came up with one more quick renovation—a row of top-dollar field boxes down both lines.

Looking to add a dash of pageantry to the start of the Series, PA announcer Art McKennan arranged for the Pitt band to march through the streets and into Forbes Field before Games 1 and 2. Berger arranged for Billy Eckstine to sing the national anthem before Game 1, though the musicians' union protested that the Pirates didn't use one of its bands. In the doldrums as well were Benny Benack and his Iron City Six, relegated for the duration of the Series to a truck platform facing Gate 6 on Sennott Street. The decision had been set in motion after Roberto Clemente complained that every time the band played inside the park, the Pirates lost.

On September 19 at Crosley Field, Vernon Law won number twenty, beating a complete-game 5-3 win over hard-luck Cal McLish. Law's feat had taken some doing—four attempts, in fact, to reach his twentieth—but the Pirate ace, more focused on the race, wasn't rattled. "I was thinking more of putting us closer to the pennant than winning number twenty," he said. "It's nice to win twenty, but frankly I don't feel any different than when I won my nineteenth." With a little more luck, Law could easily have won a lot more in 1960—of his eight defeats, four were by a single run. Law had won his twentieth in the opener of a doubleheader—and kept the Pirates six games up of second-place St. Louis. Then Mizell polished off the Reds in the nightcap with a three-hit, 1-0 masterpiece, his eleventh win. Said Cincinnati third baseman Willie Jones, "You can see the dollar signs on (their) ground balls."

* * *

But could the power of prayer help Law outpitch Moose Skowron? The Yankee slugger, a former Purdue placekicker who found himself better suited to baseball after hitting a Big Ten–record .500 as a sophomore, had become a one-man Yankee World Series wrecking crew. Skowron, now playing his *thirty-fourth* postseason game, had compiled an impeccable ability to perform in the clutch. He had nailed a game-winning grand slam in Game 7 of the '56 Series against Brooklyn and a Game 6 winning blast in '58 against Milwaukee. Hobbled by a back injury in '59, the right-handed hitter had returned with a flourish in '60 to finish with twenty-six homers and a .308 batting average—his best year yet. With his square jaw and menacing look, Moose appeared bigger than his 5'11", 195-pound frame. He even looked fierce enough to be called "Moose," though the moniker derived not from his looks, but from a shortened version of "Mussolini," the name given him as a boy in Chicago after getting a haircut that looked like the dictator's.

Looking to get the Yankees started with a hit, a walk, *anything* to get on base, Skowron took a called strike, then in an effort to catch the Pirates by surprise, actually turned and bunted the ball, which rolled down the first-base line, foul by inches. Suddenly he was in an 0-2 hole. Nearly out of options, Skowron figured that his well-known power was the answer after all—and came through. Law tried wasting a sidearm fastball outside, but left it out on the corner of the plate, and Moose met the ball solidly—drilling a line-drive bullet to right that landed in the lower deck for an opposite-field home run. The Yankees had broken through; it was 4-1.

Skowron had saved his best for when it counted. This was his second Series homer in 1960, both hit off Law in tight games; Skowron had also homered in Game 4, also to the opposite field, to give the Yankees a 1-0 lead, though the Pirates had come back to win that one 3-2. This home run was the Yankees' third hit of the day and seemed to quickly suck all the air out of Forbes Field, which had suddenly gone as quiet as a church. Rounding the bases grimly, with his

head down—hot-dog home-run trots were frowned on in 1960—
Moose accepted a quick handshake from third-base coach Frank
Crosetti, crossed the plate, and disappeared into the dugout. Taking
nothing for granted, Stengel glanced toward the Yankee bullpen,
where Coates was up again and throwing, just in case.

Was Law's ankle making it difficult for him to continue? A clue would
come with the next batter, twenty-seven-year-old Johnny Blanchard,
who had filled in for Elston Howard in Game 6—after the regular
Yankee catcher had busted his right hand—and had whacked three hits,
making it his greatest day in baseball. Law uncorked a curve that the
Yankee catcher fouled off, up and over the roof on the field's first-base
side. Next he took a ball and then took a shot at the 1-1, sending a weak
fly into center, where Virdon made the catch. One big out.

Fortunately for Pittsburgh, the Yankees had gone through the meat
of their order. Batting eighth, Clete Boyer—this time using a working
bat—tried to bunt but fouled it off. Then he swung and sent a routine
grounder toward Mazeroski, who threw to first for the second out. And
though the next batter, Shantz, gave it his best, he *was* a pitcher, after all,
and towered a 1-2 pitch into foul territory along the first-base side that
Nelson gobbled up to retire the Yanks in the fifth. So far, Skowron's
blast had been the only damage; Law had held on and led 4-1.

* * *

At the halfway point, the deciding game of the 1960 World Season
was a work in progress, a play at the end of Act I but with texture and
defining moments still to come. Rocky Nelson and Moose Skowron
had hit home runs, while Bobby Shantz had corked the Pirates' early
heroics. And yes, Law, who had retired the Yankees after Skowron in
only nine pitches, appeared to be holding up.

Pacing themselves as well were a parade of photographers, a veritable
all-star team of their own, as they maneuvered for prime locations

within Forbes Field's compact grandstand. With the advent of the on-field photo box still years away, Harry Harris of the *Associated Press* chose a traditional spot—the little photo box that hung from the first-base side of the second tier like a hornet's nest against the eaves.

Staking out a prime spot that only a local would know was Jim Klingensmith, chief photographer of the hometown *Post-Gazette.* With his teenage son in tow, Klingensmith had sweet-talked a Forbes Field maintenance man into loaning him a ladder, which he used to climb to the grandstand rooftop behind home plate. Taking the ladder with him to ensure they could get back down—and to make sure no other photographer had access to the roof—Klingensmith used his new sequencing camera to snap game photos in bursts of three.

"Kling," as he was known, had scored a small coup, finding a location that offered a vista of the field and the crowded ballpark in stark contrast to the deserted, almost pastoral scene of Schenley Park's Flagstaff Hill in the distance. Getting an edge was routine for the fifty-nine-year-old Pittsburgh native, who had been at the *Post-Gazette,* Pittsburgh's morning daily, for eighteen years. Then again, Kling had always shown a deft hand at doing the little things necessary to get that edge—such as befriending a variety of local dignitaries, from Honus Wagner and Art Rooney, with whom he traded cigars, to Bishop Wright and Governor Lawrence. Kling could also be tough as nails; as a hard drinker who preferred Canadian Club with water, he was used to softening up reluctant subjects—with what else but a drink—and once angered a group of striking steel workers by photographing them as they drove up to a picket site in their foreign cars.

Like a lot of people at Game 7, Klingensmith has vivid memories of the day—how he had to remind himself to remain objective and keep from rooting for his hometown Pirates, with many of whom he'd shared friendships. Kling was just happy to be there watching baseball with his son, considering his wife, Angeline, was in the hospital, ill with hepatitis and facing a grim prognosis for recovery. "I'd been at the hospital so much in the past few days that I jumped at the chance to be in the open air at Forbes Field with my son," Klingensmith told the *Post-Gazette*. "What could be better than that?"

Far below in the grandstand, other photographers used their "roving" media credentials to crouch in the aisles of box seats down both lines or to stand in front of a pillar. It had been in an aisle along the first-base line that seventeen-year-old Neil Leifer, a recent high-school grad covering his first Series, had snapped a memorable shot in Game 1, a play at second in which Mazeroski, stretched out like a ballet dancer, picked off Berra. *Sports Illustrated* ran the shot, in color, as a full-page in its October 17 edition—the first time the sports weekly had ever done so—in the very next week. Because the preparation of color photography generally took a week or more to appear in a news weekly in those days, Leifer's color coup was a big deal in 1960 sports journalism circles; he was fortunate to have taken the photo on a Tuesday, a full five days prior to the magazine's Sunday closing, giving editors in New York enough time to prepare. For Leifer, the photo "showed me I could compete with the big boys" and helped launch his career as one of the world's premier sports photographers.

Several of those "big boys"—*Sports Illustrated* mainstays Marvin Newman and John Zimmerman, Leifer's role models—were also at Game 7. A veteran of several World Series and just back from the Olympic Games in Rome, Newman recognized early that the game could ride on a single big play and had staked out a position in an aisle of a first-base field box, above the Pirate dugout. He had been returning to that spot on and off since the second inning, focusing his Bell & Howell Foton, fitted with the medium telephoto lens, on home plate, particularly with men on base. Framing the shot, Newman knew he had found a remarkable panorama: the batter in the lower left-hand of the lens, anchoring a sweeping view of left field, with the big scoreboard and Carnegie Library in the background.

"In picking your spots, you never know when the big moment will happen, so you have to be ready," says Newman. "It's a variation of what Leo Durocher used to tell his batters: 'Have an idea what you're going to do.' I figured if the big moment happened and I could catch it, I would have *the* picture of the game."

Newman gave credit to Leo Durocher, but in fact he was classically trained on his way to becoming one of the top sports photographers of the era. Berenice Abbott was an early mentor at Brooklyn College. In 1952, Newman became one of the first to earn a master's degree in photography, from Chicago's Institute of Design, where his master's thesis, "A Creative Analysis of the Series Form in Still Photography," explored repeated forms in a series of children's faces and inverted human shadows on the sidewalk. Newman would later work for *Life, Look,* and *Esquire.*

But of all the photographers squeezed into Forbes Field that day, *Life*'s George Silk, a New Zealand–born former combat photographer, had perhaps the day's most unusual camera angle. Without having to shoot the game itself, Silk and the other *Life* photographer, Arthur Rickerby, spent their time focusing on atmospheric photos— from the action to the field to fans dressed up outside the ballpark. Fueled by his dislike of crowds at sports events—Silk once said he "couldn't work with all that noise"—the New Zealander actually walked out of the ballpark and lugged his photography equipment clear across Forbes Avenue and into the elevator of the Cathedral of Learning, the University of Pittsburgh's skyscraper a block away. Taking the elevator all the way to the very top of the gothic, thirty-eight-story building, Silk joined a small crowd of students perched on a balcony that overlooked the suddenly tiny, almost dreamlike ballpark in the distance. Like old-time fans in New York, who watched games at the Polo Grounds by standing on nearby Coogan's Bluff, from which they could see a sliver of the field, these students shared an obstructed view but didn't seem to care. They had tuned into the game on the radio and were having a party. With no one going anywhere—certainly not to class—Silk decided to stay himself, to be in position to capture a memorable crowd-reaction shot. As with Newman, all he needed was a seminal moment.

Far below on the Forbes Field mound, Shantz was cruising, delivering a litany of slow curves and quickly disposing of Pirate batters. Sticking with Law, Murtaugh sent him to bat to kick off the Pirate fifth, and deliver a hit—"set the table" in baseball-speak—for the top of the order, Virdon and Groat, to follow.

Law gave it a good shot, swinging and missing at strike one, taking the next two for balls, and then sending the 2-2 boldly on an arc toward the left-field corner that looked like it could drop in, had it not hooked foul at the last second and landed deep in the corner just beyond the Yankee bullpen. It was as if Law suddenly had nothing left; swinging at the next pitch, he bounced out to Boyer at third.

Nor were Virdon or Groat able to get anything started. The Pirate center fielder lunged at the first pitch and sent a harmless ball to second, where Richardson easily threw him out. At least Groat took a hack, sending the 0-1 on a line shot back to Shantz, who nailed the third out and had suddenly retired seven batters in a row. The Yankee pitcher was giving his team a shot at getting back into the game; it remained 4-1 Pirates, with four innings to go.

SIXTH INNING

6

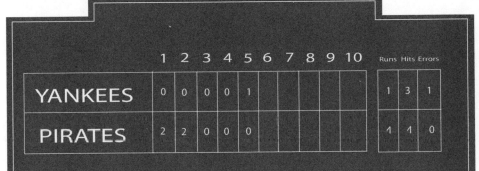

	1	2	3	4	5	6	7	8	9	10	Runs	Hits	Errors
YANKEES	0	0	0	0	1						1	3	1
PIRATES	2	2	0	0	0						4	4	0

FOR LAW, THE pressure was immense. Could he get through another inning before handing things over to Face? Murtaugh's strategy was that simple—a reminder of how much more basic managing was in the days before setup men and scholarly discourses about arm slots and velocity. Pitch counts? Not kept in those days—no need, says Groat. "The opposition let you know if you needed to change pitchers," he says with a smile. If a pitcher looked tired or was fighting an injury, you'd take 'em out, and in Murtaugh's case, call on base-ball's finest reliever.

It was almost guaranteed that the Pirates wouldn't call on any of their second-line pitchers—people like Fred Green, Clem Labine, and Tom Cheney, all of whom had been tattooed by the Yankees in those three lopsided losses. After Face—should things reach that point— Murtaugh would call on starters, either the right-hander Bob Friend, who hadn't pitched out of the third in Game 6, and Harvey Haddix, the lefty, who had last pitched October 10 in Game 5, three days ear-lier. With a welcome off-season just ahead, there would be plenty of time to rest.

Shantz was just what Stengel needed, a calming influence to shut the Pirates down and allow the Yankees time to climb back. The Yankee manager had tinkered early, but for now he had the lineup he wanted. So did Murtaugh. After facing one another for six games and part of another, neither manager could offer few surprises. How different from the start of the Series, when the Pirates had parlayed a dash of subterfuge and good fortune into an early rally.

Actually, the mind games had started some weeks before the World Series. Down the stretch, Yankee scouts Mayo Smith and Bill Skiff, a onetime Pirate, had traveled with the National League champs to develop a detailed scouting report their team would use in the Series. They watched every Pittsburgh game, got to know and like the Pirate players, and even took the team bus while on the road. Among their recommendations: no need to cover second when Virdon was on base, since the Pirate center fielder had a badly strained hamstring. He hadn't stolen a base in months and wouldn't be running.

But in the bottom of the first inning of Game 1, with the Pirates already behind 1-0, Virdon led off with a walk and, on Art Ditmar's first pitch to Groat, took off and stole second base. Behind the plate, Berra took the pitch and fired a strike to second, but remarkably, neither Kubek nor Richardson had covered the bag. The ball sailed into center field, and Virdon scooted all the way to third.

The Pirates had caught a break. All season long, Groat had signaled Virdon for the hit-and-run on his own—so confident were the Pirates in their captain's decisions that no one else, not even Murtaugh, knew the sign. But in the nervousness of his first World Series at-bat, Groat says he accidentally put on the hit-and-run sign, before deciding to take a pitch or two to calm down. But when he signaled to take the sign off, Virdon didn't see—and took off for second anyway. A moment later, Groat doubled, scoring Virdon and igniting a three-run Pirate rally. Even after the game, the Pirates didn't let on what had really happened. "We didn't want to give the Yankees any information about our signs, so we decided to simply say it was a delayed steal," Groat says. "I always say we 'outdumbed' the Yankees on that play."

But now, in Game 7, Law wasn't thinking beyond the Yankee sixth inning. That was by design—a textbook case of Baseball 101, pitching pared to the basics. Three more outs; that was all he needed. Just three more on that throbbing ankle, and the bullpen could take over. No, he wasn't nervous in his third Series start, Law professed later. Instead, he was steady and focused—"locked in," as the saying today goes—just as he had been countless times during 1960 in getting the win to stop a losing streak. "Just get through this inning," he said to himself as he headed to the mound, with the top of the order due up for the Yankees—the hot-hitting Richardson followed by Kubek, Maris, and possibly Mantle and Berra, who was hitless but had been knocking the ball well all day. It was a tall order.

Leave the nervousness to Pirate fans, who were banking on Law to erase thirty-five years of frustration with at least one more solid inning. Masterful so far, the Deacon had thrown only one bad pitch all afternoon—the 0-2 "waste pitch" to Skowron that the Yankee first baseman had dubbed into the right-field stands. If he could just get out of this inning, the Pirates' twenty-game winner would go a long way in erasing years of Pirate baggage.

* * *

It *had* been years since Pittsburghers had had much to cheer about. Anchored by the great Honus Wagner, in the century's first decade the team had been among the National League's elite. After losing to the underdog Boston Pilgrims in the very first World Series, in 1903, the Pirates bested Ty Cobb and the Tigers for their first World Championship in 1909, the year Forbes Field opened. Then they won again in '25, beating Walter Johnson in the fog and the rain—still the last time the Pirates had won a World Series.

Considering all the spirited grumbling before the 1960 Series, that Forbes Field was antiquated and too small to accommodate everyone who wanted to attend, it seems ironic that the ballpark had once been considered the crown jewel of baseball. Built some 3 miles east of downtown, Forbes at first was considered a colossal mistake: too big, with an original capacity of twenty-five thousand, and too out of the way to bring in the crowds. "They told me the Giants don't have that large a park with all New York to draw from," Pirate owner Barney Dreyfuss said later. "(It) was considered another of my follies."

But Dreyfuss, a dapper-looking German immigrant who dressed in a suit with a watch fob and a bowler plopped atop his head, knew his business. He realized that the area known as Oakland was becoming the city's entertainment and cultural center. Dreyfuss recognized that the city, hemmed in by rivers to the west, north, and south, was spreading eastward, with the neighborhoods just beyond the park—Squirrel Hill, East Liberty, Point Breeze, and Highland Park—fast becoming choice areas to live for young professionals. Streetcar lines running from downtown up both Forbes Avenue and 5th Avenue were already built and were able to deliver fans to a block from the ballpark gates. Within walking distance were Carnegie Museum, Carnegie Library, and Carnegie Music Hall, which was home to the thirteen-year-old Pittsburgh Symphony. Nearby as well were Phipps Conservatory and the first few buildings of the University of Pittsburgh, and less than a mile up Forbes Avenue was Carnegie Tech. Around the corner were countless bars and restaurants, as well as the stately orange-brick hotel where the visiting teams stayed, the Schenley (now the Pitt Student Union), with its spacious veranda wrapping around the front. "The more I looked over the property, the better I liked it," remarked Dreyfuss. "I had . . . a conviction that Pittsburgh would grow eastward."

If anything, Dreyfuss deserved a medal for the speed with which he erected his baseball palace. Breaking ground March 1, 1909, on the seven-acre property, workmen immediately had to grade 60,000 yards of dirt. They hauled in 650 carloads of sand and gravel, 130 carloads of structural steel, 110 carloads of cement, and 40 carloads of sewer pipe in throwing up a great steel-beamed triple-deck grandstand that rose 74 feet into the sooty Pittsburgh sky. In only four months, the grand new ballpark was finished. It was state of the art, among the biggest in baseball, and even had an elevator to the third tier.

To build interest, the Pirates held a contest to name the new park, and fans across the city submitted one hundred thousand entries. But in the end, Dreyfuss named it himself, calling his park Forbes Field in honor of British general John Forbes, who had led an army against the French in and around Pittsburgh in the French and Indian War. His decision was in keeping with the spirit of many streets in Pittsburgh's East End that took names from British generals and officers in that war, such as Braddock (Avenue) and Beeler (Street). But when the sign for the street along the first-base side of the ballpark went up, it was misspelled; intended to be named after another general, Henry Bouquet, a Swiss-born hero in the decisive battle at Fort Duquesne, it actually came out as "Boquet." Nobody seemed to care and "Boquet Street" it remained—usually.

The Pirates' owner had a particular dislike for "cheap" home runs, and made certain his ballpark was spacious—so much so that both left and center field were the league's most distant. Right field was originally 359 feet but was moved in gradually, settling at 300 feet by 1925 with the addition of a grandstand, an extension that expanded the park's capacity to thirty-five thousand.

To the surprise of many, people filled the park—30,388 attended Forbes Field's opening day on June 30, 1909, so many that about 5,000 had to stand behind the ropes in the outfield. The occasion was all quite grand, with folks dressed in their finery, flags rippling from the top of the upper deck, and bunting draped from the railings. Railroads offered special rates to Pittsburgh, Dreyfuss threw a big parade on opening day, and all the notables—from Pirates of the old days to U.S. congressman John Tener, a former Pirate pitcher and future N.L. president—showed up. Against the Cubs, Honus Wagner bagged a couple of base hits, but the Pirates stranded ten runners and lost, 3-2. "I'd have given my share of the gate to have won on this day," Dreyfuss said.

But the crowds kept coming, packing Forbes Field five times within two weeks. Many came to see the wondrous Wagner, a native of nearby Carnegie. At 5'11" and 200 pounds, he sported a black-smith's build, was considered too husky to have much speed, and was bowlegged—yes, bowlegged—yet he led the NL six times in stolen bases. Wagner won eight National League batting titles, too, standing deep in the batter's box with a squatlike stance that made him look like he was sitting on a barstool.

John McGraw called Wagner the best all-round player he had ever seen, better than Cobb or Ruth. When a young Giant pitcher asked McGraw how to pitch Wagner, the Giant skipper shrugged and advised him to "just pitch—and duck." Driving the ball to all fields, Wagner seldom slumped, and in twenty-two big-league seasons, com-piled a lifetime average of .329. To him, ending a rare slump was simple: "I'd look at my feet," he said, "shift my feet a bit, and the hits would start coming." In the field, Wagner was the game's most graceful shortstop, a man with the ability to go deep in the hole, and uncork both the ball and a handful of dust on a line to nail the runner at first.

Wagner and player-manager Fred Clarke topped that glorious season in 1909 with the World Series title. But only in '25, long after Wagner had retired, did the team win another Series—led by the hard-hitting, great-gloved Pie Traynor. As a player and later as man-ager, Pie became almost as beloved in Pittsburgh as Wagner, though he never managed to lead the Pirates back to a Series.

Traynor was a friendly, gracious man who some argued was too nice to be an effective manager. His '38 Pirates appeared to have the pennant in hand with a five-game lead on September 8, and team offi-cials got busy putting together a $35,000 press box (later dubbed the

"Crow's Nest") in the third deck of Forbes Field to accommodate the flood of reporters expected for the World Series. But then the Pirates fell apart, and on September 29, while clinging to a half-game lead against the second-place Cubs in the near-darkness of Wrigley Field, Gabby Hartnett hit a home run to take the game and pennant for Chicago. It was baseball's famous "Homer in the Gloamin.' "

So Pirate fans kept waiting for a pennant. At least they forgave Traynor, a Boston native who had adopted Pittsburgh as his year-round residence. Living in the King Edward Apartments on Craig Street, a ten-minute walk from Forbes Field, he became a man about town. Pie, who never learned to drive, could often be found loafing and talking shop in front of the Webster Hall Hotel, home of the Ascot Room, where fans would greet him with the declaration, "Pie Traynor, greatest third baseman of all time!"

The Depression years were a perilous time in Western Pennsylvania. The Pirates gave the unemployed free admission to Forbes Field, but crowds were scant. Without much of a team to root for, Pirate fans found pleasure where they could—reserving particular respect for homegrown stars, even when they played for somebody else. Stan Musial of the Cardinals was the most notable. He was from the nearby mill town of Donora, a fact that Bob Prince brought up seemingly every time he came to bat. How painful for Pirate fans that their team had overlooked this future Hall of Famer. And how painful for Pittsburgh pitchers, who Musial seemed to clobber at will.

A treat of going to Forbes Field in the 1930s and '40s was to arrive an hour early and watch the great Wagner, by then a coach, take fielding practice. In his first few postbaseball years, he had prospered—marrying Bessie Smith of Pittsburgh, with whom he fathered two daughters, while coaching both baseball and basketball at Carnegie Tech, and even serving a stint working for the state legislature in Harrisburg. But then came hard times—a failed partnership with Pie Traynor in a Pittsburgh sporting goods company at the outset of the Depression. By 1933, the business had left him nearly destitute when Pirates owner Bill Benswanger, Dreyfuss's son-in-law, who had taken over the teams when Barney died in 1932, asked if he'd like to rejoin the club as a coach.

Would he ever. Back in uniform, Wagner worked with the Pittsburgh infielders, and even as a white-haired man pushing sixty-five, he still had a howitzer of an arm. It became a kind of game outside the regular game—and Wagner would often retreat after practice to the grandstand, where he'd sign autographs and spin yarns, some of which were true. On the banquet circuit at just about every Kiwanis Club in Western Pennsylvania, he'd sign his name some more and tell his tall tales—making him, next to Babe Ruth, baseball's most beloved ambassador.

If Wagner is a distant memory these days in Pittsburgh, many still remembered him in 1960, including Dick Groat, who met him in his rookie year, a year after Honus stepped down as a Pirate coach. On an April morning in 1955 before the Pirates played the Reds, a crowd of fifteen hundred, including a parade of baseball icons from the old days, showed up in Schenley Park's plaza for the unveiling of a striking 18½-foot bronze statue of Wagner at bat. There were speeches, but not from the frail eighty-year-old baseball legend, who waved to the crowd from the car. How fortunate that Honus lived to see the dedication of the statue; nine months later, he died at eighty-one, hailed as "Mr. Pittsburgh" by the *Sun-Telegraph*. The statue was later moved to Three Rivers Stadium and today resides outside PNC Park, a tribute to the greatest Pirate of all.

* * *

The arrival in 1946 of a charismatic slugger named Ralph Kiner swelled Pirate home attendance. The twenty-three-year-old bashed twenty-three home runs to lead the NL—the first rookie to do so in more than forty years. That coincided with the decision of Barney Dreyfuss's heirs to sell the controlling interest in the team to a conglomerate headed by Indianapolis banker Frank McKinney, which included the Columbus real estate executive and horse breeder John Galbraith, Pittsburgh attorney Thomas Johnson, and Hollywood crooner Bing Crosby. The owners spent a lot of money, renovated Forbes Field, and even lured aging Detroit slugger Hank Greenberg, who had been ready to retire, to Pittsburgh for one more season.

The thirty-six-year-old Greenberg and young Kiner gave the Pirates a dose of sorely needed star appeal, a potent one-two punch in the batting order that almost doubled home attendance in 1947 to 1.28 million, the first time the team broke 1 million. Management moved the left-field wall in about 25 feet, to 335 feet, making it easier for the two right-handed sluggers to reach the fences. Writers dubbed the new fence "Greenberg Gardens," which stretched 200 feet toward center field, though it seemed to favor opposing sluggers, who sent a lot of home runs themselves into the Carnegie Library parking lot. Greenberg hit twenty-five homers, held down largely because NL pitchers, respecting his power, walked him a league-leading 104 times. Meantime, Greenberg mentored Kiner by getting him to pull outside pitches and refrain from hitting bad ones—and it worked. "The best thing that ever happened to me," Kiner said of Greenberg's counsel. "He just taught me some great work habits." Kiner belted fifty-one homers in '47, including forty-eight after June 1, for the second of his seven straight years as league leader.

The charismatic young ballplayer was immensely popular in Pittsburgh. He never refused an autograph to a youngster, having been brushed off as a kid in California by Dizzy Dean. Even as the team continued to lose, fans arrived early to see him in batting practice and waited until his last at-bat during the game before leaving, even when the team was hopelessly behind. For a time, Kiner dated actress Elizabeth Taylor—exotic stuff for Pittsburgh—and he became one of the first ballplayers to host his own local TV show.

Co-owner Crosby added star appeal as well, sitting in with Bob Prince on the radio when he got to town. But little seemed to help the Pirates. They were the National League's downtrodden, the butt of jokes. "You guys have a fifty-fifty team," Reds manager Roger Hornsby told a gathering of Pirate players in 1952. "You get 'em out in the clubhouse, but lose in the field." The new owners replaced Frankie Frisch with Billy Herman as manager and hired Roy Hamey, a former minor-league executive with the Yankees, as GM. Hamey sent Bob Elliott to the Braves for a forgettable foursome, and Elliott raised his batting average 54 points and was MVP. In 1948, a new manager, Billy Meyer, actually had the Pirates in contention until September, but the team finished fourth. Hamey continued to wheel and deal, sending Preacher Roe and Billy Cox to the Dodgers, where they became stars, and the Pirates went into the tank—dropping to fifth in '49, and not rising above seventh for most of the next decade.

So on a sunny November morning in 1950, Galbraith announced that he had hired the legendary Branch Rickey—architect of the great St. Louis Cardinal and Brooklyn Dodger franchises. A master innovator, Rickey had created the modern farm system, the vertically integrated pipeline of player talent beholden to a single team. He was the man who signed Jackie Robinson, ending the major-league color ban, and had even invented the batting helmet. Rickey was a true baseball pioneer, an eccentric and old-fashioned windbag with a Victorian air from whom "superfluous verbiage continually flowed," as writer Andrew O'Toole put it. Rickey asked the Pirates for a favor: patience as he began laying out what he described as a five-year master plan. "We're pointing to 1955," the Bible-quoting, tee-totaling lawyer pontificated at his Forbes Field press conference. "That's when the bells will start ringing and the red wagon comes down the street. That's when Pittsburgh folks will shout, 'By George, this is it!' "

Few people got wind of his lofty prognostication; reporters from the three Pittsburgh newspapers were on strike at the time. But the sixty-nine-year-old Rickey, who had been chased from Brooklyn by a power struggle with Dodger owner Walter O'Malley, made his mark anyway, by cleaning house and bringing in his seasoned corps of Dodger scouts: Clyde Sukeforth, Rex Bowen, and Howie Haak, along with George Sisler, the great Hall of Famer–turned–batting instructor. Rickey and his men wheeled and dealed and signed a lot of prospects, looking to mastermind a quick turnabout in Pittsburgh.

Comprising Rickey's staff were experienced baseball men, who had stuck together for years. Rickey had managed Sisler at the University of Michigan, where the future batting star was actually a pitcher—going an unworldly 50-0 before graduating with a degree in mechanical engineering. The two then served together during World War I in the Army chemical corps—Rickey was Sisler's commanding officer. Back home, as president of the St. Louis Browns, Rickey coveted his old pitcher, securing him only after a protracted and nasty tug of war with Dreyfuss of the Pirates. Sisler switched to first base and became a superstar—a two-time AL batting champion, a .400 hitter, and among the first players elected to the Baseball Hall of Fame. Dreyfuss forever regretted losing Sisler; he never again spoke to Rickey.

Rickey was a man of many sides, with a style all his own. Brilliant, vain, dictatorial, given to rambling discourses, and notoriously cheap, he wore bow ties and talked in parables that, delivered in a rich Irish baritone, were easily imitated and not easily forgotten.

Decades of experience gave Rickey his own way of doing things, a homegrown philosophy. His way of finding talent was hosting mass tryouts where he would sign promising players at bargain-basement prices. "If you scoop up enough talent," Rickey reasoned, "you can develop quality out of quantity." He checked into the personal lives of his young players, hoping they would marry and settle down, sometimes urging his staff to find them dates. As a rule, he refused to sign medical students, saying they were "already dedicated to another vocation." The same went for divinity students: With the world "in bad enough shape already," Rickey put it, "we don't want to take anyone away from the Lord's work."

Rickey's scouts delivered. They signed Law, Groat, and Maze-roski, who became the nucleus of future Pirate teams. So did the husky sinkerballer Bob Friend, who made it to Pittsburgh as a twenty-year-old in 1951 and became a star four years later when, over Rickey's objections, manager Fred Haney slipped him into the starting rotation on Sundays, the day the observant general manager didn't go to the ballpark. A former high-school halfback from Indiana, Friend was accomplished on the field and off: He became the team's player representative and was a talented pianist and a businessman who was already starting to carve out a significant role in Western Pennsyl-vania's Republican politics. Like his father and five brothers and sisters, Friend was a Purdue graduate. That he and Skowron, former Purdue students, both played in the 1960 World Series would become a point of pride on the university's West Lafayette, Indiana, campus.

Rickey had hoped to sign Groat in 1951 after his junior year at Duke, but the young ballplayer and basketball All-American asked to be given an extra year so he could graduate. As a 5'11" junior guard on the Duke basketball team, Groat set a national collegiate scoring record. Shorter and a step slower than most others on the court, he thrived with his smarts, solid fundamentals, and a relentless work ethic. As a scorer, Groat used a two-hand set-shot to hit from the out-side, and could just as easily drive in close with his stop-and-go dribble. Groat was college basketball's 1952 Player of the Year for the top-ranked Blue Devils and also led the Duke baseball team to the College World Series. The day after Duke was eliminated from the baseball finals, Groat flew home to Pittsburgh, and on June 16, 1952, he marched into Forbes Field with his father Martin and signed with the Pirates for a $25,000 bonus. "This is something I've always wanted to do—become a Pittsburgh Pirate," said Groat, who had grown up accompanying his older brothers to see the Pirates play at Forbes Field.

The signing was big news in Pittsburgh. The *Press* trumpeted the news the next day with a photo of Groat and his father shaking hands with Rickey, and the story was positioned in the middle of the sports page—underneath another piece detailing the Pirate loss in Philadelphia. The headline of the game article: "Same Sad Story—Pirates Again Beat Themselves." No question, the sad sacks of the National League had room for a new shortstop.

After signing the contract, Groat flew to New York to join his new teammates, and a day later was in the starting lineup against the Giants at the Polo Grounds. He would never spend a day in the minors, a rare feat he shared with only a handful of players, including Hall of Famers Mel Ott, Al Kaline, and Dave Winfield. Popping up in his first big-league at-bat, Groat in his next at-bat by lined a single off Larry Jaster through the box with the bases loaded to drive home two runs. By the close of '52, he had compiled a .284 batting average, better than just about anyone else on a Pirate team that lost 112 games. "Maybe it wasn't much of a ball club," Groat said, "but I wasn't worried about winning any pennants. All I was worried about was staying in the big leagues."

That fall, Groat went back to school to finish his degree, and to play more basketball by joining the NBA's Fort Wayne Pistons for a half season, which he managed by shuttling back and forth to class in Durham and meeting his team wherever they were playing. Then Groat joined the Army for two years—and on returning to the Pirates in 1955, dropped basketball, at the request of Joe L. Brown, to focus on baseball.

By 1960, Groat had become the Pirates' best all-round player. He hadn't done so with speed, with muscle, or even with hair, for that matter—Groat was bald by then. Nor did he have much power—his best production to date was nine home runs in '58. All Groat had done, said his longtime roommate and close friend Bill Virdon, was get "more out of his natural abilities than anyone I've ever seen." Warren Spahn called Groat "the player the Pirates can least afford to lose." Added Reds manager Fred Hutchinson: "He kills us. I wish to hell he'd go away."

At the plate, Groat used remarkable bat control to do just about anything but hit for power. He hit a lot of ground-ball singles; could hit in the clutch, hit behind the runner, and bunt; and he seldom struck out. At shortstop, he was rarely out of position, knew the hitters, and had a lightning-quick release. Anchored by Mazeroski at second and Hoak at third, the 1960 Pirates were the NL's best fielding infield.

Joining the Pirates in 1960, reserve catcher Bob Oldis recalled his early impressions of Groat. "The guy couldn't do anything," he said. "He didn't even look like a big leaguer to me. But then, day after day, I began to realize what he was doing out there. He was helping this team win ball games. He's a hell of a ballplayer."

No, he didn't look much like a big leaguer. Slight of build, Groat appeared more like an accountant than like the leader of the National League champions; the Pirates, by the way, were the only NL team to have a captain. For the most part, Groat was on the private side, on the road preferring to go to the movies or play bridge with Virdon rather than to hit the bars. At home, it was a quick trip from the ballpark straight to a Wilkinsburg apartment in East Pittsburgh to see his wife, Barbara, and two young daughters; the Groats had met at the Polo Grounds back in '55, where the former model had gone to see a game with her father, a big Duke basketball supporter. Bob Prince had played matchmaker, and to this day, Groat retains a special fondness for the Polo Grounds.

But inside this deceptively mild exterior, the competitive fires burned. Prince recalled a benefit basketball game in which a group of Pirates played the Steelers. For years, Groat's presence in the lineup for the Pirates had made the game a one-sided affair—that is, until

January of 1960, when the Steelers brought in a ringer: the former Pitt basketball All-American Don Hennon. The two former collegiate stars dominated the game down to the buzzer when Hennon, with his team down by three, made a field goal and was fouled by Groat. The referee: Prince, who admitted that Groat didn't really foul Hennon, but "just wanted to send the game into overtime and give the customers a show."

Groat was furious.

"Relax, Dick," Prince told Groat. "This is only an exhibition. A fun game."

"Fun, hell," Groat told him. "I'm trying to win."

After the Pirates lost in overtime, Prince said Groat didn't speak to him for weeks.

* * *

In hindsight, Rickey gets a bad rap. His ego and eccentricities could grate. He didn't win fast enough. But the '60 Pirates were largely his creation, much of the team scrapped together from Rickey's experienced hand, though he was well out the door by then. Rickey's one notable oversight was his refusal to sign a hard-throwing left-handed pitcher from Brooklyn who had accepted a scholarship to play baseball and basketball at the University of Cincinnati. Ed McCarrick, a scout Sisler had assigned to the New York area, was the first to alert the Pirates to the potential of the prospect named Sandy Koufax. So the Pirates took the young pitcher to Pittsburgh for a tryout, where he impressed Sisler enough for him to urge a contract offer. But Rickey, who insisted on final say about who received offers, thought Koufax was too wild and ungainly to make it in the big leagues. In a major mental blip, the Pirate general manager turned his back on a player who would later sign with his hometown Dodgers and end up with a plaque in Cooperstown.

Little worked for the Pirates in Rickey's early years in Pittsburgh. They were slow to sign African-American players—only the ninth of the sixteen big-league teams to integrate. No Pirate infielder in 1951 stood more than 5'6", and critics pegged the team with a derisive nickname that stuck: the "Rinkydinks." "The trouble with these guys," said Sid Gordon, an outfielder on the '51 team, "is that after you've been with them for a couple of weeks, you start to play like them."

From 1952 to 1954, the Pirates lost more than one hundred games a season, finishing last three times in a row. Looking for star appeal, the team signed a catcher, the Heisman Trophy winner Vic Janowicz, from John Galbraith's favorite university, Ohio State. The problem was, he was considerably more skilled at catching footballs than baseballs. After misplaying three foul pop-ups in a game, Janowicz was looking skyward for another when a leather-lunged voice rang out from the Forbes Field stands: "Signal for a fair catch, you bum!"

Janowicz wasn't long for the Pirates. Neither was Kiner, despite belting a league-leading thirty-seven home runs in 1952, the team's lone bright spot that year. Signing his contract for '53, Kiner was startled to receive an offer from Rickey that included a 25 percent cut from his $90,000 salary.

Asking why he deserved a cut, Rickey responded with a question of his own: Where exactly did the Pirates finish?

"In last place, Mr. Rickey," said Kiner.

"Hmmm," ruminated Mr. Rickey, a cigar planted firmly in the corner of his mouth. "Let me tell you something. We could have finished last without you."

Kiner signed anyway—players didn't have much bargaining leverage in those days—but his days with the Pirates were numbered. In June 1953, Rickey shipped him to the Cubs, a move for which the Pirate GM was never forgiven in Pittsburgh. Meantime, the Pirates kept losing in the field and in the stands, with home attendance dropping to a measly 470,000 in 1955. Not to worry, promised Pirate manager Fred Haney. "I can detect progress," he said. "The seven other clubs are growing older."

No one believed him, and out the door went Haney, who would catch on a few years later managing pennant winners with the Milwaukee Braves. In came the fiery Bobby Bragan, who guided the team in 1956 all the way to seventh place, one spot above the Cubs. But that wasn't good enough for Galbraith, by then the majority owner whose patience and dollars invested in the Pirates were running thin. The new majority owner's first significant move: sending Rickey packing.

So who could the Pirates choose to succeed perhaps the most celebrated mind in baseball history? A virtual unknown, all except for his famous name: Joe. L. Brown, the thirty-seven-year-old head of the Pirates' farm system whose father, Joe E. Brown, was a famous Hollywood actor and comedian. Deftly and decisively, the new general manager cemented his reign over a team he said had "no reason to believe they were any good."

Raised in Hollywood, Brown didn't seem much like the man to bring the Pirates back from baseball wilderness. But the game was in his blood, passed on by his famous father, who had been a decent semipro player in his day and was such a stanch baseball fan that he demanded that Warner Bros. fund a studio team. Joe E. was among the first big collectors of baseball memorabilia and owned Lou Gehrig's last glove. And he worked a lot of baseball into his routines and considered his baseball film trilogy in the '30s, topped by Ring Lardner's creation, *Alibi Ike,* his best work. Brown's most celebrated film, the 1960 classic *Some Like it Hot,* in which Joe E. plays an eccentric millionaire, even had a baseball angle; the film's director, Billy Wilder, had run into Brown so often at Dodger games at Memorial Coliseum that he decided Joe E. would be perfect for the role. His son, Joe L., may have come from privilege, but he had learned baseball the old-fashioned way, with a long apprenticeship in the bushes. At twenty, Joe L. was an end on the UCLA football team when he quit school to become assistant business manager of the Class D base-ball club in Lubbock, Texas. Over the next seventeen years, Brown did just about everything there was to be done in his minor-league apprenticeship—dragging infields, taking tickets, and developing a bona fide skill in evaluating talent. Named general manager of the Pirates in October 1955, Brown had a style all his own: Tanned, fit, and approachable, he got to know his players by roaming about the field before games and schmoozing, uninhibited by the unwritten rule in those days that GMs did not chat with the help. Not much older than most of his players, Brown made a point to find out what was on their minds. "I like to nose around," he said.

From the get-go, Brown made his presence known. He relieved George Sisler of his scouting duties and sent him to the batting cage to do what he did best: teach promising players how to hit. As one of baseball's first batting specialists, Sisler taught his batters that the key to getting base hits wasn't in shifting your stance, but in good timing and knowing the strike zone and when to make contact.

Brown made a significant trade early on, sending Pittsburgh native and journeyman pitcher Bobby Del Greco to the Cardinals for Bill Virdon, the '55 NL Rookie of the Year. Virdon went to center field, where he became a staple for the next decade—a solid leadoff hitter in the .260 to .270 range, with power and speed on the base paths and in the outfield. Wearing glasses made Virdon seem cerebral; actually, he was, and later, he would enjoy a long, successful second career as manager of the Pirates, Yankees, Astros, and Montreal Expos.

*   *   *

Bobby Bragan couldn't help the Pirates. Desperate to win, he baited his players, bruising their egos. He shrieked at umpires and pestered Brown to clean house. Figuring the Pirates could use another power hitter, he tinkered with the batting order and—get this—tried getting

Brown to trade Clemente to St. Louis for Ken Boyer. On July 31, 1957, with the Pirates more than thirty games under .500 and headed nowhere, Bragan was ejected for arguing balls and strikes, only to pop up a moment later to offer some orange drink to the umpire. That was the last straw—literally—which prompted Brown to engineer his best move of all. He replaced Bragan with Danny Murtaugh.

* * *

So what could Bobby Richardson do against Law? On a team full of big boppers, the Yankee second baseman had been the World Series' biggest, and most unlikely, slugger of all. In Game 3, Richardson had had a grand slam and six RBIs. In Game 6, he had belted two triples and three more runs batted-in—giving him an all-time Series record of 12 RBIs. "Boy blood-drinker," Red Smith had called Richardson in the morning's *Herald-Tribune*. About the only thing the twenty-five-year-old Sumter, South Carolina, native had done wrong in six and a half World Series games to date was going hitless in two at-bats here in Game 7.

So what did Richardson do? He leaned into Law's first delivery by squaring around to bunt. Yes, bunt. It didn't work, as the ball crossed the plate for a strike one. But that didn't matter; using "small" ball, he had caught the Pirate infielders by surprise, luring them to move in a tad on the next pitch and open up a sliver of the infield where he could place another base hit.

It *was* a ruse. Swinging solidly at Law's 0-1 pitch, Richardson sent a hard single into shallow center for the Yankees' fourth base hit. The Yankee second baseman was still hitting seemingly everything in sight. And could it be that Law, done in by his sore ankle, was finally starting to tire? Murtaugh wasn't taking a chance and quickly reached for the bullpen phone to get Face and Harvey Haddix warming.

There was no rest for the Pirates. Kubek, the inning's second batter, who had turned twenty-four years old the day before, was another

Yankee enjoying a top-notch Series. Hitting .370, the left-handed batter would for now play it safe—finally—and with instruction from third-base coach Frank Crosetti, laid off Law's first pitch, a ball, and the second, another ball. Better to see if a base runner might rattle the Pirate pitcher into a streak of wildness.

Behind 2-0 with a man on first, Hoak called time and trotted to the mound to offer encouragement to Law. Needing a strike, Law got one, as Kubek ran his hands up the bat as a bluff, but didn't swing—looking to take all the way. Then the 2-1 count became 3-1, with Law delivering a pitch high and outside. "(There's) an uneasy spirit for the spectators at Forbes Field," Chuck Thompson informed listeners on NBC Radio, as if they didn't know. "This is the big one, this is for all the money, the glory, and the gold of the 1960 Series."

Still not swinging, Kubek took strike two. The count was full. Stengel, his right foot back on the top step on the Yankee dugout, stared out at Law like a general trying to decipher the enemy. Slowing the game down at one of the Pirate ace's first hints of trouble all day was a sign that the Yankees were taking Game 7 pitch-by-pitch now. They were three runs down, but this was very much a contest.

With no one out, the Yankees could afford to play it safe. Richardson held at first. Into the plate came the 3-2 pitch, but Kubek still wasn't swinging. It was low for ball four, Law's first walk of the afternoon. There were two on and no outs.

Stengel continued to stand, like a sphinx, but Murtaugh bolted from his seat and walked briskly to the mound to remove his ace. Not wanting to leave, Law protested mildly, telling his manager what he admitted later was "a little white lie."

The "lie" was that his throbbing ankle was fine. "I felt I could've won with that three-run lead and wanted to stay in there," Law said. But Murtaugh wasn't buying it and, figuring his ace was too injured to go any further, turned philosophical.

"You have a lot of years left in baseball, and I don't want you to risk your arm because you have a bad ankle," Murtaugh told him. "Dizzy Dean did it and I don't want it to happen to you." And with that, the Pirate manager asked for the ball, turned toward the right-field bullpen, and stuck out his right palm, waist high and parallel to the ground. Everyone at Forbes Field recognized the sign: The call was for Elroy Face, the man Bob Prince called the "Baron of the Bullpen."

Law departed to a standing ovation. He had performed admirably— yielding one run in five-plus innings to go along with his wins in Games 1 and 4. Face had saved both those games and Game 5, too, giving the Yankees a taste of just why he had become baseball's best reliever. Of all the contributors to the 1960 Pirates, none played a greater role than this thirty-two-year-old reliever with a devastating fork ball.

Face didn't look imposing. He stood 5'8", weighed a feathery 155 pounds, and seemed smaller when photographers posed him in a fireman's hat to symbolize his stature as the National League's pre- mier reliever of the era. In '58 and '59, Face had put together a streak for ages—nabbing a 5-3 win in relief against the Cubs on June 7, 1958, and not losing until September 11, *1959,* a full *ninety-eight* games later. His final record for 1959, during which he appeared in fifty-seven games, was 18-1 and ranked as one of the greatest single seasons in history.

When Face finally lost to the Dodgers 5-4, which dropped his record to 17-1, he was humble, offering no excuses. "I would have lost a half-dozen times if these guys hadn't bailed me out with some runs," the right-hander said of his teammates during the streak. When he dropped the first game of the 1960 season—an opening-day 4-3 loss to the Phillies at Forbes Field—the laid-back, guitar-strumming devotee of country music sloughed it off, almost thankful there would be no more discussion of streaks for awhile. "*That* sure takes the pres- sure off," he drolled.

Face's comments spoke volumes. Little rattled him—certainly not base runners or sluggers, which was often what he faced when entering a game. "There's nothing you can do about the runners," he says. "The guy with the stick in his hand is the only one who can hurt you." In the bullpen at Yankee Stadium, he and the other Pirate relievers had watched the early innings of Games 3, 4, and 5 on television to get a better sense of how to pitch to the heavy-hitting Yankees. That and a few warm-up pitches were all Face needed to be ready—so unhittable was his forkball. The Pirates had come to rely on Face so often that his very presence radiated a kind of talismanic control as he calmly and steadily made the long walk from the bullpen to the mound. So it went with baseball's best relief pitcher, whose job entailed entering a game at its most crucial moment and quickly restoring order. "Let's get on with it," he seemed to be saying, "stop this nonsense and go home."

Like the knuckler, the forkball, when thrown effectively, can be virtually impossible to hit. Delivered to the plate by wrapping the index and middle fingers around the seamless part of a baseball in a facsimile of the letter "V"—more of a "U" in Face's case—it is a pitch that few can master. Buzzing toward the batter like a slow breaking ball, the forkball darts sharply in or suddenly dives straight down, a forerunner of the split-fingered fastball. Face admitted he didn't always know where his forkball was headed, "but neither does the batter." What made Face's forkball particularly effective was his cagey ability to deliver the ball with the same motion as his fastball, keeping batters continually off guard. Face also threw hard, putting his whole body into the motion with so much oomph that he seemed to quiver, a teammate said, "like a little ol' mouse shaking itself dry."

Face was just another prospect when he arrived in Pittsburgh in 1953, a draftee from the Dodgers' Montreal farm club. Destiny arrived at spring training in '54 in Fort Pierce, Florida, after Rickey told him he would need something beyond a fastball and a curve to make it to the big leagues. That spring, Face watched ex-Yankee relief mainstay Joe Page try to make a comeback with a forkball. In need of an "out" pitch, Face spent most of the year in New Orleans, where he worked hard and mastered the pitch and was soon establishing himself as one of baseball's premier relievers. As with Clemente, Rickey had stolen another future star from under the noses of his old employers, the Dodgers, which always gave him immense satisfaction. But Face had done the rest himself, without counsel or a pitching coach or a manager. "Everything I did in baseball," he says today, "I did it on my own."

The world of relief pitching was relegated to the baseball backwaters of the 1940s and '50s. Long before the world had ever heard of closers, setup men, or even saves—the term wasn't even a stat until 1959—relief staffs of the era were dominated by men who started *and* relieved, like Allie Reynolds of the Yankees, and a bunch of over-the-hill starters trying to hang on. Face was a member of the new breed of relief specialists like Page, Jim Konstanty of the Phillies, and Clem Labine of the Dodgers and later the Pirates—who threw hard, could pitch every day, and seldom got rattled. This exclusive fraternity, which included a fourth member, knuckleballer Hoyt Wilhelm, had something else: an ability to throw strikes.

That singular ability of pitchers of the era to throw a baseball where they wanted it was one of the big differences compared to the game today, Face says. Consider Game 7 as a blueprint for the way big-league hurlers of a half century ago approached their game: by throwing more strikes, which in turn got batters to commit earlier in the count and sped up the game immeasurably. "Pitchers today try to be cute," Face says, by trying to hit at the corners early and then falling behind. "What I did and others like Law and Friend did was to challenge the hitters and try to get ahead."

Pitchers who challenged hitters, he says, kept most baseball games of the era from extending much beyond two and a half hours. Pitchers not only stuck more to the strike zone, but worked faster and more rhythmically, forcing batters to be more aggressive themselves and to commit earlier in the count. See a good pitch and hit it, the feeling went; no need to work the count. And don't underestimate the power of TV to slow today's game even further, adds Maury Allen, with the current generation of players playing to the camera—all the endless digging in at the plate, adjusting and readjusting their batting gloves, and calling time. "Players in 1960 weren't as dramatic or show-oriented as they are today," Allen says. "They weren't performing, but playing the game 'as a game.' Baseball was a lot tighter in 1960, and more entertaining. The focus was on the game and the drama built."

* * *

For all of Face's success in the bullpen, the Pirates didn't convert him to a fulltime relief specialist until halfway through 1957. Set to start on July 31—the day Bobby Bragan was fired—he was shelved and sent full-time to the pen by Danny Murtaugh, the new Pirate manager. Murtaugh's signal: Meeting the Pirates from a road trip, he turned to Face's wife, Jean, and told her to make sure her husband got plenty of rest. "He said I'd be doing a lot of pitching out of the bullpen," Face recalls. "After that, I never started another game."

No wonder the Pirates had called on Face more than three hundred times in the previous five years, an average of more than sixty games a season. Working to Face's considerable advantage was that he seldom got hurt or needed much rest; during one stretch, in 1956, he had relieved in nine straight games. Nor did he need more than five or six pitches in the pen and his eight on the mound to be ready to go, he says.

Face had yet another "ace"—supreme self-confidence, a reaction to those who had told him in his younger days back home in Stephentown, New York, that he was too slight to make it in baseball. Face was used to bucking the odds—not even signing a pro contract until he was twenty-two years old. Besides, he could always go home and take up carpentry, as his grandfather, father, five uncles, and two brothers had done. "I always knew I could pitch," Face said. "Nobody else did."

Pittsburgh fans took to Face. He was the man who kept their Pirates in a lot of games. He was also one of their own: blue collar to the core. Pittsburgh native George Berger remembers his father, Harry, practically busting his buttons with pride at the 1959 All-Star Game at Forbes Field when Face, armed with a 12-0 record at the time, took the mound in the eighth and retired the AL batters. So what if he then gave up three runs via two singles, a walk, and a double? Though the Nationals held on to win by a run, the game was perhaps the only glitch of Face's magical 18-1 season. "In all my years of going with my dad to baseball games at Forbes Field, I think watching Elroy Face in the 1959 All-Star Game had to rank as one of my favorite moments," says Berger. "Elroy Face was it, one of our guys, one of our Pirates mowing down the big boys at the All-Star Game in Pittsburgh. What a moment."

Bill Virdon says Face was the difference-maker for the 1960 Pirates, one of the major reasons for their ability to come from behind in the late innings. "Having a reliever we could count on was probably as big an item as you can find," he says. "If I was going to pick a player to start a club, it would be a short reliever. If you got that guy who can shut 'em down, even if you're a loser, when you're supposed to win, you win—and that keeps you going." Agreeing with Virdon was none other than Berra, who called Face's forkball "so different it kills you." Added Stengel, "(Face) walks in and commences pounding."

That was the idea. In Box 34, a first-base field box behind the Pirate dugout, sat Face's six-year-old daughter, Michelle, who cupped the hand of her mother, Jean, as her father headed purposefully to the mound with two on and nobody gone. Then she started praying, thinking back to a conversation she'd had a few days before with her teacher at St. Bartholomew School in suburban Penn Hills Township.

"When the Yankees beat us," Michelle told a reporter, "our nun told us that maybe the Yanks prayed a little harder to win."

Michelle Face may have been nervous, but her father wasn't. Saying of the Yankees that "they put on their pants the same way we do," he had prepared for the World Series no differently than he had in sixty-eight regular-season appearances. Finishing his eight warm-up pitches here in Game 7, Face was set. Staring at Maris and barely acknowledging the two base runners—no big deal for him—the Pirate reliever blazed a strike on the inside corner. Maris, thinking the pitch was low—which it may have been in the American League—registered his displeasure by glaring at home plate umpire Bill Jackowski. Face came back with a curve that missed, evening the count. Then Maris swung and missed again—sending a high foul pop-up along third base. Backpeddling and staring the ball down, Hoak let it settle into his mitt for a big first out. Relief swept across the partisans at Forbes Field.

A more difficult challenge was just ahead. Striding to the plate was the switch-hitting Mantle, set to bat left-handed against the righty Face, and intent on driving home those two base runners. Still standing atop the dugout steps, Stengel called his big slugger back. A quick strategy session? No. Mantle, one-for-two against Law and absorbed in the moment, had forgotten his batting helmet. Nobody laughed this time; with the Yankees three runs down in the latter stages of Game 7, the tension was palpable.

In retiring Maris, Face had quickly established the upper hand. He had set down seventeen of the last eighteen Yankees throughout the Series. On the other hand, this was Mantle—*the Mick*—who was on a tear, having already smacked three long home runs in this Series to make it fourteen lifetime in the postseason. The Pirates played Mantle straightaway, because where else do you play a hitter with no apparent weaknesses? It was baseball drama in the extreme—strength on the mound against power at bat, an all-star face-off in the late innings of

Game 7. "What a ballgame, and why not?" Thompson told listeners, as if they didn't know already.

Richardson led off second and Kubek off first, both with short leads. Glancing now at both runners, and then at the plate, Face kicked and threw—and Mantle swung hard and decisively, whistling a screeching liner right up the middle, too fast for a diving Groat, and into center field for a hard single. Richardson scored easily, making it 4-2, with Kubek reaching third. Mantle's continued postseason heroics had come at a big moment—it was his second base hit of the afternoon and his tenth RBI of the Series.

With runners on the corners and only one out, Face peered toward the plate, where Berra was headed. A Yankee fixture for more than a decade, Berra's .333 World Series batting average through six games was overlooked amidst the collective team bludgeoning of hapless Pirate pitchers. But Murtaugh wasn't fooled. The toughest Yankee bat? Not Mantle or Maris, the Pirate manager said. "Our reports list Berra. He's supposed to be the tough guy." Like Mantle, Berra stepped it up a notch in the postseason—he had smashed ten home runs in this, his eleventh, World Series. And like the Mick, he was a slugger in a groove at the right time—slashing hard-hit balls around Forbes Field all day, though without a base hit.

Seated in the Yankee dugout, reserve shortstop Joe DeMaestri thought back to a conversation he'd had the evening before with Berra, his roommate on the road. After Berra had read a few of Face's comments in the paper that he considered a little too cocky for his taste, the Yankee slugger pledged to hit a home run the next day off the Pirate reliever. "Yogi took (some of Face's comments) personally," says DeMaestri. "So we're sitting in bed and watching TV, and Yogi says, 'I'm going to hit a home run off that guy.' I'll never forget it."

Despite Face's three saves, Berra had gotten a measure of the Pirate pitcher, seeing him now for the fourth time. And Yogi had taken to Forbes Field, giving credence to the theory that there is no home-field advantage in baseball. "A hitter's paradise (with a) great background, no shadows (and) no haze coming in from the stands," he had said of the old ballpark before Game 6, in which he tallied three hits in four at-bats. "Man, do we love to hit here." Overhearing his catcher's words, Stengel added a few of his own: "Berra could last five more years hitting in this park."

Here in the sixth inning of Game 7, Stengel offered some last-second advice to his slugger: "Wait for the right pitch, Yogi," he yelled. "You don't have to go for the low ball." In his third-base field box and seated within decibel range of Stengel, the equally nervous Dan Topping echoed his manager's command. "Wait for the high hard one," he shouted at Berra through cupped hands.

With a run already in and two runners on base, Face was in a jam. There was little wiggle room, giving him no choice but to throw strikes. Expecting more pitches in the zone, Berra, like Mantle, was swinging. Getting the sign, Face threw and the left-handed hitting Berra sent a ground-ball shooting down the first-base line. For a time, the ball appeared to be fair, but then it took a kangaroo bounce and hopped way above Rocky Nelson's head and into foul territory. Umpire Nestor Chylak was on it and emphatically called the ball a harmless strike.

Working rapidly, Face delivered the 0-1. Berra swung again, met the ball solidly and got some lift. This time, the ball headed high and far down the right-field line. It had plenty of distance. But would it head fair or foul? All eyes in the park and forty million pairs on TV followed the arc of the baseball. Looking skyward, Clemente headed back toward the wall, hoping to make a catch or at least get a carom off the wall. Watching intently was Berra, who trotted toward first, staring open-mouthed at the flight of the ball, as if he could will it fair. "I don't know," Thompson barked into the NBC microphone. "It is going to be a . . . home run for Yogi Berra!"

The ball landed in the upper deck of Forbes Field, not far from the auxiliary scoreboard, and fair by inches. Berra was only halfway to first when he realized the ball was gone, thrust his right hand into the air in triumph and performed an impromptu jig, "as if shot off a rebound tumbler," Arthur Daley wrote in the *Times*. As the ball disappeared into the sea of faces crowded into the right-field seats, the ballpark was suddenly enveloped in an eerie quiet, as if all 36,683 spectators were taking in a wake. In a sense, they were: Kubek crossed the plate, and so did Mantle and then Berra, plodding across the plate for his thirty-sixth Series RBI, a new record.

America caught its collective breath. The Yankees had stormed back from oblivion to take a 5-4 lead on the strength of a massive, clutch three-run homer, the kind boys hit a thousand times in their schoolyard dreams. "We always felt like we were very much in the ballgame, but we had come back, and felt we had a real shot to win," says Richardson, part of a Yankee mob who pounded Berra on the back when he reached the dugout. "By God," said DeMaestri, thinking back to his roommate's prediction. "He did it." For Face, there was a chink in the armor after all.

"In hindsight, the pitch wasn't as inside as I wanted it," says Face. "I left it out over the plate a little too much and I probably didn't have as much on it as I did at other times." And here, in his seventy-second appearance of the year, Face was just about spent. "Yeah, I was tired," he says, offering an explanation, not an excuse. "But give Berra credit: He hit it."

Yes, he did, and scattered down the first-base line, the gaggle of photographers had captured Berra's follow-through in the event the big blow would stand as the game's decisive moment. Marvin Newman got a shot, as did the group's boy wonder, the seventeen-year-old Neil Leifer, still trying to break in and feeling fortunate that he had secured a credential. Despite his youth, Leifer had certainly earned it, having already completed several assignments as a stringer for *Sports Illustrated*. Two years before, at the age of fifteen, the Queens native had snapped several memorable pictures at the 1958 NFL overtime championship at Yankee Stadium, including the famous shot of Alan Ameche of the Colts barreling into the end zone for the winning touchdown. With talent and a sizable dose of chutzpah, Leifer had worked his way into Giant home games at Yankee Stadium by volunteering to push wheelchairs of paralyzed veterans to an area just beyond the end zone. Wandering off with purpose, he had taken to joining the news photographers and become a presence.

In the fall of 1960, Leifer was still stringing but ached to move beyond his day-job delivering sandwiches from the Stage Deli and make his mark in sports photography. The week before the World Series, he decided he simply had to be there to have any hope of reaching his dream. But what he needed first was a top-notch camera with a motor drive, a device that allowed sequential photos of two or three photos per second. Though Leifer had found the right camera—a $300 Nikon F and a nifty $150 motor drive at Olden Camera on 6th Avenue at 32nd Street in Manhattan—he didn't have anywhere near the amount he needed to buy the equipment for himself. So, two days before the Series opened in Pittsburgh, he took his father to the store and convinced him to buy the camera and motor drive on credit.

Leifer's father was a postal employee, a man who had lived through the Depression, owned no credit cards, and did not believe in paying for anything on layaway. "He thought I was nuts, really out of my mind, but he agreed to go along with it, provided I pay him back the $450," Leifer recalls. "I felt I had to be there if I wanted to compete with the big boys."

Armed with a credential, with airfare provided by his benevolent boss at the deli, Leifer flew to Pittsburgh. Using his new Nikon F camera and motor drive, all the film he needed, and a "roving" media credential, he scored his memorable full-page color shot in Game 1. In Game 2, with *S.I.* photographers back to black-and-white film, Leifer shot Mantle returning to the Yankee dugout after a home run in a photo that also made it into the magazine. That two of his photos ran so prominently meant everything to Leifer, far more than a check meant. "It was a turning point in my career, something that convinced me I could hold my own and compete with men like Hy, Marvin, and John, all of whom were my heroes." Three weeks after the Series had ended, Leifer received a $450 check for his series of photos—$300 for the full-page color shot and $150 for the rest. It was the exact amount he'd borrowed from his father weeks earlier for the camera. "I paid my father immediately," says Leifer, "and he never said another word about it." Leifer had arrived; he would photograph more than two hundred *Sports Illustrated* covers and many of American sports' most iconic shots.

* * *

Realizing their team had just surrendered a three-run lead in Game 7 of the World Series, some Pirate fans grew surly. Sitting in the box behind Topping, the woman who a moment ago had been cheering wildly for the Pirates captured the gloom: "Come on Elroy, you're supposed to be a good pitcher!" she cried. "What happened?" With his team winning and feeling a tad noble all of a sudden, Topping turned and addressed the frustrated woman: "Supposed to be good?" Topping said. "He *is* good."

Throughout Forbes Field, emotions ran the gamut. Down the first-base line in the Pirate bullpen, there was no sense of panic. "We got a pretty good chance," Harvey Haddix said to himself. But in her box, Michelle Face kept praying, before stealing a glance at her mother Jean, who was taking the sudden turn of events hard. Jean Face was crying.

With three runs in and still only one out gone, the Yankees were looking for more, hoping to pour it on just as they had in their three Series victories so far. In contrast, the Pirates' goal was short-term: just stop the bleeding. Continuing the team's habit of swinging on the first pitch, Skowron sent Face's foul pop down the third-base line close to the grandstand, where Hoak drifted over and pulled it in. Two down. Then the next batter, Johnny Blanchard, actually let a pitch go by for ball before sending a grounder on a knee-high hop to first, where Nelson scooped up the ball and stepped on the bag to retire the side. But with one swing, the whole complexion of the game had changed, and the Yankees, quite suddenly staring at the prospect of their nineteenth World Series triumph, began thinking of how to preserve their 5-4 lead.

* * *

Ambling to the mound for the bottom of the sixth, Bobby Shantz faced the prospect of a brand-new game, with himself its unlikely hero. Berra may have been the batting star, but the clutch pitching of the diminutive southpaw had enabled the Yankees to claw back from the brink. Entering the game four runs down in the third, Shantz had stopped the Pirates cold for four innings: not a hit and only one base runner, Rocky Nelson, who had walked.

Shantz knew that the best strategy was to stick with what was working: his combination of slow curveballs and pinpoint control that, as one writer put it, "could tease hitters into madness." On the other hand, this was the sixth, and with their innate ability to come from behind, which gave the team a collective feeling of karma in the late innings and a belief that games ended only with the final out, the Pirates were entering territory they knew well. "Who we were playing or what the score was just didn't seem to affect us," says Virdon. "We always felt like we had a chance since we had seen it happen so many times during the course of the year. We said to ourselves, 'you never know.' " Murtaugh agreed, saying, "This club has more bounce than any I've ever been with."

But would the bounce materialize in the late innings of Game 7? Not in the sixth, when the Pirates played right into Shantz's hands—swinging early in the count and paying dearly for their lack of patience. Typically a first-ball hitter, Bob Skinner sent a fly ball fairly deep to right that Maris caught for the first out. Next came Nelson, who promptly sent the first pitch down to first, where Skowron easily scooped the ball and threw it to Shantz for the second out. Two up, two down—and fast.

In the Yankee bullpen, Terry and Coates continued throwing in the event of trouble. They needn't have bothered. With two down and the bases empty, Clemente swung at Shantz's slow 1-1 curve and tapped a weak grounder to the third-base side of the mound, where the sure-handed Yankee pitcher gobbled the ball and threw to Skowron for the third out. It had taken five pitches to dispose of the Pirates, without even the glimmer of a base runner. Shantz had retired eleven in a row. It was getting late for the Pirates, who were down to their last three innings and behind by a run.

SEVENTH INNING

7

	1	2	3	4	5	6	7	8	9	10	Runs	Hits	Errors
YANKEES	0	0	0	0	1	4					5	6	1
PIRATES	2	2	0	0	0	0					4	4	0

7

FOR THE BLIZZARD of statistics generated by a single baseball game, it was impossible to quantify the amount of the office and school work being ignored on the afternoon of Thursday, October 13, 1960. Work and regular routines could wait. By the seventh inning, office workers and students all over America had wandered from their desks in search of a television set or a radio to catch the end of this Game 7 nail-biter. Typical was the situation at Mount Vernon Junior High School in Mount Vernon, New York, where administrators, rather than face an afternoon of empty classrooms, made a sensible decision: they dismissed school at midday.

So back home to Mamaroneck, New York, hurried fourteen-year-old Ken Pearlman, an eighth-grader at Mount Vernon Junior High, to join his father, who was skipping work, to watch the game. Happy that the Yankees had stormed back, Pearlman was nonetheless baffled at how his favorite team had pounded the ball for six and a half games of the World Series but weren't yet in the clear. "No series had ever had been this way, where the Yankees were romping and couldn't put their opponent away," he says. "But, at least in this case, they'd come back."

At Lincoln Junior School in Elwood City, Pennsylvania, some 40 miles northwest of Pittsburgh, classes continued as seventh-grader Ed McConnell kept up as best he could with the action, thanks to the pocket transistor radio he had smuggled to class. "I caught the game in bits and pieces, stops and starts. It was the best I could do."

Back at Forbes Field, emotions were running the gamut. From her first-base box seat, singer Jill Corey, who admitted she didn't know a lot about baseball, was getting a crash-course tutorial from her uncle while keeping an eye on Don Hoak. Since taking up with Hoak during the summer, Corey had been to a handful of games and had caught a good chunk of the Series while in Florida filming a guest spot on the popular television show, *Miami Undercover*. "I really didn't know much about baseball, but my Uncle George was a fan and was explaining things to me," says Corey. "At the same time, I knew the basics and had picked up a few things from watching the Series. And I certainly knew we'd come to an important point."

In the Pirate bullpen, Harvey Haddix sighed to himself that the Yankees had fought back but kept the faith that his team would find a way to pull off the win, as they had so many times during the season. "We got a pretty good chance," Haddix said to himself.

In the press box, Stan Isaacs of *Newsday* figured otherwise. The Brooklyn native had grown up as a National League fan—a Giants supporter who couldn't help but root for the Dodgers, too, after Jackie Robinson joined the league—and figured he was witnessing another comeback for the Yankees, the team with a knack for finding a way. "I always thought they would win in the end," he says.

With Game 7 entering its last three innings, Isaacs and his *Newsday* colleagues, Jack Mann and Steve Jacobson, were already discussing how to divvy up their postgame duties. The only certainty at this point was that Mann would write the main game story, leaving Isaacs and Jacobson to venture into the locker rooms to get the quotes and color for as many sidebars as were needed. Would Berra's blast be the big story? Would it be Shantz's pitching that had helped the Yankees get back in the game? Would the Pirates stage another comeback? No one could tell.

Marginally good news awaited the Pirates in the Yankee seventh: The bottom of the New York batting order was due up. That presented Casey Stengel with a major decision: The Yanks were ahead but could sure use a cushion of a few more runs. Dare the Yankee manager lift Bobby Shantz for a pinch-hitter?

Nine of ten managers would have made a move. Big bats on the bench like Bob Cerv and Dale Long gave the Yankees some options. But sending a pinch-hitter to the plate would mean Stengel would have to resort to another reliever, and he had little confidence in his unsteady bullpen. So with the Yankees' first batter, Clete Boyer, stepping in to bat against Face, Shantz went to the on-deck circle.

Elroy Face had gone to the mound in the seventh looking like his old self by throwing strikes and pitching quickly, as if he needed to be somewhere. Staking Clete Boyer to an 0-2 count, he got the Yankee batter to sky his next pitch deep into left-center field, and Virdon drifted over to make the catch. One gone.

Stepping to the plate, Shantz dug in to polite applause, the custom in those days afforded to an opposing pitcher on a roll. Shantz was a right-handed batter and presented a bit of a challenge for an opposing pitcher: at only 5'6", there wasn't much of a strike zone. The prospective hero of Game 7, Shantz wasn't such a bad hitter either—for a pitcher, anyway—though he had batted only twelve times all season.

Taking ball one, Shantz took a hack and sent a foul ball straight back into the stands. Letting ball two pass, he chopped at Face's 2-1 delivery and sent the ball on a kangaroo hop toward third base, over the head of Don Hoak, and into left field for a single. Things were going right for the diminutive right-hander who was delivering big on the mound—and had just gained his first World Series base hit.

The Pirate infield took a collective step toward the plate in the event that the next batter, Richardson, delivered a ground ball that could then be converted to a double play. Stengel signaled "bunt," which for most batters was purely conventional—perhaps too much so, considering the Yankee second baseman had been slugging everything in sight.

Looking for an edge, any edge, Face threw quickly to first base, nearly catching Shantz, who was not used to being there, leaning the wrong way. In the Pirate dugout, Murtaugh figured his ace was just about out of gas and called to get two of his starters, Bob Friend and Harvey Haddix, working. Squaring to bunt, Richardson took a ball inside and then ran his hands up the bat for one strike.

With the Pirate infield still drawn nearer to the plate, Stengel pulled a switch, signaling to third base coach Frank Crosetti to direct Richardson to swing away. Lashing at the 1-1, the Yankee second baseman shot a ball down the right-field line that hooked foul by about three feet. Advantage Face. The infield remained in, but on the 1-2, Richardson took another hack, shooting a sharp grounder directly to third base, where Hoak handled the ball and rifled it to 2nd, forcing Shantz. There were two down, with a man on first.

These days, the late innings of close games often slow to a crawl, with managers stalling to get relievers warm, pitchers nibbling at the corners and hitters going deep in the count to wear them down. But not this game—still short of two hours and moving briskly. Remarkably, no one, including the next batter, Tony Kubek, had struck out. Not about to slow things down, the Yankee shortstop took a ball inside before jumping on the next pitch and sending a line shot to right field, where Clemente, playing him perfectly, grabbed the ball for the third out.

* * *

"What a ballgame, what a series," Chuck Thompson barked into the NBC Radio microphone as the sides changed, preparing for the bottom of the seventh with the Yankees clinging to a 5-4 lead. Not that his listeners had to be reminded of the drama: Well above Thompson in the third-tier press box, sportswriters were meeting every big play with a clattering chorus of typing that might—or might not—be the lead to their game stories. "Even after the three lopsided Yankee wins, I can't recall whether there was ever a feeling of who was going to win this game," says Maury Allen. "It was such a back-and-forth, up-and-down game. Whoever was up at the time was the team you thought was going to win."

Thompson and his NBC-TV colleague, Mel Allen, were old school—minimalists, content to describe the action and provide the stats, but not with the endless analysis, graphics, and babble of today. Each had a color man but did most of the talking himself and even handled the pregame show. No need for studio hosts, a third announcer in the booth, or another in the stands, all of them breaking down a baseball game like Middle East peace talks.

But it was Allen himself who was most responsible for broadcasting pared to the basics. His style and mannerisms amounted to a blueprint that he had created back in 1939, the year the twenty-six-year-old University of Alabama Law School graduate joined the Yankee radio team and became baseball's preeminent voice. Allen was a master of the airwaves who could build excitement with the simple anticipation of a slugger walking to the plate. He deftly exploited the rhythms of baseball and of his soft Southern cadence to create a series of expressions known throughout the land: A full count became "3 and 2, what'll he do?" while busy bullpens were "alive" in Allen-speak, third base coaches "chirped" instructions, and batters sent "looping" fly balls into the outfield. A ball streaking toward home-run territory was "Going . . . going . . . gone!" and a truly big play was met with his trademark, "How about that?" Sponsors

adored Allen, especially because he shamelessly plugged their products by describing a homer (pronounced "hummah") as "a Ballantine blast" or a "a White Owl wallop."

The tape of NBC-TV's Game 7 broadcast of the 1960 World Series
is lost; only the audio of the the game's last four innings exists.
Though Allen comes through loud and clear, the technology used to
broadcast the game is crude, particularly with the microphone picking
up voices in the crowd but muting the collective roar. "Come on,
(Bobby, Bob, Tiger, Smoky, Maz . . . fill in the blank), home run
here," implores one Pirate fan in a constant stream of chatter clearly
audible to the forty million viewers.

So who better to get things going than one of the objects of that
fan's exhortations, the grandly named Forrest Harrill "Smoky"
Burgess? The rotund catcher, "shaped like a bench rider on a fat
man's softball team," as *Time* magazine called him, was a reigning
baseball oddity who could seemingly roll out of bed and hit, despite
his girth. How often it seemed that the 5'8½" left-handed hitter—
given another nickname, "Spanky," by teammates after the tubby kid
in the *Our Gang* comedies—started a patented late-inning Pirate rally
with a big base hit.

Burgess took Shantz's curve for a strike. In the bullpen, Coates and
Terry continued to toss. Then Shantz delivered another curveball that
Burgess knocked back through the middle into center field for a
single. The crowd, quiet for most of the last five innings, seemed to
wake up at once to cheer their burley catcher as he returned to the
dugout, replaced by a pinch-runner, Joe Christopher.

Was this the start of something? Ironically, the Pirates had won
those three Series games after grabbing early leads and holding on,
not by giving the Yankees a chance to experience their late-inning
heroics. From the on-deck circle, Don Hoak turned back to the
dugout and loudly encouraged his teammates to step up, and do it
soon. Heading to the plate, Hoak, a patient hitter, had a plan: take

Shantz's pitches for as long as possible. The odds were that Shantz, into his fifth inning of relief, was tiring.

Hoak's hunch was on the mark. Shantz delivered the first one way inside, tumbling the Pirate batter back from the plate. Then came ball two, also inside. In the Yankee bullpen, Coates and Terry delivered their tosses with more pop. Stepping to the top of the dugout, Stengel stared long and hard at Shantz as if he were looking for smoke signals. At the plate, Hoak hardened his strategy: Better to let Shantz dig his own grave than to try anything rash. On the 2-0, almost always a good hitter's pitch, he was still taking and barely lifted his bat. Shantz's delivery was inside again, sending the count to 3-0.

Hoak then rested his bat in taking the obligatory strike at the knees for a 3-1 count. Coming up next was an even better hitter's pitch, but looking toward third base coach Frank Oceak for a sign, Hoak got a small surprise designed to catch the Yankees off guard. To get men on base, he would have to bunt. But squaring around to do so, Hoak fouled off the pitch, making the count full.

The pace was quickening. Trying to slow it down, Shantz opted for an age-old pitcher's trick, throwing to first to send pinch-runner Joe Christopher—"from the Virgin Islands, a speed merchant," Allen reminded viewers—back to the bag. Then Hoak unleashed *his* little mind game by calling time. "If I have to wait on you," said Thompson, encapsulating the Pirate third baseman's thoughts, then "you gonna wait on me a spell." Finally, the Pirate batter was set, and he sent Shantz's next pitch on the fly into left field, where Berra hauled in the ball and tossed it back to the infield. There was one down.

It was getting to be the late show, the Pirates' special time. Could Mazeroski be the hero? At twenty-four years old, the Pirate second baseman was in his fifth big-league season, and it seemed as if he had been around forever. Still developing as a hitter with some pop,

Mazeroski was noted as a fielder without peer, already the league's premier fielder at second base. What Groat, Maz's double-play partner, recalls about Mazeroski's game above anything else was his "marvelous range, great instincts, and never (throwing) to the wrong base." Virdon raves as well, saying, "Nobody ever played 2nd base like he did, and I've been in the game fifty years." Few balls hit anywhere near second base got by; Virdon cannot recall ever having to back Maz up in center and actually getting a ball.

Born in the nearby West Virginia Panhandle town of Wheeling, Mazeroski grew up across the Ohio River in rural southeastern Ohio, where his family lived without electricity. Mazeroski's father, Lew, was a coal miner and an athlete himself, who at seventeen had earned an invitation to spring training with the Indians but tragically never made it when he lost part of his foot in a mining accident. Though Lew was alcoholic, he still found the time to teach his son the basics of baseball.

In the field, Mazeroski seemed to gobble up baseballs so smoothly that many assumed his abilities were God-given. Far from it, said Mazeroski, whose father had fed him field tennis balls thrown against a concrete wall for hours to hone his quickness and ability to meet erratic bounces. Do all you can to be a ballplayer, Lew counseled his son, sounding a lot like Mickey Mantle's father, Mutt. It was better than being a miner.

To pay for his first baseball glove, Mazeroski dug an outhouse for his uncle, who later became his coach. By the time Bill was a sophomore at Warren Consolidated High School in Tiltonsville, Ohio, he was the team's all-purpose baseball star—its best pitcher, catcher, second baseman, and shortstop. In the summer before his junior year of high school, Mazeroski took a well paying job on a highway construction crew, but his father put an end to it, thinking the work would leave him too muscle-bound for baseball. "If you want to work eight or nine hours a day," Lew told him, "do it on a ball field."

Just as good at basketball, Mazeroski was offered scholarships by Ohio State, Duquesne, and West Virginia. But Lew urged his son to focus on baseball and got him to one of Rickey's mass tryouts. Liking what they saw, the Pirates gave Mazeroski a $4,000 bonus and sent him to Williamsport, Pennsylvania, of the Class A Eastern League, where it took him a while to get his footing. Playing short-stop, he hit only .225 and hardly shined on defense, earning the "good glove, no hit" moniker that would unfairly mark his early professional years.

But spring training of 1955 was a revelation: Filling in one day at second, Mazeroski performed a perfect pivot in making a double play, impressing Rickey so much that he decided right there and then that Maz had found his position. Sent to Hollywood of the AAA Pacific Coast League as a second baseman, Maz batted only .170 and was sent back to Williamsport, where he hit his stride, batting .293 and turning a league-leading 108 double plays.

Back in Hollywood, Mazeroski kept hitting—his final batting average there was .306—and earned himself a midseason promotion to the Pirates at age nineteen. Soft-spoken and lacking confidence, Mazeroski molded himself into a big leaguer that winter in the Dominican Republic league: "That season is what made a man out of me, both on and off the baseball field," he told writer Bill Sur-face. "I knew after playing there that no matter what happened on the field, no matter how much you were booed or cursed, no matter how silly you felt for striking out, the world went on the same as always."

Never flamboyant or acrobatic, Mazeroski performed his fielding duties with a remarkable blend of economy, deft footwork, and the physical toughness to stand in on the double play against hard-charging base runners. Dubbed "No Touch" by his teammates for his technique of ricocheting the ball from his glove to his bare hand, Mazeroski built his arm strength by playing catch with his right elbow planted firmly against his side. Looking to collect on a $100 bet from his teammates for taking out Mazeroski at second, Vada Pinson of the Reds once wound up limping off the field, to much cackling from his own dugout.

Total Baseball uses a complex but fair formula in rating fielders, and Mazeroski is judged as not only the best ever at his position but as the best fielder ever—anywhere. Hall of Famer Joe Morgan, a better all-round second baseman, considers Mazeroski second-to-none in the field: "Mazeroski instinctively knew where to play every hitter," he told ESPN's Steve Wulf, "including those he had never seen before." Mazeroski did so by using the same tiny, patched MacGregor G119 glove, with his signature and the big scripted "M" on the inside pinky, for most of his career. At least once a season, Maz hauled the mitt to the pre- or postgame broadcast to show it to Bob Prince, and a generation of Pirate fans grew up with the sense of wonder at how a baseball player could perform so much with so little.

The abrasive Bobby Bragan didn't do much for Mazeroski's confidence. But thanks to Murtaugh's soothing demeanor and George Sisler's batting instruction, Mazeroski had continued his great second-half rally at the plate in 1960 all the way through the World Series. He was batting .286 through the first six games of the Series, second among regulars to Clemente, and had swatted that lone Pirate home run back in Game 1. The hometown fans hoped he could keep producing: "Come on Maz, (hit one) over the clock," yelled the man sitting near Mel Allen.

Eying another of Shantz's big roundhouse curveballs, Mazeroski swung hard and sent a shot down to third base, where Boyer fielded the ball and quickly fired it to Richardson, who stepped on second for one out and fired down to first for a bang-bang, inning-ending double play.

Later, Mazeroski chastised himself for getting sucked in by another of those slow curveballs and swinging too hard. "I had gone for the long ball and I overswung," he told *Baseball Digest* in 1961. The next time up—if there was a next time—he needed to demonstrate more discipline at the plate, he said. All Schantz had done was slither out of trouble to complete his fifth inning of stellar relief, this time with heads-up fielding that even Mazeroski could admire. The Yankees clung to a 5-4 lead.

EIGHTH INNING

8

	1	2	3	4	5	6	7	8	9	10	Runs	Hits	Errors
YANKEES	0	0	0	0	1	4	0				5	7	1
PIRATES	2	2	0	0	0	0	0	0			4	5	0

OF THE FLOOD of memories about October 13, 1960, one of the most powerful for right-handed pitcher Bob Friend was the glorious Indian-summer weather. Leaving his Highland Park house that morning, Friend remembers what a great day it was for baseball. "It was already beautiful and 70 degrees," he recalls. "The sun was out. What a day."

Parking his car at the corner of 5th and Boquet in the lot at Elmer Stuckert's Esso Station, which took care of the cars of most of the Pirate players, Friend walked the last two blocks toward Forbes Field past the early arrivals and wondered if Danny Murtaugh might let him pitch. Sure, he had had two rough outings in the Series and hadn't lasted three innings the day before, but this was Game 7. "We were all ready to go," Friend says. "Everybody was available. We had all winter to rest."

Friend wanted to pitch. For that to happen, the normally unflappable Elroy Face would have to run into further trouble. With his ace clearly tiring, Murtaugh had taken precautions in directing Haddix and Friend to loosen their arms. With Maris, Mantle, and Berra—the heart of the best order in baseball—due up, the Pirate manager would be taking it batter by batter.

Maris went down easily. Peering in at the new Pirates catcher, Hal Smith, Face fired a forkball that Maris drilled on a rope into the right field corner for a foul ball. Batters seldom waited long on Face, whose forkball looked so tempting—like a big, fat, off-speed fastball— before it fell like a bird shot from the sky. Still hacking, Maris lunged at the 0-1 forkball and got a piece. The ball dribbled perhaps thirty feet toward the third-base side of the mound, where Face gobbled it up and threw to first for a quick out. One gone.

Yankee players would say later that Face's forkball felt heavy, as if they were hitting a shot put. That's what Mantle found out as he laid into the 1-0 pitch and lashed the ball on a line toward shortstop, where Groat was perfectly positioned. He barely moved and made the catch. Four pitches had yielded two outs.

But there was little rest for the weary. To the plate stepped Berra— "the man with the big blow," Thompson informed radio listeners, referring to his "three-run home run," which stood to make him the Game 7 hero. With two down and the bases empty, Face had earned some wiggle room. He threw high for a ball, setting Berra up for a good hitter's pitch on the next one. But then Face decided he could waste another one and let Berra know that he was still in charge by buzzing the 1-0 high and tight, thrusting the right-handed batter backward. "Sometimes," said Thompson, "that pitch carries a rather authoritarian message."

For most pitchers, a 2-0 count is tricky—putting them in a position to have to throw a strike. But Face had the forkball, which he could throw well within the strike zone and still expect a batter to have trouble connecting. Swinging at the 2-0, Berra sent a long, high foul ball that struck off the first base grandstand and bounced back on the field down the line. Still committing, he popped another foul into the netting behind home plate. Face had drawn even at a 2-2 count. But then he threw two more balls high for ball four, giving Berra a free pass to first base.

There was one on with two down. Face had been in worse jams many times. But when Skowron sent his first pitch on a kangaroo hop

Vernon Law delivers to Bobby Richardson—and Game 7 of the 1960 World Series is underway. (United Press International)

A key moment in Game 7: Bill Virdon's sharply hit ground ball in the eighth inning has just taken a bad hop and struck Yankee shortstop Tony Kubek on the Adam's apple, turning a routine double play into a run-scoring single and keeping an improbable Pirate rally alive. Here, Kubek is tended to by second baseman Bobby Richardson. (United Press International)

Hal Smith's dramatic three-run home run caps the Pirates' eighth-inning rally. Yankee manager Casey Stengel is already headed to the mound to lift his beleaguered pitcher, Jim Coates. (National Baseball Hall of Fame Library, Cooperstown, NY)

No wonder Bill Mazeroski is so happy as he rounds third base in the bottom of the ninth inning. He has just won the 1960 World Series with the only Game 7 walk-off home run in baseball history. (AP/ Wide World Photos)

An impromptu welcoming committee waits at home plate for Bill Mazeroski, who has just won the 1960 World Series for the Pirates. Note the tackle-sized umpire Bill Jackowski as he positions himself to make sure that the Pirate second baseman touches home plate. Virtually ignored amidst the growing bedlam is Casey Stengel, number 37, as he makes his way off the field for the last time in a Yankee uniform. (National Baseball Hall of Fame Library, Cooperstown, NY)

Let the party begin! Maz nears home plate in a classic shot from Harry Harris of the Associated Press. (AP/Wide World Photos)

Is it snowing in mid-October in downtown Pittsburgh? That's confetti in honor of the Pirates having just won the 1960 World Series. This is the scene outside Kaufman's Department Store at the intersection of Fifth Avenue and Smithfield Street. (National Baseball Hall of Fame Library, Cooperstown, NY)

Big man, big bat: Bill Mazeroski pays tribute to his game-winning bat, Louisville Slugger 125 Pro Model. (National Baseball Hall of Fame Library, Cooperstown, NY)

It is twenty-five minutes after the dramatic end of Game 7. Headed to the left-field exit gate at Forbes Field, Byron Oertel snaps a photo of his daughter Jean in what looks like a very lonely ballpark.

In the streets of downtown Pittsburgh, winning the World Series meant paper, paper, and more paper. City officials would estimate the cleanup cost at $10,000. (Photos taken by Byron F. Oertel, courtesy of Dr. Jean Oertel)

There was once a ballpark here: Pittsburgh's "wailing wall," as one fan puts it, the
remaining section of Forbes Field in Oakland.

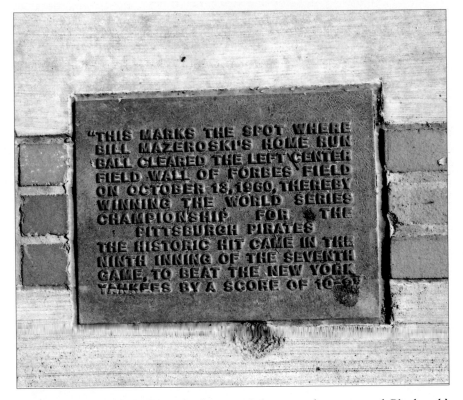

A plaque in the sidewalk marks the spot of the event that prompted Pittsburgh's greatest party ever. (Photos by Jim Reisler)

Forty-five years from the day the Pirates won the 1960 World Series, the believers gathered in what was once left-center field of Forbes Field to listen to the broadcast of Game 7 and remember. That's Herb Saul wearing the tie.

toward third base and Hoak had to wait on it to drop, things began getting dicey for the Pirates. That wait took a millisecond, but it was long enough: Bare-handing the ball, Hoak rifled it to second for the force out, but was late. Berra was safe, as was Skowron. Was it a fielder's choice? A base hit? The bipartisan trio of official scorers—Joe Trimble of the *Daily News,* Jack Hernon of the *Post-Gazette,* and Edgar Munzel of the Chicago *Sun-Times*—figured Skowron would have been able to leg out a peg to first, and gave him an infield single, his twelfth 1960 Series base hit.

Could the Yankees take advantage and drive at least one of the runners home? Blanchard, on a streak of his own with those three hits in Game 6, was at bat to try. Committing to Face's first pitch, he lifted a pop-fly ball down the first-base line. In an effort to disrupt Blanchard's timing, Face was working more quickly than usual, barely giving him time to set himself. So the Yankee catcher fought back, sort of, and stepped out, giving everyone a chance to catch their breath. Composing himself, Face threw the 0-1 and Blanchard popped a short fly toward right that sailed beyond Mazeroski but short of Clemente and dunked in for a bloop single. It wasn't pretty, but the Yankees would take it: Berra scooted home, making it 6-4 Yanks, with Skowron reaching third.

Face was in trouble, and the Pirates had started ahead but fallen behind late—hardly a script the 1960 team had followed to date. Getting loose in the Pirate bullpen, Friend and Haddix both added some zip to their warm-up pitches, giving rise to the oddity that they could be called on to relieve the game's best reliever. Face kept at it, but things were unraveling fast as the next batter, Clete Boyer, ripped at his first pitch—sending the ball down the left-field line into the corner of the outfield, near the base of the big scoreboard. Skowron scored, Blanchard went to third, and Boyer coasted into second with a stand-up double. With two down, the Yanks had ignited and stretched their lead to three runs, 7-4.

Even better for the Yankees, pitcher Bobby Shantz was due up, giving Stengel the golden opportunity to bring up a pinch-hitter, several of whom were available on the Yankee bench. A blowout seemed imminent: Should the pinch-hitter walk and load the bases, the Pirates would be facing Richardson, the batting star of the Series. It seemed like an obvious move, especially to the substitute-happy Stengel. But then the Yankee manager pulled a "Stengel" and did what few expected: Figuring the left-hander who had already pitched five shutout innings, was strong enough to go six, he sent him to bat.

In doing so, Stengel was following his gut—his lack of faith in the rest of the Yankee bullpen, and Shantz's career as a pitcher who could hit. The unorthodox decision nearly paid off: Shantz took Face to a 3-2 count before sending a soft fly to right that Clemente gathered to retire the Yanks. Maybe Stengel could have grabbed another few runs. But his team was leading 7-4 and Shantz was headed back to the hill for the eighth, giving even the never-say-die Pirates a steep challenge. As Roy Terrell of *Sports Illustrated* would write: "This seemed to be the end."

* * *

Starting the Pirates' eighth down by three runs, Danny Murtaugh tinkered. With Elroy Face due up, he called on a pinch-hitter, Gino Cimoli. Another member of the deep Pirates bench, Cimoli had batted .267 for the year, subbing for Bill Virdon in center while playing all three outfield positions, and keeping the clubhouse loose with his pranks.

Cimoli got to the majors with the '56 Dodgers and appeared briefly that fall in the World Series against the Yankees. He became a fan favorite in heavily Italian Brooklyn but two years later was dealt to St. Louis, and then in '59 to Pittsburgh for pitcher Ronnie Kline. Cimoli, a right-handed batter, hadn't wanted to go to Pittsburgh, figuring

Forbes Field's distant left-field wall would deprive him of home runs. Cimoli's trepidation was warranted; of his eighty-two base hits in the 1960 regular season, none were homers. But he had gotten on base so often that the Pirates valued him as another of their batters who seemed to come alive in the late innings. Subbing for the injured Skinner throughout the Series, Cimoli had managed four base hits in nineteen at-bats, demonstrating his value all over again. That went over partic-ularly well in and around Oakland, the Little Italy of Pittsburgh—a neighborhood that, as in Brooklyn, took to "Gino" (his last name was seldom used) as one of its own.

Choosing his bat from the corner rack of the Pirates' dugout, Gino felt weak in the stomach; he slowly climbed the four steps that led to the field. Digging in at the plate, he peered out at the mound and cocked his bat, ready for what would probably be another off-speed curveball like the kind that had bedeviled the Pirates most of the afternoon. Working deliberately, Shantz looked in, got the sign, and took aim with—you guessed it—a slow curve on the outside at the knees. Cimoli stepped for-ward, thinking for a fraction of a second about committing, and held back. Umpire Bill Jackowski's hand shot up. Strike one.

With the count on his side, Shantz wasted a high fastball, tempting Cimoli to chase it. He didn't, and the count evened at 1-1. Down the third-base line in the Yankee bullpen, Ralph Terry and Jim Coates continued to throw, with Shantz now pitching into his sixth inning of work. Also loosening in the pen was shortstop Joe DeMaestri, due to enter the game as part of a late-game defensive maneuver; he was to go in for Kubek, who would then move to left in place of Berra. That first pitch had been a good one, thought Shantz, so he tried it again, thinking another off-speed pitch might get Cimoli to muster only a weak swing. But the Pirate batter wasn't swinging, and the pitch, a screwball, broke down and away, nicking the corner for strike two. Finally, on the 1-2, Cimoli swung—fouling a curveball straight back, keeping the count in Shantz's favor.

It was a cat-and-mouse game, with Shantz trying to tempt the Pirate batter and Cimoli holding back, patient, and waiting for a good pitch—anything that he could fight off to get on base. "(It's) a tense, taut crowd," Thompson told the radio audience. "The fans here at Forbes Field are sitting as if they are on a keg of dynamite. You can feel the explosion that could happen should Cimoli get it started." Shantz wasted another one, up high, evening the count at 2-2. Then the Yankee pitcher made a mistake, trying to surprise Cimoli with a ball right down the middle. Cimoli pounced on it, sending a looping fly over the infield and into short right field, not far from the spot where Blanchard had delivered his base hit in the seventh. Richardson turned and started for the ball. Maris started in, but as happens in the final innings, he had been positioned close to the line, making it too far a run to reach the ball. Cimoli's arching fly fell to the ground for a single, and the Pirates had a base runner.

"Now Forbes Field becomes a little more lively," Thompson told NBC Radio listeners as Bill Virdon, at the top of the order, stepped to bat. If Game 7, now exactly two hours old, had ended right then and there, Virdon would have to be satisfied with his earlier performance—a two-run single back in the Pirate second to put them up 4-0. But that seemed like an eternity ago, as Virdon took a quick fastball on the outside corner for a strike.

Then, taking a solid cut at the 0-1, Virdon cracked a hard, skipping ball down toward shortstop. From his seat in the Pirate dugout, Danny Murtaugh winced as he saw a routine double play about to happen. Across the way in the Yankee dugout, there was just the opposite reaction—relief that they would soon have two outs and nearly be rid of these pesky Pirates once and for all.

Baseball fans have felt the sudden emotion of the 6-4-3 double play a thousand times. It's the tidy, efficient play that personifies the yin and yang of a tight baseball game—crushing for the offense by quickly snuffing out a promising rally, while for the defense, an affirmation that yes, a tired pitcher should be able to escape a jam after all. At its most basic, the DP is one of baseball's signature plays, a mix of motion, athleticism, and teamwork, with all parts having to work seamlessly to nail both runners, and the last one usually by just a half step.

* * *

Virdon's ball skipped once as Tony Kubek moved a half step into position and bent low, his glove ready to take in the baseball. The Yankee shortstop had done this a thousand times, a routine double play in which he'd flip the ball to second base, where Richardson would take care of Cimoli, before throwing to Skowron to nail the batter at first. Then the ball skipped again and hit an obstruction in the infield—at first, everyone thought it was a pebble embedded into the hard Forbes Field infield, but it was in fact a spike cut. In an instant, the ball changed course—ricocheting upward and higher than Kubek's outstretched glove and, like a cannon shot, slamming the Yankee shortstop squarely on the Adam's apple. The force of the ball drove him backward as he instinctively clutched at his throat and crumpled to the ground, "flip(ped) over like a fish out of water," as Thompson said.

The ball dribbled six to eight feet to Kubek's left, toward second base, and both runners were safe. Kubek, still on the ground and with blood now visible in the corners of his mouth, leaned on his right elbow like a groggy sleeper waking from a nap. Looking toward the third-base dugout, Bobby Richardson picked up the baseball with his glove hand and signaled for help with his left. He needn't have bothered; recognizing the violence of the injury, Stengel and the Yankee trainers, Gus Mauch and Joe Soares, had broken from the dugout like sprinters and were already on their way.

The trainers tended to the Yankee shortstop. Within a minute, Kubek was sitting, but he was still dazed and clutching his throat as teammates gathered around in a loose semicircle. It took another thirty seconds for Kubek to get to his feet and start walking as if to pace off the pain, while telling Stengel in croaking whispers that he wanted to stay in the game.

"I can't talk, but I can play alright," Kubek said. "Let me stay in."

But Stengel wouldn't hear of it. Kubek was still spitting up blood and in no condition to continue. Turning toward the bullpen, Stengel signaled for Joe DeMaestri to take over at shortstop. Then the manager, the Yankee trainers, and Kubek, his larynx badly bruised, all trudged deliberately to the dugout. Under the stands, Kubek was examined by the team physicians, Dr. Sidney Gaynor of the Yankees and Dr. Joseph Finegold of the Pirates, both of whom recommended immediate transport to Presbyterian Hospital, where the ballplayer could be properly treated by an ear, nose, and throat specialist. But Kubek wouldn't hear of it until the end of the game, which he sat down to watch on a portable black-and-white TV set up just outside the Yankee clubhouse. So the doctors told their patient to keep from talking and called the hospital, asking that the specialist, Dr. Henry Sherman, get to Forbes Field to make the call himself.

What happened? "I hit the ball well," concedes Virdon. "But it was hit right at (Kubek) and was the type of ball that if you're a shortstop, you want me to hit because if it doesn't take a bad hop, it's routine and we're probably done."

Instead, the Pirates were very much alive in the eighth inning of Game 7, with Cimoli standing on second and Virdon, with his second big base hit of the day, on first with no outs—and with the heart of the Pirate batting order due to bat. Could they take advantage of the big break? Stepping to bat, Dick Groat surveyed the field, thinking how best to punch through a single to bring home at least one. Right field was the best target because a ball hit that way would be behind the base runners and would provide extra seconds to run the bases.

But that's what Shantz was thinking, too, so he decided to jam the right-handed Groat, to coax him into sending the ball to left, where the Yankee infield could make the force at second or third.

Up by three runs and anchored by a veteran pitcher on top of his game, the Yankees still commanded the upper hand. But Groat sensed, from the Virdon at-bat, a crack in the Yankee armor that he could exploit. Virdon's drive was the Pirates' first hard-hit ball off Bobby Shantz all afternoon, so maybe Shantz was tiring after all, he told himself. Wise to the Yankee pitcher's tactics, Groat took a fastball strike on the inside corner at the letters, then a ball. Both pitches were inside, and it became clear to Groat that Shantz would jam him all day if he had to; neither man was about to back down.

So Groat stepped out of the batter's box and took stock. "My biggest fear in baseball was, because I didn't run well and was basically a ground-ball hitter, that I'd hit into a double play," he recalls. "So I said to myself, 'Dick, you just aren't going to hit one to right, so you had just better swing the bat and hit it as hard as you can.' That was against all my beliefs. I didn't do that very often."

Groat figured right. Shantz's 1-1 pitch was in on the fists, again, and the Pirate batter took a level swing—sending the ball not to right, but pulling it about two feet off the ground on a line through the infield between third and short, too far for Boyer to make a play. Cimoli scampered home, closing the gap to 7-5, with Virdon advancing to second. The Pirates were still in business, with the Forbes Field crowd thundering its approval. "The stage," said Mel Allen, "is set for more dramatics."

There were two base runners and still no one out, sending Stengel to the mound again, but this time not just to chat. He called for Jim Coates, a right-hander, though the next batter, Bob Skinner, swung lefty. Stengel was throwing the percentages out the window again, thinking that Skinner would be bunting, which was almost a certainty with Murtaugh's propensity to play the fundamentals. So in one sense, it made almost no difference who was pitching. But knowing that Shantz was the best fielding pitcher in baseball—he would win the fourth of his eight Golden Gloves that fall—wouldn't it have been better to leave him in the game?

Coates, a slider and sinkerball pitcher, had been throwing since the fifth and was more than ready. He took his warm-up pitches mostly to get used to the mound and hoping to quiet the crowd, which had come to life again. It was a tight spot, but the twenty-eight-year-old, 6'4", string bean of a Yankee pitcher had proven himself in the Series, having already pitched more than five innings of solid relief. Lost in the drama of the moment was the performance of Shantz, who stood to be the winner, having pitched like Cy Young—five-plus shutout innings before that last run, and allowing the Yanks to claw ahead.

Everyone knew what was coming next. The Yankee infielders moved a few steps toward the plate as Coates threw and Skinner bunted—a well-placed sacrifice down the third-base line, with the base runners breaking on the pitch. Scooping up the slow-moving ball, Boyer made his only play—firing a strike down to first to nail Skinner—with Virdon taking third and Groat, second. The sacrifice had worked; two runners were in scoring position with one down.

In the Yankee bullpen, right-hander Ralph Terry continued to throw, joined this time by Luis Arroyo, a left-hander. Stepping to the plate, Rocky Nelson knew his job. He needn't hit a home run, as he had back in the first; a single, which would score two runs, would certainly do. Coates, sticking to the Yankee scouting report, threw inside on the Pirate batter, but low, so low that for a split second, the ball seemed like it might be a wild pitch. But Yankee catcher Johnny Blanchard heaved his body in front of it and probably saved a run. Then, on the 1-0, Nelson swung hard at a slider but got only a piece of the ball—sending it on a soft fly into shallow right field, where Maris made the catch and quickly fired to Blanchard, standing on the plate.

Virdon had thought for a moment that the ball could drop, but headed back to third; Groat stuck to second.

In securing two quick outs, Coates was coming through with the poise of a veteran. Facing Roberto Clemente, hitless in three at-bats after hitting safely in all six games, the Yankee pitcher again followed the advice of their scouts: pitch the free-swinging Pirate right fielder outside the strike zone, as a way of tempting him to chase a bad ball, his weakness. "Outside, that's the thing," Coates thought to himself. "He'll swing at anything." Clemente *was* anxious, ready to hack at just about everything thrown his way.

Watching the game at home in Mamaroneck, New York, fourteen-year-old Yankee fan Ken Pearlman remembers a "foreboding feeling" as Clemente strode to the plate. "The Kubek play was one thing, but this was a big at-bat," he says. "Clemente was a contact hitter who seldom struck out. You were always afraid of what he could do." The Yankee strategy, however, appeared sound: Rapping at a high fastball, the Pirate batter sent a towering foul ball back over the Forbes Field roof. Advantage New York.

Popping out from the visitor's dugout, Stengel headed to the mound to advise that his young pitcher not stray *too* far from the strike zone, since this was no time for a wild pitch, which could score two runs. The old sage's advice: Jam Clemente, a right-handed batter, by throwing to Blanchard's glove hand and forcing the Pirate batter to the send the ball toward third base, the more populated part of the field where there could be a play.

Setting himself, Coates delivered the 0-1, sticking to the script with another high, hard one, up near the bill of Clemente's hat. But Clemente, appearing to fight the ball off, swung and lofted another foul ball up and over the roof onto Sennott Street. Playing the percentages, Coates had gone ahead with two strikes.

"This is (a) peak moment of World Series drama," Mel Allen told his forty million viewers. In the hole at 0-2, Clemente kept swinging—sending another foul, this one trickling down the first-base line. Then he swung again, fouling off another and breaking his bat at the handle.

Batboy Bobby Recker plucked a fresh bat from the rack, walked to home plate, and offered it to Clemente. But the Pirate right fielder wanted a different bat and walked over himself to the dugout and made a selection. It slowed things down a tad, giving everyone a chance to catch his breath. Clemente, as Chuck Thompson told listeners, "has a couple of ducks on the pond right now that he'd dearly love to knock in."

Armed with his new Louisville Slugger, Clemente actually let one go by, a ball low and outside to make the count 1-2. Matching analogies, broadcasters Allen and Thompson set the scene: "Hearts pound and pulses race here in this last half of the 8th inning," Allen told viewers. Added Thompson: "In typical World Series fashion, this one appears to be going right down to the wire." Coates set himself again and threw, with Clemente swinging again—this time chopping a roller toward the right side of the infield about 12 feet to the left of the first-base bag. Playing deep, Skowron was a fraction of a second slow in reaching the ball, and when he finally did and turned to flip it to the pitcher at first base—another routine play out of Baseball 101—no one was there. Inexplicably, Coates, "probably so busy trying to figure out what his share of the winners' purse would be," joked Arthur Daley of the *Times,* had reacted slowly and not reached the bag in time to take the throw. Skowron just held on to the ball and watched helplessly as Virdon, who broke for home plate on contact, scored, Groat scooted to third, and Clemente dashed safely across first. The Yankee lead had narrowed to a sliver, 7-6.

So add a dash of luck and a sprinkle of fairy dust to another improbable Pirate rally, helped by sloppy fielding at the wrong time. "It's not just the pitcher who failed to cover the bag," thought Pearlman, watching at home, "but Skowron didn't seem to move."

So give Clemente a single—not the most artistic of all time, but a big one at a crucial time, which gave him a base hit in all seven games. Whether the Yankees, with a cleanly fielded ball, would ever have caught Clemente is another matter. It would certainly have been close. There were still two down, with Pittsburgh's ability to continue its comeback resting squarely on the bat of catcher Hal Smith.

Smith was playing Game 7 as an afterthought—a defensive replacement in the seventh for Burgess, who had been lifted for a pinch-runner. As a right-handed batter, he wasn't Murtaugh's top choice for batting duty. But the twenty-nine-year-old backup catcher was a good man to have at bat: With eleven home runs and a .295 batting average in seventy-seven regular-season games, he had both pop and steadiness and had won a half-dozen games with big pinch hits in the late innings. Signed by the Yankees, Smith had been swapped to Baltimore and then Kansas City before landing with the Pirates in 1960. He fit in, particularly with Face and Haddix, as part of a guitar-strumming trio who kept their teammates loose with impromptu country tunes. Smith, Face, and their guitars had even scored some gigs in Monroeville at the Holiday House nightclub—a profitable sideline that would earn them a tidy $10,000 after the Series. About the only issue with being Harold Wayne Smith of the 1960 Pirates, a native of West Frankfort, Illinois, was that there happened to be a couple of other notable Hal Smiths, one a veteran character actor who had debuted just ten days before on a new TV hit, *The Andy Griffith Show*, as the small-town drunk, Otis Campbell. Unfortunately, the other Hal Smith was another National League catcher who was the same age, about the same height, and even resembled his Pirate namesake. Harold Raymond Smith of the Cardinals, a Barling, Arkansas, native, even shared a passion for country music, writing songs memorable for titles like "I Got a Churnful of Chitlins and a Belly Full of You." No wonder the two men were continually confused for one another.

But all of that was forgotten amidst the immediate challenge: With two men on base in the eighth, Harold Wayne Smith's goal was to work the Yankee pitcher to a favorable count to get a good ball to drive. So Smith took a strike right down the middle of the plate and waited out a ball up high, not swinging—yet. The count was 1-1.

Jim Coates needed to be cautious and throw strikes. This was no time to work at the corners and risk the chance of walking Smith and loading the bases. So Coates threw the 1-1 pitch right down the middle of the plate—sending it in a tad slower and just enough to prompt a swing. It was a good pitch; the Pirate batter swung hard, a split-second late . . . and missed. "(He) really pulled the trigger," Thompson said of Smith, "gave it the big ripple, the Sunday punch, and couldn't find it." Smith had been fooled, sending the count to 1-2 and the momentum, ever so slightly, back to the Yankees.

What to do now? On the mound, Coates thought to himself, "I'll go a little higher this time." So in came a 1-2 fastball, and Smith pumped his left leg forward, ready to commit, before holding back at the last instant. The pitch *was* high—ball two—and Smith had made the right choice. He probably would have missed the ball completely had he not checked his swing, and stalled the Pirate rally. Instead, the count evened at 2-2 and the pendulum swung back to Smith.

It was imperative for the Yankees that Coates deliver his next pitch in the strike zone; a pitch on a full count would send the runners, giving the Pirates precious seconds to wreak damage on the base paths. The only question was where Coates should try to put the pitch. Smith had seen his high, hard heat and had lain off. So the Yankee pitcher changed course, just a little: Looking to first to check the runner and then going into his stretch, Coates delivered another fastball and kept it low—right in his "wheelhouse," in baseball-speak, where the Pirate catcher could reach full follow-through and get some lift on the ball. This time, the Pirate batter swung hard, connecting solidly.

* * *

Watch enough sports movies, and it becomes clear that there's always the epic moment, a fraction of a second at most, when something big is about to set off an explosion of crowd noise, but it's still quiet. It's the moment when the players, the spectators, and the millions crowded around TV sets are too absorbed in the moment to yell.

Smith's ball "climbed over the infield like a rocket shot," Myron Cope would write the following day in the *Post-Gazette*. Coates himself jerked his head around to watch. So did the Pirate dugout, its occupants bouncing from their seats as if on springs. The ball continued on its flight, headed toward center field, just to the left of the 406-foot mark. In left field, Yogi Berra eyed the ball as well and started to drift after it, but he knew from experience that there would be no play. It was gone.

The baseball cleared the ivy-covered wall by a good 30 feet and landed near the entrance to Schenley Park; no one was exactly sure where, because the ball was never claimed. The crowd exploded and Smith, running hard and only realizing what he had done once he had passed second base, broke into long exuberant strides like a triple jumper loping down the runway. Forbes Field had become a rocking carnival of noise that could be heard all the way to Squirrel Hill.

Inexplicably and improbably, the Pirates had sprung back from the dead, scoring five times in the eighth to regain the lead, 9-7. In the stands, silver streamers floated through the air, and men hugged the nearest available women, who didn't seem to mind. Everyone stood and hollered as Groat danced across the plate, followed by Clemente bouncing down the line. Jumping from his seat in the second tier behind home plate was Abe Cimoli, Gino's father, in such a state of feverish excitement that he threw his coat, hat, and glasses into the air; all were quickly returned.

Even cynical sportswriters who had seen it all cheered. This was one for the journeyman who had saved his biggest moment for the biggest stage. A giant smile "crinkl(ed Smith's) face into a hundred happy lines," wrote Roy Terrell of *Sports Illustrated,* "that stretched all the way back to Kansas City and Quincy and Ventura and Twin Falls and all the places in baseball where he has been."

"Pandemonium (had broken) out at Forbes Field!" cried Mel Allen. On the radio, Thompson outdid everyone, making a memorable call that is still rebroadcast on baseball retrospectives: "Forbes Field is at this time, an outdoor insane asylum!" he yelled above the crowd noise. "We have seen and shared in one of baseball's great moments." After the game, in the locker room, Smith would cherish the moment but take the long view, admitting that his greatest baseball experience hadn't been this memorable World Series home run, but the trade that made him a Pirate. "When you're playing with a pennant contender, you get plenty of publicity," he said.

Overlooked in all the excitement was the stunned Yankee reaction. Like Abe Cimoli, Jim Coates had something to throw—his mitt—which he tossed in frustration 10 feet in the air as Smith bounded around the bases. Before the mitt even landed, Stengel was on his way to the mound to relieve his fourth pitcher with a fifth—Ralph Terry, who had been warming up seemingly forever, actually five separate times. As Terry entered the game, most of the Yankee infielders, hands on their hips, stood stone-faced and stared. At least for the Yanks, their pitcher quickly got his batter, Don Hoak, when the Pirate third baseman sent a 1-1 pitch on a lazy fly to left field, where Berra made the final out.

What an inning! Of the five Pirate runs, three were charged to Shantz and the last two to Coates, who stood to be the loser. Had the game ended right then and there, Game 7 would have been memorable enough, with Hal Smith's bat probably bronzed and displayed in Cooperstown. Behind by two with an inning to go, the Yankees were down to their last shot. As it turned out, the 1960 World Series was far from over.

NINTH INNING

9

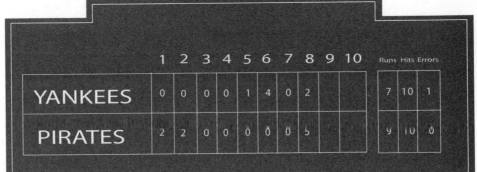

	1	2	3	4	5	6	7	8	9	10		Runs	Hits	Errors
YANKEES	0	0	0	0	1	4	0	2				7	10	1
PIRATES	2	2	0	0	0	0	0	5				9	10	0

9

"**THREE OUTS, THREE** more outs," Dick Groat told himself as the Pirates took their positions for the ninth. With his team ahead in the latter stages of a game, the Pirate captain often repeated those words like a mantra, staying focused by counting down the game's final outs.

Normally, the Pittsburgh pitcher would be Elroy Face, but Murtaugh had removed him for a pinch-hitter. So in from the Pirate bullpen trudged the hard-throwing right-hander Bob Friend, anxious to wrap things up and atone for his hard-luck World Series performances to date—two starts and two tough losses. But Friend was a good choice—a dependable veteran right-hander with steadiness appropriate to the situation. There was no need for the proper righty-lefty matchup that you get today. Friend was ready, relatively fresh—having gone less than three innings in Game 6—and the best Murtaugh could offer.

But these were the Yankees, the team that always seemed to find a way—especially during the 1960 World Series, when not just the sluggers but the role players were having their way with Pirate pitchers. A case in point was the hot-hitting Richardson, who was leading off a Yankee inning for the fourth time of the afternoon and looking for his eleventh hit of the World Series. Taking no chances, Murtaugh kept Haddix warming in the bullpen and, just in case, added another backup—lefty Vinegar Bend Mizell.

Friend started Richardson with a strike, and a roar went up from the expectant crowd, sensing victory. But then Richardson—"the pest," as Myron Cope had coined him—did what he'd been doing throughout the Series, delivering a timely base hit, this one a fly-ball single that dunked into shallow left-center to raise his Series batting average to a stratospheric .367. That gave Stengel some options; instead of the light-hitting DeMaestri, who was due up, he could resort to one of the big Yankee bats on the bench as a setup for the powerful heart of his team's order. So the Yankee manager called on thirty-four-year-old Dale Long, whose left-handed power had suited the short porch at Forbes Field back in '56, when for the Pirates he had knocked those eight home runs in as many games. Hitless in two at-bats in his first World Series, Long was anxious to reach base.

In this case, Long's goal was decidedly modest: get a good pitch and drive it into right field to put two runners on base for the big boppers. He fouled off Friend's first pitch, then let a high one go by, evening the count at 1-1. Then Long took a hefty roundhouse hack, as he'd done a million times in batting practice and lashed the ball on a line. The ball went skipping exactly where he wanted it—into the right-field corner, where Clemente played it on a hop off the wall. Standing on first base, Long took stock of the fact that despite 101 lifetime big-league home runs and a reputation as a slugger, he had just delivered his first World Series base hit—a 300-foot single to keep the Yankees alive.

With two runners on base, there wasn't time for reflection. That's because Danny Murtaugh was headed to the mound to retrieve the struggling Bob Friend. The Pirate ace wanted to scream, having just added a final exclamation point to his 1960 World Series frustration: He had run into a buzz saw of a team on a streak, one of the few downsides of a distinguished career. Gazing toward the Pirate bullpen and surrounded by his infielders, Murtaugh selected his new pitcher: Haddix.

In retrospect, Stengel should have countered with a move himself.

Just why he didn't remove the lumbering Long for a pinch-runner has never been adequately explained. Long hadn't stolen a base for two seasons and was about the last man the Yankees would want on base in the late innings of Game 7 of the World Series. Bob Cerv was available, but he wasn't fast, and Stengel would want to hold him out in the event of extra innings. But the other available bench player was McDougald, who at thirty-two had lost a step, but who knew his way around the bases and could always stay in at second, third, or short. Watching from his seat in the auxiliary press box, broadcaster Nellie King thought to himself, "McDougald should be in there."

Haddix would be pitching on three days' rest, having gone six and one-third innings in his Game 5 win at Yankee Stadium. At 5'9½", the Pirate lefty looked almost too slight to take on the heart of the Yankee order, seemingly as much a mismatch as a Little Leaguer facing the high school varsity, but he entered the game confident and "cool as ice," as Hoak put it. Standing on the mound as the new Pirate pitcher arrived, Hoak urged him on. "Dammit, Harve, we've come this far," the third baseman told him. "Let's get those two guys out of here and go home."

Haddix just chomped on his gum and pared the situation down to the basics: "Well, I've got Maris up there," he said to himself, "and I just better pitch him low and see what happens." As Haddix took his warm-up tosses on the Forbes Field mound, there came a jarring reminder of how tantalizingly close the Pirates were to sewing up their first Series title in thirty-five years: an announcement from PA man Art McKennan that all uniformed officers on the second and third tiers should report to the bleacher gate, from which they would ring the field after the game. The prospect of a postgame celebration! That unleashed a roar from the Forbes Field faithful. Standing on second, Richardson turned to Mazeroski: "It's lucky we don't play ball games like this one all the time," cracked the Yankee second sacker to the Pirate second sacker. "Every player in the country would have ulcers."

Haddix started Maris with a ball, low, then jammed him on the fists, hoping to coax a swing and a pop-up. Maris committed, a little too late, and sent a towering pop behind home, where Smith circled under it perhaps 10 feet back off the plate, threw away his mask, and made the catch. The Pirates had secured one precious out in the Yankee ninth as the crowd roared its approval. Upset with himself for going hitless in five tries in Game 7, Maris flung his bat to the ground, and stalked back to a seat in the dugout.

Two on, one gone—and to the plate stepped Mantle. Batting right-handed, Mantle was just the man the Pirates did not want to see. Crouched at bat, like a cat waiting to uncoil, Mantle let a low, outside pitch go for ball one, then lined a decisive single into the right-field alley, his third base hit of the game and his tenth of the Series. Richardson sailed home and the slow-footed Long ran to third, barely ahead of Clemente's throw. Suddenly, the Pirates were clinging to a 9-8 lead.

Both managers tinkered. Murtaugh started right-hander George Witt warming in the Pirate bullpen; Stengel dispatched Game 6 winner Whitey Ford to throw for the Yankees. Seeing the close play at third and taking hold of his senses, Stengel opted for speed—finally—and sent McDougald into the game to run for Long. In the press box, King wondered what had taken him so long.

Though McDougald, a ten-year big-league veteran, hadn't said anything publicly, he and his wife, Lucille, had already decided he would retire after the Series. With four young children at home and a growing business, and weary of the travel, McDougald was making it the last of his 1,389 games in the majors—53 of them in the World Series. "I was saying to myself, 'Wow, this is really it,' " he says.

Haddix stuck to the scouting report, which advised to keep the ball low against Berra, a devastating high-ball batter. Looking for a double-play ball to end the game, Haddix threw low but kept it inches off the plate, hoping to coax Berra into lunging and sending the ball somewhere toward the infield. But Berra was taking and got what he wanted: a ball. In the stands, the man who had been yelling in the vicinity of Mel Allen's microphone most of the afternoon cheered on his team's pitcher: "Come on Harvey, let's get two."

That's just what Haddix was thinking. Sending the 1-0 in so low that it was almost in the dirt, the Pirate pitcher was still looking to tempt Berra. But the Yankee batter took again, working the count to 2-0, a good hitter's count. On the mound, Haddix shifted his chewing gum under his lower lip and figured his moment of reckoning had arrived: He had no choice but to throw a strike this time. "Got to give him something now," he said to himself. "Got to take a chance."

The 2-0 pitch was in the strike zone. Berra lashed at the ball, meeting it squarely and sending a cannon shot on one hop toward first base, where Rocky Nelson, playing three steps from the line, scooped up the ball and stepped on the bag for the second out. What the Pirate first baseman could have done next was throw to second, double up Mantle, and close out the game, but what he did instead was straighten up and try to tag Mantle for the double play.

The odds favored Nelson. Stranded a good ten feet from the bag, Mantle was in a base runner's "no-man's land" as he faced Nelson, whose arm was still cocked to throw. What happened next was one of those rare plays that didn't made the box score, but offered a glimpse of an extraordinary athlete at the top of his game: Realizing he'd be out by a country mile if he turned to second and drew a throw, Mantle quickly turned the other way and dived safely back into first— "wriggling like a snake" to get there, as Red Smith put it in the *Herald-Tribune*—to elude the Pirate first baseman's frenetic tag. Mantle's left hand had found the bag a split second ahead of Nelson's tag. The play allowed McDougald, who had broken from third with the crack of the bat, to score, tying the game at 9.

Few ballplayers but Mantle possessed the combination of skills, quick thinking, and intuitive feel for the game to have done that. Mel Allen recognized a case of baseball artistry right away: "An amazing turn of events! . . . Mantle, with quick thinking . . . slid underneath the tag and got back to first as (the Yankees tie). . . . How about that!" Nelson had done his best to apply the tag, but his thirty-five-year-old instincts were a split second late in arriving at the bag in a heap—and at the feet of first base umpire Nestor Chylak, who flapped his hands outward with an emphatic call of "Safe!" The Yankees had stormed back. Both runs were charged to hard-luck Friend, who closed out his Series with an unfortunate 13.50 ERA.

Nearly a half century later, Maury Allen calls Mantle's quick-thinking one of the most dramatic plays *ever* in a World Series. "It only took an instant—it was bang, bang and over—but it was so significant, so unique, and so typical of the great athlete Mickey Mantle was," says Allen. "What made it unique is that the 1st baseman was Rocky Nelson was so named because he made plays that were 'bonehead' plays. All he had to do was throw to 2nd to force Mantle. But what we got instead was a classic 'Rocky' play, with Mantle just sliding around and making it back to the bag."

Watching the drama unfold from behind home plate was the most dejected man in America. That would be Hal Smith, whose titanic three-run blast minutes before had, with the score now deadlocked, abruptly and unceremoniously been reduced to just another home run. So there would be no bronzed bat or magazine covers after all for the Pirate catcher. Broadcaster Nellie King remembers Smith's body language as one of the most powerful visual images of the entire 1960 Series. "As McDougald crossed the plate to tie the game, Smith's shoulders just slumped, like finding somebody had died," King says. "He knew his home run meant nothing. I can still see it."

Back and forth the two teams had gone all afternoon, zigzagging, thrusting, and parrying like boxers, only to be deadlocked in the late rounds. One would think that Haddix would be crushed, having come so close to being on the mound as his teammates closed out the Yankees. But he wasn't, he admitted later; he was too much of a seasoned professional to let anything but the present bother him. "That would have been a nice double play," Haddix later admitted. But this was no time for reflection: Moose Skowron was stepping to the plate.

So Haddix went back to work—his mind eased somewhat with the bases suddenly cleared—and threw a ball low. Looking at the 1-0, Skowron sent a shot down the third-base line, where Hoak stabbed the ball and threw to first base for the final out of the ninth. The Yankees were finally snuffed, but they had come back, just as the Pirates had done all year, and deadlocked Game 7 in the ninth. Collectively, they had gone through the 1960 World Series hitting .338 and compiling fifty-five runs, ninety-one base hits, ten home runs, and even four triples—all records. But the 1960 World Series, headed to the bottom of the ninth in Game 7, very much up for grabs.

* * *

In hindsight, it all happened so quickly. The game itself had just passed two hours and thirty minutes, an almost unfathomable speed by today's standards, considering the number of pitchers, Kubek's injury, and Stengel's many rambles to the mound. Keeping track of the time was easy—the 25-foot-high rectangular clock atop of the left-field scoreboard read 3:32 PM.

In most cases, the break between the innings is a chance for spectators to grab a beer or visit the snack bar. Here in the bottom of the ninth, most people at Forbes Field were bolted to their seats, unwilling to run the risk of missing something big. But not twenty-five-year-old Herb Saul from Squirrel Hill. Cutting work that day, he had begun his afternoon in the reserved section behind the Pirate dugout but started moving some innings before, as if by instinct, ever closer to the action, and was now ready to spring from his new spot in the box seats to the field should the game suddenly end. Forbes Field usher Dom Verratti had the same idea but for a different reason:

With the Steelers set to take on the St. Louis Cardinals in three days at Forbes Field, his task was to keep people like Herb Saul off the field at all costs.

Preparing for *their* moment was the army of photographers positioned around the field—that is, with the exception of *Life* magazine's George Silk, who had found his way to the south-facing balcony, atop the Cathedral of Learning, where students were drinking in their obstructed-view piece of the action. Attaching his camera to a powerful telephoto lens, Silk framed the partying students with Forbes Field looking hazy and dreamlike in the distance, similar to the memorable last scene of the film *Field of Dreams*. Sticking to the grandstand rooftop with his sequencing camera able to shoot at three-second intervals was Jim Klingensmith of the *Post-Gazette*. Crouching in the box seats just above the Pirate dugout was Marvin Newman of *Sports Illustrated* with his Bell & Howell camera focused on home plate, as well as on the big left-field scoreboard, which offered the time, score, and even the count. A section or so toward right field were Neil Leifer and his Nikon F, equipped with a motor drive, taking in home plate with a background of the jammed third-base grandstand. Knowing the game could end with a single big moment, most photographers were shooting on every swing; there would be no second chances.

Much of America was at a standstill, caught up in the drama of a baseball classic tied in the ninth inning of Game 7. In offices, prolonged coffee breaks continued. Bartenders kept the taps flowing. Kids, many on the East Coast just now getting out of school for the day, clustered around transistor radios. All day long in front of an appliance store on Grant Street in downtown Pittsburgh, a crowd had watched the action on a TV in the storeroom window—giving at least some life to the otherwise deserted downtown, a surreal scene for a Thursday afternoon. Also on Grant Street, the Clerk of Courts had been shut tight since 12:30 PM, with employees long scattered to bars or offices in search of TV sets. The lone remaining employee was a bond clerk, stoically remaining on duty for the benefit of anyone posting bail.

On NBC Radio, listeners absorbed a ditty pitching the "space, bunk and . . . room in the trunk" of Chevrolet's new '61 Corvair. Then came a thirty-second station identification, which, in the case of the sole remaining recording of the event, from station WGY "810 on your dial" in Schenectady, included the weather forecast for upstate New York: "mostly fair and cool with scattered frost tonight, with low overnight reading in the 30s and low 40s." It was a chilly omen that baseball's winter break lay just ahead.

Both teams scrambled in preparation for the bottom of the ninth. As expected, McDougald went to third, with Boyer shifting to short. Back to the mound with a new lease on life trudged Terry, a twenty-four-year-old right-hander, another of the Yankee minions who had beaten a track to the Bronx from Kansas City. Working in Terry's favor was a respectable 10-8 record in 1960, his best season to date. More impressive to Stengel was the poise he had shown as the starter in Game 4, the 3-2 Yankee loss.

Terry's immediate challenge was just getting comfortable with the new mound. Entering the game in the eighth, he had been startled to discover that the mound on the playing field was 6 inches lower than one in the bullpen, where he'd been throwing for most of the afternoon. But there wasn't much he could do about it now, with the Pirates' eighth hitter, Bill Mazeroski, due to bat. Maz was in a bit of a state himself, having jogged off the field after the half inning, so absorbed in his thoughts that he actually forgot he was first up for the Pirates. Snapping him to reality was a reminder from Pirate coach Lenny Levy to get ready and do it fast: "Maz, grab a bat," Levy thundered, "you're the leadoff hitter!"

For all the millions of words written about the 1960 World Series, Mazeroski has spent a great deal of time avoiding much talk of it. But with the years and the growing legend of the 1960 Pirates, he finally gave his thoughts to Nellie King after a 2002 charity golf tournament. So why was he so lost in thought heading into the bottom of the ninth? Growing up as a Cleveland Indians fan, Maz knew all about Yankee heroics, he told King, and how they seemed to somehow pull the Series out every year. "Those damn Yankees are going to do it again," Maz thought to himself. "They always seem to win the big games."

Striding quickly to the bat rack, Mazeroski selected his Louisville Slugger 125 Pro Model with pine tar slathered one-third of the way down the handle. Seated nearby, Murtaugh offered encouragement: "We're almost in," he told the Pirate second baseman. "Just need one to go home." His teammates concurred. "Give us a start, Maz," yelled one, as another, Dick Stuart, moved into the on-deck circle to ready himself to bat for Haddix.

Walking purposely to the batter's box, Mazeroski focused on the essentials. "The time before, in the 7th, I had gone for the long ball and I overswung," he told *Baseball Digest* in 1961. "This time I kept saying to myself, 'Don't overswing. Just meet the ball.' " Was he on edge? No. "I thought I'd be more nervous this time, but I wasn't a bit," Mazeroski said.

Settling in at the plate, Mazeroski, his jaw filled with the ever-present, baseball-sized plug of tobacco, took a practice swing and steadied himself. Terry leaned in, took the sign, and buzzed in a pitch, shoulder high for ball one, nowhere near the target set low in the strike zone by Johnny Blanchard, the Yankee catcher. Blanchard, who had played against Mazeroski in the minor leagues and remembered him as a murderous high-ball hitter, sensed trouble. Emerging from his crouch, Blanchard stalked 20 feet toward the mound, close enough for a quick word, and yelled at Terry as he returned the ball with an extra snap for emphasis: "Keep the damn ball down on this guy! He's a good high-ball hitter."

Apparently, the low mound was still giving Terry fits. With little slope, the angle was causing him to plant his foot early; without maximum follow-through, he was throwing high in the zone, which was too close, much too close in Blanchard's view, to Mazeroski's strength. So the Yankee catcher set another low target, very low, and got down on one knee with his mitt perhaps 10 inches from the ground, and waited for Terry's next pitch.

It was 3:35 PM. In the bowels of the ballpark, near the doors to the clubhouses, NBC-TV announcer Bob Prince prepared to board the elevator on his way back to the booth. The ninth had already been an odyssey for Prince, who was due to interview players in the winning locker room. In the top of the inning, with the Pirates up by two, Prince had headed toward the Pittsburgh locker room. But when the Yankees tied it up, he was ordered back to rejoin Mel Allen for what the NBC producer figured would be extra innings. Several feet away in the radio booth sat Chuck Thompson, who set the scene in a hurry. "A little while ago when we mentioned that this one, in typical fashion, was going right down to the wire," he said, "little did we know."

Little *did* Thompson or the rest of America know at that very moment. Taking both Blanchard's snap throw and his admonishment, Terry considered his options. Blanchard called for another fastball, but the Yankee pitcher shook him off once, twice, and then a third time. He wanted to throw the slider, despite a warning from Yankee pitching coach Eddie Lopat not to do so. "It's not working," Lopat had told both Terry and Blanchard in the dugout before the half-inning. "It isn't sliding, okay?" But Terry was insistent. Setting himself, he pumped and threw, sending in the pitch, this one a little lower, about an inch above the letters, in the strike zone. In left field, the scoreboard clock read 3:36 PM as a beautiful Indian summer afternoon blazed away in Pittsburgh.

All these years later, there is an enduring mystery as to what kind of pitch Terry did throw. Blanchard insisted it was the slider—against Lopat's wishes—which he had finally called for in exasperation after being repeatedly shaken off. Mazeroski said it was a fastball, adding that he was thinking fastball and guessed right. "As Terry wound up,

I was thinking to myself, 'Fastball! Fastball!' " he told *Baseball Digest*. "That's what I wanted." Terry himself won't say.

The pitch arrived belt-high. Stepping forward with a quick, compact swing, the Pirate second baseman met the ball solidly, sending it on the fly toward left-center—the same direction Smith's ball had headed in the eighth. Rounding first, Mazeroski looked for clues that would tell him how far the ball had traveled—the distance that Yankee left fielder Yogi Berra was drifting back to catch it, and a possible signal from second base umpire Dusty Vargas.

Many in the Forbes Field crowd had already jumped to their feet to watch the flight of the ball. In bars, diners, offices, factory lounges, gas stations, and dens across America, television viewers watched, too. So did the photographers, who snapped away—including Marvin Newman and Neil Leifer from the first-base line, Jim Klingensmith from the grandstand roof, and George Silk on the balcony of the Cathedral of Learning. All four would capture the moment— Newman most notably, with his extraordinary image of Mazeroski following through as the ball headed out over the infield. It was *the* panoramic picture that Newman had carefully planned for all afternoon, one of sports' most memorable photos. Leifer caught Mazeroski on the follow-through as well, but lower to the ground, and with the third-base crowd in the background, a few feet away from Newman's truly timeless image. On the roof, Klingensmith, the lifelong Pittsburgher whose good friend Mazeroski had just hit a mighty wallop in the World Series, forgot himself for a fraction of second— "jumping up and down" in excitement—before catching himself and remembering that he had a job to do. "I said to myself, 'What the heck, I'm supposed to be working,' " Klingensmith told the *Post-Gazette,* as he focused on Mazeroski romping around the bases and snapped a memorable series of images now owned by the National Baseball Hall of Fame. Securing the moment's most unusual photo, which ran in *Life* and is now a well-known poster, was Silk, who captured a group of perhaps a dozen college students as they raised their hands in excitement and absorbed the moment.

"I thought I might get three bases as Berra . . . might have trouble playing the ball off the wall," Mazeroski would say later. Berra chugged back toward the wall in left-center, following the flight of the ball, and was joined by Mantle, swiftly heading from center field. The ball wasn't traveling with the authority of the Smith blast, but the real indication of its path would come from the outfielders.

All of America watched. Leaping to his feet in the Pirate dugout, Hoak reportedly yelled, "Get out of here, you rotten, stinking, beautiful baseball!" though the language was probably a tad more colorful. As the ball started to descend near the 406-foot-mark in left-center, Berra stopped on the inner edge of the warning track and stared at the ivy to gauge if there might be a play. Mantle just kept running.

But neither outfielder had a play. The ball disappeared into a backdrop of trees well over the fence, and the crowd erupted like the takeoff of a spaceship. Steaming toward second base, perhaps twenty feet from the bag, Mazeroski saw Vargas, the umpire, thrust his index finger in the air and move it in a circle—the sign for a home run. Suddenly, the mild-mannered Pirate second baseman was whirling his hands in the air, shouting to the heavens and waving his faded helmet.

The Pirates had done it—they had beaten the Yankees, 10-9, with a home run in the bottom of the ninth of Game 7 of the World Series. Rounding second, the leaping, joyous Mazeroski was joined on the field by a couple of kids, then by a stream of them. Vaulting the first base railing, Herb Saul ran toward home plate—to this day, unable to remember his feet carrying him, as if he were on air. Nearby, nineteen-year-old Howard Singer did the same and joined the mob of Pirate players headed to home plate to meet the new home-run hero. Mingling with the throbbing, gathering crowd, Singer reached out to grab the cap of a player, any player. The hat he came up with was Clemente's, size 7, which didn't fit him; years later, Singer returned to Pittsburgh from his home in California and sold the hat for more than $18,000.

Facing the left-field wall as the ball disappeared into Schenley Park, Berra, with the big number 8 on his back, formed one of the most memorable images of the wildest World Series ever. Berra insisted forty-five years later to Murray Chass of the *Times* that he thought the ball would strike the inside of the wall and stay in play. "I didn't think it was going over the wall," he said. "I thought it was going to bounce off the wall. That's why I turned around. If I knew it was out, I wouldn't have turned around and looked." But seeing the ball sail over the fence, Berra turned and started jogging toward the dugout with what looked like a studied nonchalance. What else could he do? Turning himself and walking slowly off the mound with his head down was Terry, virtually ignored amidst the growing bedlam.

Touching third base with his headgear now firmly in his right hand, Mazeroski had just passed umpire John Stevens when the first fan to storm the field reached him. It was Fritz McCauley, a twenty-two-year-old Hilton doorman, who had been at the ballpark since 8:30 AM, admitted by a friendly Pinkerton "security guard." Watching the game from the third-base line, McCauley told Pittsburgh writer Jim O'Brien that he knew the ball was gone the instant Mazeroski had swung. He knew from the sound. Dressed in his work attire, a dark blazer with a white shirt and a tie, McCauley hurdled the waist-high iron fence to the field and ran—"blinded with delight."

So did Forbes Field usher Dom Verratti. As the stream of people storming the field became a flood, there wasn't much he could do to stop them. Jumping out of the first-base stands, Verratti, a balding man in his midthirties and dressed in a windbreaker, tore diagonally across the infield toward Mazeroski, who was now past third. Holding his usher's cap in his left hand, Verratti laughed and yelled as he followed Mazeroski home, his a toothy smile of delight forever etched in a memorable photo taken from the press box by Harry Harris of the Associated Press.

Blanchard knew better than anyone that the ball was a home run the moment Mazeroski swung. He was already inside the locker room, angry at himself that he hadn't called time before the pitch as Terry repeatedly shook him off. The Yankee catcher was particularly angry that he had essentially given in and called for the slider. "Maybe I should have gotten Eddie Lopat out there" to the mound, he recalled. "But I didn't."

Crossing the plate, Mazeroski was engulfed by fans and teammates. It was pandemonium, an explosion of joy, Pittsburgh's version of Times Square on New Year's Eve, of New Orleans at Mardi Gras. Overlooked in the quickly growing mob, which from a distance looked like a rugby scrum, was home plate umpire Bill Jackowski, as he dutifully wedged in front of Clemente at home plate to make sure Mazeroski actually touched home. Everyone else just assumed he did, as strangers hugged and people yelled, overcome at the finish and overjoyed that the Pirates were suddenly, shockingly, champs once again after thirty-five years. More people streamed onto the field, well ahead of the phalanx of policemen who were now steaming toward the commotion in a belated effort to keep order.

Among all the joyful images of the moment captured in film and video, several have endured. For some reason, a videographer decided to turn his camera away from the dramatic home-run moment to focus on a blond twenty-something woman in the front row of a third-base box. Dressed in black and wearing a stylish red beret and sunglasses, the woman follows the path of the fateful home-run ball and joyfully thrusts her arms skyward in triumph as the game ends. Her spontaneity has become one of the better-known images of documentaries about the 1960 World Series, but to this day, her identity is unknown—she is the mystery woman of Forbes Field.

What a contrast she presents to the plight of the Yankee players and coaches, quickly overwhelmed and ignored as they threaded though and around a sea of rampaging, happy fans still pouring from the stands. Most of them walked off silently, holding their mitts, ignored as if the grays of their road uniforms had transformed them into shadows. Ironically, the Yankees were headed the same place as the victorious Pirates: the first-base dugout, where both teams would walk down a tunnel before heading to their locker rooms. This served as another reminder both of the limitations of cramped old Forbes Field, where the visiting teams didn't even have their own exit, and of the fact that there are just as many great sports photographs of the losers as there are of winners. Most poignant of all was Herb Scharfman's *Sports Illustrated* shot of Stengel sidestepping the raucous celebration as he trudged off the field for perhaps the last time.

For reasons lost to history, NBC Radio's Chuck Thompson blew the call, the only blemish in a crisp, virtually spotless broadcast. It was as if he had been momentarily distracted in the fraction of a second before the fateful pitch, perhaps picking up a pencil or swigging a beer. "Art Ditmar throws and here's a swing and a long fly ball going deep to left" is how he described it as the ball took flight. "This may do it! Back to the wall goes Berra . . . and it's over the fence—home run! The Pirates win!"

Art Ditmar? It was Ralph Terry. Then, after saying nothing for thirty-five seconds of sustained crowd noise—very effective—Thompson came back with a businesslike game summary and blew it again. "Ladies and gentleman, Mazeroski has hit a 1-0 pitch over the left-field fence at Forbes Field to win the 1960 World Series for the Pittsburgh Pirates by a score of 10 to nothing." Huh? "Once again, that final score," added Thompson, quickly catching himself, "the Pirates, 10, and the Yankees, 9."

Not that anyone much cared. Thompson, the voice of the Senators, would soon leave Washington for Baltimore, where he would spend a long, distinguished career as the voice of the Orioles. Years later, in an interview with Curt Smith, Thompson 'fessed up to his erroneous calls, which were mostly forgotten until the 1985 World Series, when a Budweiser ad featured the sound bite, prompting hundreds of viewers to call the brewery and point out the reference to Ditmar. As for giving the wrong score, Thompson attributed it to the excitement: "It was about the wildest crowd I've ever seen in my life," he told Smith.

Actually, Pirate team officials took note of the broadcast miscue shortly after the Series as they prepared a postseason commemorative record album that featured the call. PR Director Jack Berger asked Thompson if he wanted to do a voice-over correction of the call, but to his considerable credit, the broadcaster said not to bother. "I just told 'em, 'Hey, I said it, so keep it in.' " In 1961, when Thompson went to Pittsburgh to broadcast the NBC *Game of the Week,* the album was playing everywhere. "I kept hearing the wrong score," Thompson told Curt Smith, "but somehow it seemed to fit into the confusion of the occasion."

He got that part right. After touching home plate—probably—Mazeroski was hugged, embraced, crushed, and pounded on the back, all the while holding on, somehow, to his batting helmet. By then, a cordon of state troopers had muscled their way toward Pittsburgh's new toast of the town and escorted him toward the dugout, but not before they had a whack themselves and pounded the Pirate second baseman on his back a few more times. In the stands, people threw hats in the air, and strangers hugged and danced in the aisles. Leaping from his seat as he watched the ball disappear over the ivy, Mayor Barr nearly decked his wife, Alice, with an uppercut as he threw his arms into the air in triumph.

The climactic moment had happened so quickly that from his seat in Section 23 of the bleachers, Byron Oertel was momentarily stunned. "What happened?" he asked his daughter, Jean, as the ballpark exploded with noise. "Dad, Maz hit a home run and we won!" his daughter told him. "What you have to remember is that there were no postgame fireworks in those days, no scoreboard flashing, 'Home Run . . . We Win!' You watched with your own eyes. It was no-frills baseball."

Just like that, concession sales, nearly dead for the last few tense innings of the game, shot up. Going particularly fast were the $1 Pirate pennants, with many happy fans throwing $5 bills at the vendors and leaving vendors with generous tips. One Pirate fan, dressed in a regalia eye patch, bought a Yankee pennant and solemnly marched onto the field behind the backstop, where he methodically dug a 6-inch hole—and carefully buried his new purchase.

Anything not bolted down at the ballpark became fair game for souvenir hunters. Alec Demao stole first base, intending to find an honored spot for it at his bar in Arnold. Harold Baird of Dormant laid claim to a greater prize—home plate—thanks to a shovel and pliers he had smuggled into the ballpark. Working with great efficiency, Baird dug up his treasure in minutes, though he ruined his $85 sport jacket in the process. It was a small price to pay for the sudden notoriety that followed, as officials quickly whisked him inside the Pirate clubhouse to pose for photographers.

Even the well churned soil around the batter's box was claimed. Within minutes, an enterprising soul was roaming Sennott Street, advertising his wares by yelling, "Get your pay dirt here." Unloading a scoop for $5 to a fan who simply dumped it in his suit coat pocket and kept walking, Forbes Field's newest entrepreneur pocketed his earnings and headed back inside the park for more dirt.

So who came up with the game-winning home-run ball? Disappearing into a sea of people hanging around just beyond the left-field wall, the ball was quickly claimed by what seemed like half of Western Pennsylvania. The *Pittsburgh Press* reported the owner as hooky-playing fourteen-year-old Chris Montgomery from the Hill District. But the *Times* said that another fourteen-year-old, Andy Jerpe—the *Herald-Tribune* spelled it "Jerpo"—had retrieved the ball and taken it to the Pirate locker room, where he tried giving to Mazeroski, but the Pirate second baseman had signed the ball and told him to keep the souvenir himself.

By the time the day was over, ownership of the ball was claimed by another half-dozen people, several of whom, Mazeroski would say later, approached him and demanded $100 for the ball. But Maz turned them all down, not sure of anyone's claim and not really caring if the real ball ever appeared at all. To this day, the home-run ball has never been authenticated. It is among baseball's most renowned absent treasures, joining Bobby Thomson's 1951 playoff home-run shot at the Polo Grounds and Bucky Dent's 1977 playoff home-run ball into the left-field netting at Fenway Park as the sport's most valuable missing balls. In 2005, *Sports Illustrated* placed the value of the Mazeroski ball at $100,000.

Watching the ball disappear over the wall, Pirate owner John Galbraith stood in his box seat by the Pirate dugout and immediately hugged everyone in sight. "Nobody ever did anything like this before," he laughed. "It's never been done—never until now."

As if on cue, another scrum of policemen appeared on the field in front of his box to ensure that Galbraith, his son Dan, and co-owner Tom Johnson safely reached the Pirate dressing room. Latching on to the belt of a burly cop, Galbraith and the other two were an odd site— a kind of middle-aged, white-collar conga line—as they steadily pushed ahead, forcing their way through the mayhem into the clubhouse.

Across the field in his third-base box seat, Yankee owner Dan Topping was almost too stunned to move as he absorbed the Yankees' shocking defeat. "It was when Kubek got hit with that ball," he said of the game's turning point. "That was the beginning of the end for us." Staring at the wild scene in front of him, Topping grew reflective. "I guess thirty-five years is a long time to wait for this," he said before disappearing into his team's clubhouse.

Steadily, the throbbing mass of fans hit the streets of Oakland.

Some headed straight to streetcars and buses and were stuck in traffic for hours. Others milled about, headed nowhere in particular, and absorbed the atmosphere. "The thrill of thrills," one fan called out. "Game of a lifetime," another yelled. A half mile or so east of Forbes Field on Craig Street, nine-year-old Pete Kirby had just been dismissed for the day from his fourth-grade classroom at St. Paul's Cathedral Grade School when one of his baseball-mad teachers, Sister Mary Carmine, started yelling. She had just heard the home-run call on the transistor radio embedded deep in her robes, sending her into an uncharacteristic whoop of triumph.

"The other nuns looked over at her with disdain, but all the kids got excited," recalls Kirby, who lived on Atwood Street, so close to Forbes Field that the glow from the light standards shone through his bedroom window at night. Headed home, he and his next-door neighbor got caught up in the pandemonium—and the traffic—just outside the ballpark.

"I remember all the noise and the confetti, but the image burned into my memory is of the thousands and thousands of 'Nixon-Lodge' and 'Kennedy-Johnson' flyers that littered the field and the street," Kirby remembers. Presidential campaign workers, adorned in skimmers, had been a presence around the ballpark throughout the Series and continued passing out flyers even after the game had ended. But most spectators just threw their flyers away right then and there, which quickly accumulated into a pile of trash so thick that Kirby and his friends took to sliding on them across the sidewalk. For Kirby, the contrast of the earnest campaign workers and the giddy fans created a vivid image that endures. "You don't forget things like that," says Kirby, who later became an usher at Forbes Field. "We saw all these happy adults, caught up in the excitement, so we got happy, too."

Byron and Jean Oertel headed from their seats in the bleachers toward the exits in the left-field corner. But first, Byron paused to snap some shots of the crowd, whom the security guards had managed to quickly and ably clear to the perimeter of the diamond after all. In another shot, Jean holds her father's overcoat as she poses in front of the big left-field scoreboard in the background. Half a block away and headed across Forbes Avenue to a reserved table at Gustine's was former Pirate and Cincinnati slugger Ted Kluszewski, now a member of the White Sox, who called the home run a typical Pirate finish. "It's almost unbelievable," said Big Klu. Under orders not to clamp down on the celebrants but simply to keep them from getting out of hand, police watched the evolving postgame shenanigans out on the streets of Oakland with a collective policy of benign neglect.

*　*　*

By then, eight-year-old Bob Costas, who had skipped school to watch the game on television at home in Redondo Beach, was in full-throttle despair that his beloved Yankees had lost, and at the sudden, dramatic way the game had ended. "I shed tears, I really did," he says, "and went into my bedroom and threw myself on my bed when the game ended." In his disappointment and "because I could scarcely contain my sadness and rage" at the result, Costas decided on a form of protest—declaring a moratorium against speaking, a self-imposed silence that he intended to continue all the way until opening day of 1961.

That evening, there was the usual conversation around the Costas's dinner table, but young Bob didn't participate, choosing to communicate with nods and shakes of his head. But things grew a bit sticky the next day at school, when he was forced to respond to the taunts of his classmates, most of whom were reveling at the Yankee misfortune. "They were making inane comments that had to be debated and set straight," Costas recalls. "And so ended my silence."

(Costas, however, would have the last laugh: His Yankees would go on to play in every World Series through 1965, winning three of them. By 1963, Costas was back on Long Island, where Mr. Tomasee, "a very wise sixth-grade teacher who understood that the World Series was more important, at least for one day, than any school lesson," hauled his television from home into school so students could watch Game 1 of the Series against the Dodgers. "This may sound sexist, but the general reaction was that the boys were delighted and the girls thought, this is stupid," says Costas. "The handful of girls who wanted to follow it have forever ranked high in my esteem.")

Descending on the Pirate locker room after the customary five-minute cooling off period, reporters and cameramen got the obligatory champagne bath. Delivery of those cases of champagne and beer wouldn't go to waste after all. "Everybody was dodging the beer cans that sailed through the air and one needed a raincoat to stay dry," wrote Jim McCulley of the *Daily News*. "And nobody had a raincoat." Dick Stuart, on deck when Mazeroski hit the winning blast, blasted writer Dick Schaap and his guest Lenny Bruce with a mixture of champagne and beer. As was his custom, pinch-hit master Gino Cimoli grabbed the first hat he could find and squashed it onto his head, before belting out perhaps one of the most memorable lines of all about the 1960 World Series: "They set all the records and we won the Series," Cimoli laughed. "Let 'em stuff that on their mantelpieces."

Standing with his back to his locker before a forest of microphones and popping flashbulbs Mazeroski, sweating and animated in the steamy surroundings, did his best in responding to questions as quickly as they were delivered. "Yeah, a high fastball," he said over and over of the home-run pitch he had hit, contradicting what Blanchard insisted was a slider. Not that it mattered. "Yeah, I was swinging for the fence," Maz added. "What did I think? I was too happy to think." Posing for photographers, he kissed his bat perhaps a dozen times for photographers. Then Mazeroski grew reflective as he remembered the man who had hit him all those ground balls, his

father, Lew, who had died of cancer the year before: "I only wish my
dad had been alive to see it," he said.

Harvey Haddix, the improbable Game 7 winner, insisted he had
been the first Pirate to the plate to congratulate Mazeroski. Haddix
beamed when asked to compare this game with his "lost" perfect
game of 1958. "We lost that game," he reminded reporters. "This
game we won. This is wonderful. There's no better feeling."

Calling this one "a typical Pirate victory" was team captain Dick
Groat, already putting things in perspective. "We've been doing this
all year," said Groat, who would finally be able to let his throbbing
wrist heal properly. "Today's result did not surprise me. I imagine the
Yankees are the most surprised people of all. I know some of them
thought we weren't a very tough team. We showed 'em today how
tough we can be."

Then Cimoli poured champagne on Murtaugh's head. Nearby, a blizzard of wet towels—shocking purple Turkish towels that were standard
fare in the Pirate clubhouse—went flying through the air, with one hitting Joe L. Brown squarely in the face. Then pitcher George Witt threw
another towel that landed smack on the back of Tom Cheney's head.
"Witt," Cheney yelled, "you never threw that straight in your life!" Stan
Isaacs in *Newsday* cleverly called them the "Lavender Towel Mob." A
knowledgeable insider nodded agreement. "That's the Pirates," he said.
"They always throw towels. They think it's good luck."

"Pirate power!" somebody else roared.

"We don't have any power—remember?" countered Hal Smith.

A Yankee comeback followed by Mazeroski's big blast may have turned
Smith's eighth-inning shot into World Series footnote status, but the
happy Pirates hadn't forgotten it. "Smith hit the big blow that won the
game for us, no doubt about it," said Rocky Nelson, sitting with knees
crossed and a big cigar in one hand. "Maz's hit was anticlimactic to me."

Nelson had knocked a big home run himself, back in the first, but fresh in people's minds was how Mantle had eluded his tag in the eighth to keep the Yankees alive. "Mantle made a good slide and got away from me," he said. "He made a great play, that's all." Even Elroy Face was upbeat, not letting his first subpar Series performance affect his mood. "I felt pretty bad for awhile," he said. "But we won and that's all that counts."

A gaggle of suits shoehorned their way behind a wedge of cops into the middle of the wild scene, courtesy of Joey Diven, who had materialized as an impromptu clubhouse gatekeeper. You would think that at nearly 300 pounds, Joey would have been intimidating enough to keep the locker room relatively clear. But Diven just had too many friends, most of whom gained entry, among them Mayor Barr, who at first looked a little out of place in a suit, until Dick Stuart doused him with a bucket of champagne. The Mayor took his impromptu bath in stride. "I wore an old suit anyway," he said.

Meantime, Stuart targeted other victims in suits, a practice that, as one wag noted, he was more skilled at than hitting a baseball. Few suit-types were spared: John Galbraith got drenched, as did United Steelworkers Union president David McDonald, police superintendent James Slusser, and even the Most Rev. John Wright. "That," said the Most Rev. Wright, a future Cardinal in the church, of the game's dramatic finish, "was the answer to a prayer."

Dodging the beer cans and lavender towels, Murtaugh made his way around the room to congratulate his happy ballplayers. "This club never gives up," he said. "It has been this way all year. We've snapped back time and again." So who stood out? "The whole group," the Pirate manager answered magnanimously, "everyone who played today and at any time this season." Murtaugh's wife, Kate, would say later than she had never seen him so happy as he was directly after the 1960 Series. Danny agreed: "(Say) you had been standing on one side of me, and Mazeroski on the other side, and I had to kiss one or the other," he told her. "It wouldn't have been you."

Holding court in the steamy scene was Bob Prince, grabbing whoever was available for postgame interviews in front of the NBC cameras. "How does it feel to be a member of the World Champions?"
Prince asked Mazeroski. "Great," Maz replied. And that was that, as
the Gunner briskly moved on to other players. Not only had Prince
missed Mazeroski's big home run, but he claimed later to have had
no idea how the Pirates had actually won. Hours later, while eating
dinner with his wife, Betty, at the Pittsburgh Athletic Association,
Prince casually inquired how the game had ended.

"You're kidding," Betty said. "Bill Mazeroski hit a home run."

With the celebration in full throttle, Bob Skinner and Bill Virdon,
two of the more reserved Pirate players, had each grabbed a bottle of
champagne and stashed them in their lockers—to be enjoyed later.
Even so, Virdon, who seldom drank much of anything, realized he had
ingested just a little too much of the bubbly. Forty-five minutes later,
as the locker room cleared out, Virdon realized he still needed to
shower and asked his friend Nellie King a question rarely heard in a
big-league clubhouse.

"Nellie," he said, "would you take a shower with me?"

Startled, King asked why.

"I've had too much to drink, and I'm afraid I'm going to fall on
my rear in the shower and get hurt," Virdon said. "I don't want to
miss the team party."

So King complied and joined Virdon for a shower. Then Virdon
attended the party at the Webster Hall with King and their wives.
Both men were fully clothed.

* * *

Anyone doubting the heart of major-league ballplayers need only have
paid a visit down the hallway to the cramped, steamy locker room
serving the Yankees. They were decimated, stunned, and shattered by

the loss that they felt had been given away. "Everybody had their heads down; there wasn't much conversation," says Richardson. "We had a good ball club and thought we should have won the Series. But all of a sudden, it was down to that last inning, and all of a sudden, we'd lost. It was almost like a funeral."

The Yankees had outscored the Pirates 55-27, out-hit them 91-60, out-homered them 10-4, and anchored by Ford's two shutouts, out-pitched them, too. As a team, the Yankees had taken three lopsided games, batted .338 to the Pirates' .256, and bludgeoned the Pittsburgh staff into an ERA of more than 7, still the highest mark in Series history. Richardson finished with a batting average of .367. The rest of the lineup had hit just as handily—from Skowron at .375 to Berra's .318, Howard's .462, and Blanchard's .455—all for naught. Even after *Sport* magazine editor Ed Fitzgerald hurried into the locker room to congratulate Richardson on winning the magazine's World Series MVP award, not one Yankee offered so much as a word.

"Nobody said 'congratulations,' because we'd lost the Series," Richardson says. "It was over. There was no joy, no excitement." At least the Yankee second baseman would win a car for his award, and be honored with a parade back home in Sumter, South Carolina. These days, the winner of the 1960 World Series MVP is the answer to a good trivia question, still the only player from a losing team to be so honored.

But no one had performed better in the 1960 World Series than Mickey Mantle, whose .400 batting average, three home runs, eight walks, and eleven RBIs demonstrated why he was baseball's most complete player. Reaching the locker room, Mantle retreated to the trainer's room, where the combination of a stinging, sudden loss and the jarring sight of his close friend, Kubek, still coughing up blood while lying on the trainer's table with a towel over his face, made him do something his teammates have never forgotten.

Mickey Mantle sobbed.

"That's the one thing I remember as vivid as it can be," says Joe

DeMaestri. "Seeing Mickey crying was almost more crushing than losing the game. I would never had thought it would bother him like that."

Richardson calls losing the 1960 World Series "Mickey's biggest disappointment." Years later, Mantle would do so as well, calling it, "the first time I lost a Series when I know we should have won."

But sportswriter Maury Allen says it was the loss *and* the sight of Kubek *and* the realization that the ear, nose, and throat specialist had not yet arrived that set Mantle off. "Mantle walked into the trainer's room, and there was Kubek, forty-five minutes after he was hurt and still spitting up blood—and the doctor still hadn't shown up," he says. "Neither the Pirate or the Yankee team doctors were skilled enough to deal with that kind of injury. So the writers enter the clubhouse and there's Mickey Mantle who is sitting by Kubek and very emotional and wondering out loud, 'Where's the f–ing doctor?' "

In front of his locker sat Blanchard, still annoyed at the way he'd handled himself behind the plate in the ninth, and he was crying, too. Berra, the team's elder statesman, settled him down: "You'll be in a lot more of these things, and break some of the records I've been breaking," he told him.

Crossing the plate in the eighth, Berra had scored his thirty-ninth run in a World Series, an all-time record. The Yankee catcher had broken a slew of other Series records as well in 1960—the most games played, at-bats, base hits, and total bases. In Game 7, Berra had even hit the home run he had guaranteed the night before. But for now, the records meant little: Next to Berra and holding an unopened can of beer sat Maris, whose booming bat had crippled the Pirates in the three Yankee wins, but who had gone a frustrating 0-5 in Game 7. "What in the hell happened to us, for cryin' out loud?"

"We just got beat, Roger," said Yogi, his round form wrapped in a towel, "by the damndest baseball team that me or you or anybody else ever played against."

In hindsight, Berra was quietly showing the kind of leadership in the

somber clubhouse that he would draw on later as a big-league manager. With a combination of genuine humility and an innate ability to
get along with everyone, Berra would become one of baseball's great
ambassadors, "truly one of nature's noble men," as Bob Friend would
call him. Knowing he was taking off his uniform for the final time, Gil
McDougald said he was struck with an overwhelming desire to dress
as quickly as possible and leave the cramped locker room.

"(The loss) didn't upset me the way it upset a lot of the guys," he
says. "I was disappointed, but had a different feeling than if I was
going to stay with the club. Deep down, I was happy for the Pirates.
In a town like Pittsburgh where they don't win that often, it's a big
thing. We'd had our share."

Other Yankees had even less to say. Staring at his locker and
stewing was Dale Long, the ex-Pirate with the big pinch-hit. "The
best team lost," he said. "Imagine, Hal Smith hitting a homer."
Feeling their pain—and his own for that matter—was Kubek, who
was finally being examined by Dr. Sherman, the ear, nose, and
throat specialist, who advised immediate hospitalization. The
Yankee shortstop was diagnosed with a bruised larynx and vocal
chords, and internal bleeding. Flying was out, so he was only now
showering and dressing for his ride in an ambulance to the hospital,
where he would spend the night. Still under orders from Dr.
Gaynor to not even try to talk, Kubek responded to a reporter's
question—sort of.

"Would Virdon's grounder have been a double play were it not for
the erratic bounce?" asked the reporter.

"Yes," nodded Kubek.

The sting of defeat was apparent, but the Yankee regulars had performed admirably in piling up all those base hits and runs. Stengel put
the rap squarely on his pitchers: "The infielders and outfielders fought
like hell to come back and win this one and those guys with the ball

let it get away," he sighed. "They were told not to throw high to these hitters. Maybe they'll learn their lesson someday."

By the time that the writers reached Stengel, the Yankee manager had already comforted a distressed Ralph Terry, giving him the advice that may just have helped the young pitcher get over the stigma of yielding a famous home run. In the clubhouse, Stengel had summoned Terry to his office right away, curious to find out the home-run pitch he had thrown Mazeroski. "How were you trying to pitch him?" he asked him.

"Breaking stuff, low and outside, but I couldn't get the ball down," Terry said. "I just couldn't get it where I wanted to."

Stengel, his pants already down around his shoes and his shirt unbuttoned, presented a comical sight, but he chose his words wisely. "As long as you pitch, you're not always going to get the ball where you want it," he told Terry. "That's a physical mistake. As long as you weren't going against the scouting report, that's okay. Otherwise, I wouldn't sleep good at night."

Then came the moment that writer Ed Lucas figured probably saved Terry's career: "Forget it, kid," Stengel advised his hard-luck pitcher. "Come back and have a good year next year." So the twenty-four-year old right-hander did—several, in fact, in winning thirty-nine games over the next two seasons, including twenty-three in '62. That fall in the World Series against the Giants, Terry won Game 5 and then tossed a complete-game, 1-0 victory in Game 7 to earn MVP honors.

Facing renewed questions about whether he would be back as Yankee manager, Stengel avoided the subject by focusing on the game and graciously crediting the Pirates. "Your boys fought very good," he told Pirate general manager Joe L. Brown. "We had to come from behind and get that momentum so we got thinking we were pretty good, and we are pretty good." Addressing the writers, Stengel felt their pain—"You musta written 50 leads," he said, before offering his analysis of the game itself.

The turning point? The bad hop to Kubek: "He was all set to field it, and it jumped up and cracked him," Stengel said, forever making his point without mentioning a single name. The best Pirate in the Series? "You gotta say that the man who hit the ball last was the payoff guy." That would be Mazeroski. "But the center fielder (Virdon) had us in trouble all year." All year? "And until today, those two pitchers (Law and Face) gave it to us good." Then Stengel summed up his team's frustration. "It looked like we were going to win it but we didn't get that last thing done."

* * *

That "last thing"—a walk-off World Series Game 7 home run—had never happened before and has not happened since. It was an exclamation point to the best game ever—one that was crisply and briskly played, had only one error, and displayed a combination of sparkling and startling plays—and remarkably, not a single strikeout. Around the country and the world, people reacted to what they had just seen, many reveling that the underdog had won. In Fairview, Alberta, the Pirate victory brightened Duncan Cameron's 101st birthday party, since, as Mr. Cameron explained, "I didn't particularly want the Yankees to win." Nor did people in Havana, given the New Yorkers' unpopular nickname, which reeked of American imperialism and had inspired a barbershop there to put up a sign in its window: "Pittsburgh Sí, Yankees No." In El Cerrito, California, sixty-seven-year-old Ray Kremer, the winning Pirate pitcher in games 6 and 7 of the 1925 Series, called this one the "funniest" of all the World Series, adding that it appeared for a time that Game 7 would end 9-7 Pirates, just as it had thirty-five years ago at Forbes Field. "That was a slugfest, too," Kremer recalled of his late-inning dual with Walter Johnson. "They sure had me sweating today. But wasn't that homer of Mazeroski's wonderful?"

Stunned that the Yankees had somehow lost the World Series, Ken Pearlman of Mamaroneck, New York, thought to himself, " 'How could the Yankees have scored fifty-some runs and lost?' " But he also remembers thinking that even though they had been beaten, there would be other seasons and other Series for the Yankees. "Sure, it was a downer they'd lost, but it was certainly not depressing," says Pearlman. "The whole approach to sports was different in those days when things weren't so overanalyzed and rehashed, and everyone just moved on. Besides, I remember thinking that the Pirates had done something unbelievable in winning. It had been an exhilarating World Series."

Even Chief Justice Earl Warren of the Supreme Court went on the record about the outcome. Late that afternoon when somebody referred to "Yankee ingenuity" in a patent case, the chief justice offered a quick retort: "According to the information I have just received," the chief justice said, "you should have spoken of *Pirate* ingenuity."

In Pittsburgh, the real party was just beginning. Downtown, which had been a virtual ghost town for most of the afternoon, steadily filled with people. Some came barreling out of bars, where they'd been watching the game. Some hopped in cars and drove about blaring their horns. Others, holed up in office buildings, flung open the windows and tossed out paper—quickly filling the air with what looked like an October snowstorm. People threw any kind of paper they could find, wastepaper baskets full of it—and in one case on Grant Street, a red wastepaper basket itself, which landed on the street with a thud, thankfully hitting no one. A spokesman at the Bessemer & Lake Erie Railroad office in the Frick Building said later that a whole room of company records had gone missing, tossed out the window in giddy celebration.

At first, city officials feared that mobs would wreak havoc. Police and firefighters stood by, but there was little to do, with most of the untold thousands content to drive or walk around, wave signs, and smile at strangers. For the most part, vandalism was minor; of the twenty-eight celebrants arrested, twenty were for excessive drinking and the rest were for disorderly conduct. Thinking quickly, managers of downtown variety stores dipped into their Halloween stock of horns and rattles and did a landmark business. As darkness descended, the lights in the windows at Bell Telephone headquarters on Stanwix Street snapped on to spell out the phrase, a favorite of Bob Prince, "We Had 'Em All The Way." Standing on Smithfield Street and shaking his head in wonder as a Buick convertible full of flag-waving girls rambled by was Annab Natayan, a Duquesne University exchange student from Bombay: "I was told Americans like to live it up," he said. "But all this? I'm flabbergasted."

So was Joe Falls of the *Detroit News*. Headed back to the Hilton to write his piece, "I saw a celebration in the streets that has never been matched in all the years that have followed," he said. "It seemed as if nobody went home but instead clogged the streets of downtown Pittsburgh so that it was almost impossible to walk."

Falls noted that paper was knee-deep on some downtown streets. Amidst a din of whistles, bells, horns, firecrackers, and people yelling, he made it back to his hotel room, ready to write his stories, but faced another decision in the meantime. Keep the windows open to get some air, but continue to be distracted by the noise? Or close the windows for some peace and quiet, but (in those days before air conditioning) sweat? Falls closed the window, perspired, and wrote his story—forever remembering the intensity of the celebration.

The party had become a story unto itself. Stan Isaacs of *Newsday* already planned to file news stories about Hal Smith's home run, Kubek's injury, and the rowdy celebration in the Pirate locker room. But seeing the commotion on his way back to the Hilton, he got his notebook out again to interview celebrants for yet another piece. "Everything but the Monongahela River spilled over in this happy town," Isaacs wrote. "Fans who had waited a long time to celebrate let go with a vengeance. . . . Beer bottles littered main streets. Girls grabbed strangers and kissed them. The men got into the act by kissing strangers. That caused a few fist fights."

In and around Forbes Field—the "eye of the storm"—the impromptu party went on for hours. Swarms of fans stuck around, wandering the field and serenading the ballplayers. Even at the normally staid Pittsburgh Athletic Association dining room two blocks away, happy members tossed tablecloths and plates, with new revelers bursting through the revolving door every few seconds. Throughout Oakland, there was bumper-to-bumper traffic, dancing, and a lot of drinking.

Threading through the throngs was the challenge faced by Pirate ballplayers in trying to reach their cars parked at Stuckert's Esso. But when a cop shoved Hal Smith into a big black Cadillac as delirious fans swarmed around the car, the Pirate home-run hero realized he was in the wrong car. Eventually finding the right one, Smith drove off. So did Elroy Face, who managed to reach his car and head east on Forbes Avenue, before he was directed by a cop to turn right, toward downtown. But Face lived in the eastern suburbs and wanted to reach Fifth Avenue, a more direct artery. "Hey buddy, this is a crowded ballpark," yelled the cop. "Don't you know your way around here?"

Dressing quickly and not partaking in the hijinks was Vernon Law, intent on getting to a postgame television appearance. So how exactly to dodge the frenzied crowds outside the ballpark? Law had an ace in the hole—the U.S. secretary of agriculture, Ezra Taft Benson, a family friend. A fellow Idahoan and a future LDS president, Taft, along with his wife, Flora, had watched the game from the third-base box where they were pictured in the next day's *Press,* staring intently at the field and eating popcorn—"consuming farm products and rooting for Law," the paper wrote. Meeting Law in the clubhouse, Benson became his escort and suggested they take a back door to a stadium alley out in deep right field, where the secretary's chauffeur whisked them away.

Most fans behaved themselves. Some did not and ripped down the Forbes Field admission signs and swatches of the red, white, and blue World Series bunting. Outside Gate 6 from atop the truck platform, Benny Benack and his Iron City Six played on . . . and on . . . with many revelers sticking around, in no particular hurry, as revelers added their own impromptu titles to old standards—"Taps" after someone yelled "Casey Stengel" and the Dixieland "Death March" in honor of Mantle.

At the Oakland Café on Forbes Avenue, a man pushed through the mob, and waving a hastily printed bulldog edition of the *Press* with the banner headline "PIRATES WORLD CHAMPS," handed it to the bartender, who promptly tacked the front page over the bar to thunderous applause. Surveying the festive scene along Craig Street, retired electrician Ray Evans cracked, "You would have thought we won the World Series." Gus Miller, who once headed the ushers' union at Forbes Field, and operated a newsstand at Forbes Avenue and Boquet Street for more than forty years, recalled Pittsburgh's last Series celebration, in 1925, though that one "was like an old ladies' knitting circle compared to this." (Gus Miller himself is gone now, but his newsstand lives on.)

The Pirates were planning a party for that evening at the Webster Hall, a few blocks away on Fifth Avenue, which gave the players a few hours to soak in the atmosphere. In the late afternoon, with shadows starting to creep across the streets, Roberto Clemente didn't head toward his car but went on foot across the Panther Hollow Bridge into Schenley Park to be among the fans. Writers and all those who mocked him be damned, Clemente thought to himself as he shook hands with happy Pittsburghers, who had appreciated him from the start. "(I) saw all those thousands of fans in the streets," he would say. "It was something you cannot describe. I did not feel like a player at the time. I felt like one of those persons, and I walked the streets among them."

Consumed by the crowds and still not completely comfortable with his teammates, Clemente didn't attend the party. Mazeroski did, but not before heading to Schenley Park himself, where he and his wife, Milene, found a secluded spot and took in the sudden and welcome solitude. "There was nobody there," Mazeroski told writer Jim O'Brien. "Not any cars. Not a soul. It was so quiet. Even the squirrels had disappeared. Maybe they were out celebrating."

Sitting in their black Lincoln, the Mazeroskis didn't discuss the home run. "It was just another home run," Bill told O'Brien. "I didn't think it was such a big deal. I didn't realize then the proportions it would reach."

That evening, the Pirates had their Webster Hall celebration, a boisterous and boozy affair. On television, Senator Kennedy and Vice President Nixon focused the third of their four debates—a nifty spilt-screen affair with Kennedy in New York and Nixon in Hollywood—on a protracted discussion of whether the Democrats would let the Communists take over the Pacific island of Quemoy and Matsu. Nearly 61 million people watched, though Western Pennsylvanians had other things on their mind.

It was as if no one in Pittsburgh wanted October 13, 1960, to end. Traffic clogged the streets, which didn't seem to bother anyone—not even those gathered at the Syria Mosque for a scheduled 8 PM concert with jazz great Gerry Mulligan. The only glitch was that by 8:45 PM, Mulligan had not shown up, delayed by traffic-choked streets, remembers Pirate fan and jazz aficionado George Berger. Finally, at 9 PM, Mulligan sauntered to the stage and apologized for his tardiness—offering the offhand joke that considering all the traffic, "Maybe they should ban baseball in Pittsburgh."

"It *was* a joke," concedes Berger. "But obviously, Gerry was not a baseball fan."

By 9 PM, downtown Pittsburgh was packed with some three hundred thousand people—"saturation point," said Safety Director Louis Rosenberg—causing city officials to shut off inbound traffic from both major feeders, the Fort Pitt and Liberty tunnels. As darkness fell and the stores downtown closed, impromptu celebrations continued to break out. A three-piece combo comprised of a bugle, paint bucket, and soup spoon belted out "There's No Tomorrow." Two brothers from the Northside, Archie and Louie Lidey, maneuvered their car slowly along Smithfield Street, periodically pausing to bash in the roof of the car with sledgehammers. "We sold this heap today for $25," explained Louie. "We got to deliver it in the morning, and I don't know what the owner's going to say when he sees it."

"Everybody loved it," Isaacs wrote of the celebration. "Well, almost everybody." When a University of Pittsburgh student said she had to go home to study, a friend couldn't believe anyone would want to leave.

"I have to study for this test," the student answered. "My prof hates baseball."

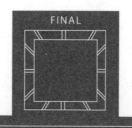

FINAL

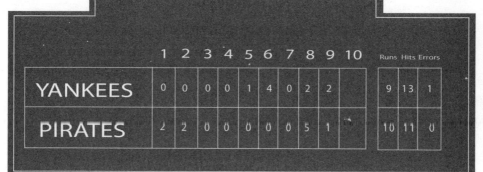

	1	2	3	4	5	6	7	8	9	10	Runs	Hits	Errors
YANKEES	0	0	0	0	1	4	0	2	2		9	13	1
PIRATES	2	2	0	0	0	0	0	5	1		10	11	0

AND THE NEXT DAY . . .

ON FRIDAY, OCTOBER 14, the first day of the rest of his life, Bill Maze-roski flew back to New York on his way to Jersey City. That evening at Roosevelt Stadium he drove in two runs in the Ernie Banks National League All-Stars' 5-0 exhibition victory over the Roger Maris American League All-Stars. Whitey Ford, the AL starter, gave up two runs in the fifth, with Don Newcombe of the Reds earning the victory for the NL.

Ford was still brooding over the way he felt Casey Stengel had mishandled him throughout the World Series. Snubbing Stengel on the plane ride back to New York, Ford felt he should have been given the opportunity to start a third game in the Series. "I know I would have beaten them three times, and we would have been World Champs again," he told writer Tony Castro. "But Stengel was stubborn." Still stewing, Maris would say little about what he thought, but three weeks later, would earn the first of his two straight AL MVP awards.

Back in Pittsburgh, groggy fans stumbled off to work or school on Friday morning. Meantime, city officials took stock of exactly how much of a cleanup was ahead and put sanitation crews quickly to work. By the afternoon, Bangy Ambrose, superintendent of the city's Bureau of Bridges, Highways, and Sewers, said that 50 tons of garbage and litter had been cleared already. Bangy put the cost of the removal at $10,000—a hefty amount, but just a fraction of the $3.5 million the Series had added to the city's economy revenues.

Tony Kubek flew home to Milwaukee on Friday, but not before he received a visitor in his room at Presbyterian Hospital. Dressed in street clothes, Dick Groat was visiting the hospital to get his wrist x-rayed, and decided to stop by to say hello. The two men had exchanged pleasantries numerous times over the previous few weeks, but as Groat walked into Kubek's room and said, "Hello," the Yankee shortstop had no idea he was being addressed by the Pirate shortstop. "I'd always talked to Tony with my cap on," Groat says with a grin. "He didn't know I was bald." Kubek would make a complete recovery from his throat injury and go on to a successful second career in talking, as NBC's leading baseball analyst.

On Saturday morning, Marvin Newman, by then at a hotel room in Iowa City to shoot that afternoon's Iowa-Wisconsin college football game, called *Sports Illustrated* picture editor Jerry Astor to make sure they had received his Game 7 film. Foremost on Newman's mind was whether the editors might have use for his panoramic shot of Mazeroski's home run.

Use it? "Marvin," said Astor, "you got the greatest baseball picture I've ever seen."

Not only had Newman caught the moment, but he had done so with stunning precision—actually freezing the ball as it climbed over the infield on its historic flight into Schenley Park. "Nobody has ever done that before," Astor said.

"That made my day," Newman says. "Yes, I knew I'd taken a good shot. But I had no idea (it was that good)." The photo would run across two pages in the October 24 edition of *Sports Illustrated* under the headline, "It Went All the Way!" with an arrow pointing to the ball. Today the print, signed by Newman, sells for thousands.

By the weekend, things in Western Pennsylvania had started returning to normal. The area's local race track, Waterford Park, resumed its card at 3 PM sharp on Friday after a two-day layoff. Pitts-burgh Home Furnishings announced that the 1961 Frigidaire Washer with its "Somersault Washing Action" was now available for $214 with "easy terms." Presumably wearing a different suit, Mayor Barr announced a series of new streetlights along East Ohio Street on the Northside. That Friday evening, Western Pennsylvanians got back to a particular preoccupation of theirs—a nearly full schedule of high-school football games, though it was a rare bye week for the Beaver Falls Tigers and their star quarterback, Joe Namath. At the Syria Mosque, the Pittsburgh Symphony launched its thirty-fifth season with Beethoven's Seventh—"Symphony," not "game"—before a full house of thirty-six hundred.

On Saturday at Pitt Stadium, the Pitt Panthers flattened archrival West Virginia, 42-0, on homecoming day, with Mike Ditka grabbing a touchdown pass and sending many in the crowd of thirty-one thou-sand into Oakland's bars and restaurants—again—to celebrate. And though the weather had cooled to more seasonal temperatures, Sen-ator Kennedy figured Western Pennsylvania was again safe to visit. Stumping through seven Western Pennsylvania counties, he ham-mered away at Republicans on a series of economic issues, while joking about complaints from Vice President Nixon that he had used notes in their Thursday debate.

"I understand that Casey Stengel wants to replay the 9th inning of the seventh game," Kennedy said in Johnstown, "because Danny Murtaugh had notes." The seven thousand people crammed into the fifty-two-hundred-seat Cambria County War Memorial roared with laughter.

Two nights later, Elroy Face and Hal Smith, this time joined by Bob Prince and a Hungarian dancer named Dita Aldo, donned light-blue dinner jackets, string ties, and gray Texas hats to resume their guitar picking at the Holiday House in Monroeville. The seven hun-dred customers applauded their music generously, the *Press* reported, "but if anyone had any doubts as to whether they were cheering the singers or the ballplayers, the finalé straightened it out." That's when Face and Smith broke into the Pirate fight song and were joined by the crowd "with such gusto," the paper wrote, "that it almost seemed like last Thursday all over again."

A few days later, Face left for Fort Myers, the Pirates' spring-training home, to relax on his boat. Others weren't headed so far; after his barnstorming trip, Mazeroski went to the North Hills section of Pittsburgh, where he was building a home and doing a lot of the work himself. That most ballplayers still worked in the off-season is a sign of how long ago it all was; Stuart, a resident of East Liberty, spent the winter as a car salesman, and Friend as a stockbroker. Groat would rejoin Jessop Steel, but not before vacationing with his wife, Barbara, in Hot Springs, Virginia, where he could finally admit how much pain his wrist was still giving him. Pulling out a pocketful of change for cigarettes, Groat still couldn't straighten out his fingers, and the coins spilled onto the carpet of the lobby hotel.

Others left for their hometowns—Hoak to Roulette, Pennsylvania, to hunt for turkey, and Virdon to West Plains, Missouri, where he and ex-Yankee Jerry Lumpe operated a sporting goods store. Smoky Burgess had joined Mazeroski on the barnstorming circuit in Jersey City and then Syracuse, before heading home to Forrest City, North Carolina, where he ran a service station. Clemente went home to San Juan, Puerto Rico, where he would play part of the winter-league season.

Out-of-town sportswriters continued to marvel not only at how the Pirates had won but at the intensity of Pittsburgh's postgame celebration. "Washington in '24 was boisterously buoyant (and) St. Louis in '26 was a big one," recalled syndicated columnist Joe Williams. "Even so, neither St. Louis nor any of the others managed anything remotely resembling the gigantic blast generated by Pittsburgh. This was a roar, the others faint whispers."

Jimmy Powers of the *Daily News* called the Pirates' victory "a popular national victory . . . a win for the poor little guys against the big rich guys swollen with past loot and overladen with records. (It was) one of the greatest Series finales ever."

Arthur Daley of the *Times* agreed, saying that the dramatic finish brought back memories of Bobby Thomson's 1951 pennant-winning home run for the Giants. "Hysterically happy fans streamed out of the stands," he wrote of the scene at Forbes Field. "This was New Year's Eve, the Mardi Gras and Armistice Day jammed into one boisterous package. Bands played and screaming singers repeated the same mad refrain over and over again until the needle had become stuck."

* * *

From the moment Game 7 ended, New York writers got back to the core question that had consumed them throughout the World Series: Was 1960 the end of the line for Casey Stengel? "If this was Stengel's last game as Bomber manager, the old geezer didn't even have the privilege of going out with the flourish he deserved," Daley wrote. "He almost had it won. Then it slipped from his eager grasp."

On Tuesday, October 18, the Yankees called a press conference at the Savoy Hilton in Manhattan, where a few minutes after noon, Stengel appeared, looking a tad nervous in a blue suit and striped tie. In a sense, it was all for show, since the Associated Press and United Press International had already reported the Yankees had fired their longtime manager. A gaggle of writers appeared anyway, firing questions as Dan Topping stepped forward and began reading from a prepared statement.

"Casey Stengel has been—and deservedly—the highest-paid manager in baseball history," Topping began. "He has been—and is—a great manager. Two years ago Casey quite reluctantly signed a new two-year contract . . . with the understanding that after the first year he could retire if he wanted to." On Topping went, "circling the subject," as Stengel's biographer Robert Creamer wrote.

"Do you mean he's through?" someone interrupted. "Has he resigned?"

Topping didn't answer and gave way to Stengel. His hands stuffed deep into the front pockets of his jacket, Casey stepped to the microphone: "Mr. Webb and Mr. Topping have started a program for the Yankees," he said. "They want to put in a youth program as an advanced way of keeping the club going. . . ."

"Casey," a reporter demanded. "Were you fired?"

"No, I wasn't fired," Stengel fired back, his irritation growing. "I was paid up in full." People laughed, but Casey wasn't trying to be funny. "Write anything you want," he spat. "Quit, fired, whatever you please. I don't care."

So that was it; the wire services had been right after all. "What do I care what the AP says," Stengel said. "Their opinion ain't gonna send me into a faint."

A few minutes later, as Stengel gave a last few sound bites to the horde of print and television reporters, Topping ran damage control. The real reason for the decision to replace Stengel with Ralph Houk was their concern about Stengel's health.

Nobody believed it for a minute. "I'll never," Casey rebutted, "make the mistake of being seventy again."

So this was the sendoff for a baseball legend, the man who had delivered ten AL pennants and seven World Championships in a dozen years. The press conference suddenly finished, Stengel and his wife, Edna, disappeared into the midtown pedestrian traffic, just another elderly couple, as they headed back to the Essex House on Central Park South, their New York residence.

Shock waves swept through the baseball landscape. Even Senator Kennedy took note, slyly using the news to jibe at Republican assertions that he lacked the background to be president. "The worst news for the Republicans this week was that Casey Stengel has been fired," Kennedy noted. "It must show that perhaps experience does not count."

For all the Yankee aura of button-down efficiency, the team had been sloppy in handling Stengel's dismissal. Topping's real intention had been to get in some new blood and purge the old guard. That became apparent all over again two weeks later when the Yankees dismissed General Manager George Weiss, who had been with the team since 1932 and had built its great farm system.

No one showed much sympathy for Weiss—Mantle actually poured himself a celebratory drink when he heard the news in mock honor for all those torturous contract negotiations. But the same writers who had so maligned Stengel twelve years before when the Yankees hired him now lamented his firing. Stengel hadn't just won, but he'd made it a lot of fun with his rambling discourses and ready quotes.

The forty-one-year-old Ralph Houk was a decided contrast to Stengel. With twenty-three years' experience already in the Yankee organization, the new manager was eminently qualified for the position; he had spent eight of those years as a Yankee backup catcher to Berra, absorbing the game and learning. Gruff and hierarchal, Houk was a decorated Army Ranger veteran of World War II and just the sort of no-nonsense leader that Yankee executives felt they needed to motivate their veteran team. Topping in particular was taken with Houk's war record, harboring the admiration of a Marine who hadn't seen combat experience for a soldier who had. Nor was Houk a man who took any lip, having once decked actor Gordon McRae for making a pass at his wife. He even punched a drunken teammate, pitcher Ryne Duren, for smashing his ever-present cigar into his face on the rowdy train ride home from Milwaukee after winning the '58 World Series.

Houk would put his own stamp on the Yankees. He hired the four-time twenty-game winner Johnny Sain, a former teammate, as the team's new pitching coach. Sain, who had retired in 1955 and had already developed into a respected pitching guru, convinced Houk to direct the Yankee starters to pitch more frequently—every four days on the calendar and instead of four starts. Then Sain taught Whitey Ford a new pitch that alleviated pressure on his elbow and broke sharply. The results gave Ford, who had never won twenty games in a single season under Stengel's platooning system, a chance to wrack up some big numbers. Pitching nearly one hundred innings more in '61, Ford had his best year ever, going 25-4.

Most things went right for the 1961 Yankees. Houk flip-flopped Mantle and Maris in the lineup with spectacular results: Batting third, Mantle seldom saw a bad pitch and hit fifty-four home runs. Batting cleanup, Maris broke Babe Ruth's single-season record with sixty-one home, a record that looks better every year in light of this generation's inflated, steroid-fueled power numbers. The Yanks started slowly in '61, but coasted to the AL pennant with 109 wins and dispatched the overmatched Reds in five games in that fall's World Series. Not that the season was devoid of drama, especially in the case of Maris, for whom the media glare was decidedly unwelcome. Never approaching Mantle—or the Babe, for that matter—in the hearts of Yankee fans, Maris broke the home-run record on the season's final day at Yankee Stadium before a paltry crowd of only twenty-five thousand, many of them crammed into the right-field grandstand for a shot at catching the home-run ball.

The pressure of the chase tore at Maris, who had little patience with the swarm of reporters who trailed after him—quite a contrast to Mantle, who was developing more of an affable, self-deprecating demeanor. That Maris broke sports' most hallowed record in 162 games—big-league owners had added the additional eight games before the season—convinced Commissioner Ford Frick to rule that a notation be added to explain that Ruth had attained his record in *only* 154 games. Frick resented that the mark broke the record of his old friend Babe Ruth, for whom he had ghostwritten newspaper articles. The ruling became the basis of the asterisk that the papers placed after the "61" in the record books, as if the new home-run mark were stained. The asterisk made it all the way to 1991, when acting Commissioner Fay Vincent reversed the ruling and recognized Maris as an official record-breaker.

Back on top of the baseball world, the Yankees repeated in '62, beating the Giants in seven games behind Ralph Terry. Twice more the Yankees reached the Series—getting swept by the Dodgers behind Sandy Koufax in '63 and losing to the Cardinals in '64 in 7 games—before things hit rock bottom. In 1965, the greatest dynasty in sports unraveled—falling with a thud to sixth place in the American League.

How things deteriorated so quickly for the Yankees would require a dissertation. There were devastating injuries. The team's stars were aging. So the front office tinkered by naming Houk general manager in '64, and replacing him with Berra, who provided lots of good quotes but couldn't motivate his players. Hovering just below the surface of the team's sudden demise was its imperious insistence on ignoring top African-American prospects, many of whom were becoming the foundation of other big-league teams. That trend became crystal clear in the '64 World Series, in which the Yankees faced a St. Louis lineup with a core of dynamic black players like Bob Gibson, Lou Brock, Curt Flood, and Bill White. The Yankees would take another twelve years and another change in ownership to get back to the Series.

Baseball changed in profound ways after the 1960 World Series. As the election of John F. Kennedy swept new ideas into Washington, big-league baseball owners took big, brash steps of their own, ushering in their first expansion in sixty years. Forcing their hand was a forceful group of baseball executives pushing a renegade idea—a third major league, called the Continental League. Though the concept of this new league, headed by Branch Rickey, never got off the ground, major-league owners got the message. They needed to expand as a way of building on the recent financial successes of the West Coast and in Milwaukee and Baltimore. With an eye on America's shifting demographics and the recent successes of pro football, owners looked to a variety of cities as potential homes for new baseball teams. That went for New York, too, where a dynamic thirty-eight-year-old attorney named William Shea was appointed by Mayor Robert Wagner to help lure a new NL franchise to the city.

The owners moved quickly. The American League awarded franchises in '61 to Los Angeles and Washington, D.C., followed by the National League, which agreed to expand by two in '62 to New York and Houston. The AL franchise in Washington would replace the Senators, who were moving to Minneapolis-St. Paul, an area particularly eager to land a big-league team, having just lost its basketball team, the Lakers, to Los Angeles. Leaving Washington was a shrewd move for Twins owner Calvin Griffith, though a tinge of old-style racism figured into the decision; years later, Griffith admitted he went to Minnesota because of Washington's large African-American population. "Black people don't go to ballgames," he said.

Stocked with castoffs, the expansion clubs were predictably poor. To bolster the new clubs, a draft was held in which the established clubs sent two players to the teams in their league. So the Yankees shipped Bobby Shantz and Dale Long to the "new" Senators and Bob Cerv to the Angels, but when they tried sending Gil McDougald to the Senators, the thirty-two-year-old ten-year veteran instead retired to New Jersey to run his janitorial-supply business. Anything was preferable to playing for Washington, for as the saying went, "First in war, first in peace, and last in the American League."

The owners' decision to bring back National League baseball to New York was shrewd. The legions of old Dodger and Giants fans, who never took to the Yankees, welcomed the Mets with open arms and flocked to the Polo Grounds to see them play, especially against the California teams. Helping attract the crowds was none other than Casey Stengel, lured from a restless retirement by his old Yankee comrade and new president, George Weiss, to manage the Mets. Introduced at a press conference, the seventy-two-year-old Stengel proclaimed it was "a great honor for me to be joining the Knickerbockers."

The early Mets were dreadful. Not that anybody was particularly upset about it, especially the writers, who were thrilled to have Casey back in New York. Stengel got into form quickly, saying of a journeyman catcher named Hobie Landrith, the Mets' top pick in the expansion draft, that "you gotta have someone back there to catch the ball, or you're gonna have a lot of passed balls." The Mets were soon outdrawing the Yankees, thanks in part to a lot of one-time Dodger crowd-pleasers like Gil Hodges, Duke Snider, and Billy Loes. Stengel stuck around for three seasons—the first two at the Polo Grounds, and then a year at spanking new Shea Stadium, which he heralded as a gleaming, futuristic ballpark. "We got fifty-four restrooms—twenty-seven for the men and twenty-seven for the ladies, and I know you will all want to use them now," Casey said. "And the escalators. No stairs. I tell you, you'll all keep your youth if you follow the Mets." Though the Mets lost their opening game at Shea and many more after that, they were on their way; five years later, the team startled the sports world by winning the World Series.

* * *

For the Pirates, the post-Series glow continued for months. Two days after the Series ended, Murtaugh was named baseball's Manager of the Year in a rout, collecting 127 of 193 first-place votes, and easily outdistancing Solly Hemus of the Cardinals. In early November, Vernon Law won the major leagues' Cy Young Award on the strength of his twenty wins during the season and two victories in the World

Series (until 1967, the Cy Young was a single award, not given to the top pitcher in each league as it is today). Then, on November 17, Dick Groat was named the National League's MVP, beating out Don Hoak by taking sixteen of the twenty-two first-place votes, and succeeding Ernie Banks, who had won the award the last two seasons. Groat was elated, saying that "next to being a member of the World Champion Pirates, this is the finest honor I've ever had."

Reading the news in a Puerto Rican newspaper, Roberto Clemente was bitterly disappointed—not that he had failed to win the award, but at how distant he'd finished in the balloting. Though Groat had out-hit him .325 to .314 during the regular season, Clemente felt that his ninety-four RBIs next to Groat's fifty should have earned him better treatment, as should his nine hits and .310 batting average in the World Series, next to Groat's .214. Seeing he had placed not third or fourth in the balloting but a distant eighth, behind several players of significantly lesser abilities who were more popular with the voting writers, Clemente became angry. "I was very bitter," Clemente recalled years later. "I'm a team player—winning the pennant and the World Championship were more important to me than my average— but I feel I should get the credit I deserve." In 1961, his teammates, by now more comfortable with Clemente as he was with them, gave him a new nickname: "Mr. No Votes."

Some athletes would have sulked at the news and remained in a funk. Not Clemente, who used the disappointment of the MVP voting as motivation. Determined to earn more respect, Clemente went to spring training in February 1961 at Fort Myers a changed man—not full of the usual complaints about his physical ailments, but healthy and composed of an inner fire designed to demonstrate the way he could play the game. Continuing to work with Sisler, Clemente became more selective at the plate and switched to a heavier bat, which slowed his swing a fraction of a second and improved his wrist control. In 1961, Clemente's batting average soared, so much so that pitchers began knocking him down, which made him even more driven. At the All-Star Game, Clemente, who was hitting an NL-leading .357 at the time, was the league's starting right fielder. Many watching the game at Candlestick Park took stock not just of Clemente's emerging greatness, but of the contributions of other talented non-white players, especially in the National League, for which minorities comprised 36 percent of the All-Star roster. Though African-American and Hispanic players comprised only 17 percent of the NL teams by '61, seven of the league's top ten hitters and its four leading batters were non-white.

Clemente maintained his torrid pace in '61, compiling a .351 batting average and earning the first of his four NL batting titles. Also working with Sisler, Dick Stuart became more selective and broke through with a top-flight season in '61, batting .301 and powering thirty-five home runs. It was a big year for Big Stu, but sadly for the Pirates, an otherwise forgettable year.

The '61 Pirates stumbled to sixth place, four games under .500 and a distant eighteen games back of the pennant-winning Reds. Pitching was the main culprit. Law's ankle continued to hurt, so much so that he altered his mechanics and injured his shoulder in the process—struggling through eleven games before landing on the disabled list. There was talk that the thirty-one-year-old ace was finished. But Law had a lot of baseball left in his right arm, winning another sixty-seven games and retiring in 1967 after sixteen big-league seasons, all with Pittsburgh.

In 1962, the Pirates rallied to win ninety-three games. But the team finished only fourth—a sign to many, including Joe Brown, that a number of its mainline players were aging. After the season, Brown began disassembling the team that had gone so far just two years before. Groat went to the Cardinals, where he spent what he describes as his "three happiest years in baseball." In 1963, Groat batted .319 and placed second in MVP balloting. In '64, he anchored another

World Series–winning team—taken again in seven games against the Yankees. The Cardinals not only paid Groat a higher salary than he earned in Pittsburgh but "busted their butts to take care of my family," he says. When Groat's third daughter was born, the team sent him back to Pittsburgh with time off and a plane ticket. "You don't forget things like that," Groat says. After moving on to the Phillies, he finally closed his career with the Giants, retiring in 1967 with a .286 career batting average.

Brown kept dealing. Stuart went to Boston, where in '63 he enjoyed a career year by hitting forty-two home runs, thanks to a right-handed swing that perfectly suited Fenway Park's left-field Green Monster. But when Stuart, still bedeviled by all those strike-outs, slumped in '64, the Sox shipped him to the Phillies. In 1965, Stuart managed to improve his fielding enough that he did not lead or tie or lead the league in errors for the first time in eight years. But his reputation preceded him, and by then he had taken on a new nick-name, "Dr. Strangeglove," after the Peter Sellers film *Dr. Strange Love*. Playing out the string with the Dodgers, Mets, Taiyo in Japan, and finally the Angels, Big Stu retired in 1969 with 228 home runs.

In December 1961, Hoak and the singer Jill Corey were married by Mayor Barr. A year later, the intense Pirate third baseman became part of Brown's rebuilding program himself—shipped to Philadel-phia, where he played two seasons and retired. Then Hoak joined Prince as a Pirates broadcaster for two years before returning to the field, as a Phillies coach in '67 and for the next two years as a man-ager in the Pirates' farm system.

Hoak flourished as a manager. His team won the Carolina League in 1968, and he was the league's manager of the year. Promoted in '69 to AAA, Hoak took the Columbus Jets to the finals of the play-offs before falling to Syracuse. "His players loved him," says Corey. "Don treated everyone the same—that is, he was hard on all of them, and they did well."

Hoak seemed destined to be named manager of the Pirates when the team fired Larry Shepard after the '69 season. But on the morning of October 9, 1969, the Pirates rehired Danny Murtaugh. That afternoon, Hoak died of a heart attack while chasing a relative's stolen car in the Shadyside section of Pittsburgh. He was only forty-one, and he and Corey were the parents of a four-year-old daughter, Clare.

Hoak, or at least his memory, made a notable cameo of sorts in the 1991 film *City Slickers,* about a New Yorker (played by Billy Crystal) who tackles his midlife crisis with a cattle-driving vacation out West. When actress Helen Slater wonders aloud why men pay so much attention to baseball and all its endless statistics, she throws out a trivia question to prove her point: Who played third base for the 1960 Pirates? "Don Hoak!" blurts Crystal, a fraction of a second before his two friends, played by Bruno Kirby and Daniel Stern, both answer correctly. As a passionate Yankee fan, Crystal would have strong memories of the 1960 World Series. Watching the film in a theater in New York, where she now lives, Corey stood up and yelled, "That's my husband!" (In New York, she explains, "You can get away with stuff like that without them thinking you're crazy.")

Joe L. Brown continued to dismantle his '60 Pirates. Six weeks into the 1963 season, Skinner was traded to Cincinnati for Jerry Lynch. Later, he managed the San Diego Padres. Virdon became a big-league manager as well after his retirement in 1968, and became a two-time *Sporting News* Manager of the Year, in 1974 with the Yankees and in 1980 with Houston. Others hung on—Friend until '66 and Face until the middle of '68.

Clemente took his second batting title in 1964, but the Pirates continued to struggle. After the '64 season, Murtaugh resigned because of ill health, though some whispered he was forced out. But in 1970, he came back and led the Pirates to the NL East Crown, and in '71, to another Series title.

In the meantime, the Pirates became Clemente's team. Finally named MVP in 1966, the great Roberto would stage a highlight reel for the ages in that '71 Series. A marvel on the field, Roberto Clemente had become one of baseball's great ambassadors and role models off the field as well. After his death on New Year's Even 1972, the Baseball Hall of Fame waved the five-year rule and voted him in on the first ballot as the first Hispanic player to reach Cooperstown.

Bill Mazeroski's road to Cooperstown took considerably longer. After years of waiting for the call, the unassuming second baseman was selected to the Hall of Fame in 2001 by baseball's Veterans Committee. Unassuming to the end, Mazeroski was a seven-time All-Star and eight-time Gold Glove–winner in his seventeen-year career. How good was Mazeroski in the field? More than three decades later, he still holds big-league records for second basemen for most double plays in a season and a career, and for most years leading a league in double plays (eight) and assists (nine).

Stepping to the microphone to give his remarks after making the Hall of Fame, Mazeroski summed up his long and arduous trip to Cooperstown. In a moment as moving as any in the memory of those who attend induction ceremonies, he dissolved into tears and quickly cut it short. "I thought having my Pirates number retired was the greatest thing that ever happened to me," Maz said. "I didn't think I would make it into the Hall of Fame." Then, pausing as tears welled, he held up his prepared remarks and said, "I think you can kiss these twelve pages down the drain." At the postceremony press conference, Mazeroski admitted he had always been emotional—"I even cry at the sad commercials," he once said—adding that with family, friends, and more than fifteen former teammates in attendance, he figured he might not be able to finish. "I felt for Maz," said fellow inductee Kirby Puckett. "If you can't cry for a guy who couldn't even start his speech before he started crying, you don't have an emotional bone in your body."

These days, Mazeroski lives in Panama City, Florida, where he plays a lot of golf and fishes for striped bass. Forever humble, he rarely talks about the past, introducing himself at spring training, where he still coaches Pirate prospects, as "an old second baseman." His famous glove, along with the Louisville Slugger 125 Pro Model that he used to hit his famous World Series home run, is at the Hall of Fame.

* * *

The anniversaries come and go, as do the ESPN documentaries and the periodic calls to players for remembrances of the famous Game 7. They are older men now, just as apt to brag about their grandchildren as their exploits long ago in baseball. After all, several of the men who played in the famous game have children who made it to the big leagues; Bob Skinner's son, Joel, played with the White Sox, Yankees and Indians and now coaches for the Indians, and Vernon Law's son, Vance, was the Pirates' shortstop for several years and is now the baseball coach at Brigham Young University. Yogi Berra's son, Dale, became a Pirate *and* a Yankee, while another son, Larry, returned kicks in the NFL. Still others, like Clemente, Mazeroski, and Mantle, have sons who played in the minor leagues.

The march of time continues to claim men who played critical roles in Game 7 of the 1960 Series, some of them, like Hoak and Clemente, at young ages. Danny Murtaugh died in late '76 of a heart attack at age fifty-nine. Smoky Burgess and Dick Stuart made it to the '60 Pirates' thirtieth anniversary in Pittsburgh but died shortly thereafter—Burgess in late '91 at the age of sixty-five and Big Stu in 2002 at seventy. Sadly, several big Yankee stars are gone as well—Howard died in 1980 at the age of sixty-one, Maris from cancer at only fifty-one in 1985, and Mantle in 1995 at sixty-five.

Though the Pirates were a consistently strong team throughout the '70s—following up their '71 Series win with another in '79, neither team and none since have resonated like the 1960 club. The

Pirates of the '70s played in Three Rivers Stadium, one of the era's colorless, multipurpose ballparks that were hard to like. The Pirates also faced an unfortunate case of lousy timing: having to compete for the affections of Pittsburgh fans with Art Rooney's team, the Steelers, which, after forty years in the desert, finally found it to football's promised land. The Steelers won four Super Bowls in six years, the last in that run coming early in 1980, making the two teams champions at the same time. "City of Champions," Pittsburgh boldly proclaimed.

In the years since, fanfare over the Steelers has eclipsed all interest in the Pirates, who have now endured a drought of twenty-six years without returning to a World Series. Not only have the Steelers assembled great teams made up of a colorful cast of great players—men like Mean Joe Greene, Jack Lambert, Lynn Swann, Franco Harris, and Terry Bradshaw—but the team has won the public relations battle as well, and with it, the hearts and minds of Pittsburgh fans. Steeler players are everywhere in demand in Pittsburgh—visiting sick children in hospitals, cutting ribbons for new stores in malls, and generally building up a generation of goodwill, helped considerably by many players who established year-round homes in the city. Contrast that to the Pirates, most of whom over the years have departed for other places the minute the season had ended.

Even Bob Prince couldn't help the Pirates. Forever irreverent, the Gunner continued to amuse listeners but never quite satisfied Joe Brown, who told him after the '74 season that he needed to "sell" the team better. But Prince ventured too far in 1975 when, sharing the press box at Three Rivers Stadium with Westinghouse Broadcasting visitors who were rooting openly for the visiting Cubs, he blurted out on the air that "we've got some idiots in the box rooting for Chicago." After the season, Westinghouse, which owned KDKA Radio, fired Prince after twenty-eight years, along with Nellie King. Pirate fans were outraged and even held a downtown parade in their honor. Willie Stargell likened the unceremonious dumping of Prince to "the U.S. Steel Building falling down."

The Gunner caught on for a time with the Houston Astros and ABC's short-lived *Monday Night Baseball,* but his style was lost on just about anyone beyond Western Pennsylvania. Cut loose from both jobs after a year, he returned to Pittsburgh, picked up jobs where he could, and eventually wandered back to baseball by calling Pirate games for a time in the early '80s for a cable station. On May 3, 1985, Prince, by then suffering from cancer, returned to Three Rivers Stadium to announce three innings of a Pirates-Dodgers game. So weak that he lasted only two innings, Prince was greeted with several standing ovations, as the last-place Pirates inexplicably rallied to win 16-2, giving the Dodgers their worst drubbing in a decade. The Gunner died five weeks later; in 1986, he was posthumously awarded the Ford Frick Award for Broadcasting by the National Baseball Hall of Fame.

Even during the good years in the '70s, Pittsburgh's relationship to its baseball team never again amounted to anything approaching its love affair with the 1960 Bucs. Not that attendance was bad, it just wasn't very good—as if Pittsburgh took its team for granted. During most of those years, the Pirates drew between 1.1 million and 1.5 million—middle-of-the-road among NL teams, and nowhere near the more than 2 million Red fans in Cincinnati who flocked to watch the era's other NL power. Hard times didn't help the Pirates, and when Western Pennsylvania's steel industry dipped into a prolonged recession in the late '70s and early '80s, it grew harder for many families to justify the expense of a day at the ballpark. The plight of the Pirates and of the city mirrored one another. Pittsburgh's population sagged, dropping precipitously to 334,000 by the year 2000, slightly over half of the 1960 figure; whereas Pittsburgh was the sixteenth biggest city in the U.S. in 1960, by 2000 it was only the fifty-first biggest city.

* * *

Names of the men who played so long ago in Game 7 of the 1960 World Series still evoke magic. In 1997, the late Roger Maris again commanded headlines as Mark McGuire and Sammy Sosa staged a stirring race to eclipse his single-season home run record—one that looks better all the time in light of alleged steroid use in more recent times. Ensuring that Maris's accomplishments remain in the public eye was actor-turned-filmmaker Billy Crystal, whose gripping 2001 film, *61**, captures the humility of a reluctant hero.

A hopeless Yankee romantic, Crystal in 1999 paid $239,000 at Sotheby's auction house for Mantle's 1960 glove. The Rawlings-model glove, which Mantle signed, still has the classic deep-well pocket design with all-original stitching and Mickey's famed number 7 appearing on either side of the company label on the wrist guard. The item was among the nearly one-hundred thousand pieces from the collection of New Jersey printing executive Barry Halper, considered the largest private assemblage of historical items related to baseball ever sold.

In Pittsburgh, images of Mazeroski steaming around the bases after his big World Series home run appear periodically on commemorative Iron City Beer cans, as well as in faded black-and-white photos behind bars and as part of a mural on the ramp of the Boulevard of the Allies Bridge. There's another painting of Maz—and a trunk's worth of other 1960 reminders that includes the Game 7 Forbes Field pitching rubber, dug up by a groundskeeper and resembling a big slab of cheese—at the John Heinz Pittsburgh Regional History Center on Smallman Street.

But like Mazeroski's missing home-run ball, the actual television broadcast of Game 7 has yet to surface and may never be found. Television networks in 1960 didn't keep copies of the shows, partly due to the expense and because the large reels of film took up too much room.

Though a few clips of big moments were filmed and saved, there is next to nothing before videotape was introduced in the late 1960s.

Actually finding a broadcast of Game 7 would be a real coup for Doak Ewing, whose company, Rare Sportsfilms, Inc., is in the business of tracking down old film of famous sporting events and preserving them on DVDs for home viewing. Broadcasts from the 1950s and early '60s that do exist are kinescopes, from a process in which a motion picture camera was set up in front of a TV monitor. In an agreement between major-league baseball, the networks, and the U.S. Armed Forces, the films were then shown to U.S. troops overseas and were supposed to be destroyed after showing.

Ewing, who recently found a kinescope of Don Larsen's perfect game in the '56 Series, soldiers on anyway as he continues to track down any and all leads on the 1960 broadcast. A few years ago, after hearing that the family of Danny Murtaugh may have owned a copy, Ewing contacted the manager's widow and son, who checked and found that they had only a Series highlight film. "I'm pretty much convinced that Game 7, or any of the games of the 1960 World Series, does not exist anywhere," says Ewing. "But we can always hold out hope. I've been surprised before."

Memories of Game 7 of the 1960 World Series are preserved and kept very much alive by the players themselves. Mazeroski and other former 1960 Pirates and Yankees are frequent guests at baseball-card shows, which have contributed more than anything since the 1980s to keep their names on the lips of baseball fans, young and old. "You get a guy in his seventies who is with his son in his fifties and his grandson in his twenties, who meet Mazeroski or Moose Skowron at a show and can relate to what happened in the 1960 World Series," says Maury Allen. "The stories get passed down from one generation to the next generation. The names stay vivid and so do the faces. That's what separates baseball from every other sport, so players from 45 years ago are as clear to young people today as (to) the fans who went to see them in 1960. Baseball is the only sport in which this happens."

Something else contributes to keeping the memories fresh: the box score, one of journalism's great inventions. "Fifty or one hundred years from now, somebody will be able to pick up the box score of Game 7 of the 1960 World Series and see exactly what happened," says Allen. "They'll see Mazeroski's home run, see exactly what happened, and get a vivid and emotional sense of the event that they couldn't have in any other sport. The box score keeps these names alive forever."

In 2005 when the Pirates met the Yankees for three intraleague games in New York, as they have in the teams' spring-training games since 1960, newspaper columnists ran a fresh batch of "Where are they now?" features on the last time the teams had met. Predictably, the Yankees swept the overmatched Pirates in a fitting symbol of baseball's payroll disparity.

Periodically, the surviving players from the 1960 World Series gather to play golf or for reunions, especially in the years ending with zeros and fives. Some, like Groat and other Pirate players, still relish talking about it: "That '60 team, believe it or not," Groat says, "is so beloved to people, more than any team in the history of Pittsburgh." Others, like the snakebitten Bobby Shantz of the Yankees, would rather forget. "I really don't remember too much about the game," he writes in respectfully declining a request for an interview, "except we should have won that World Series."

As the man who threw the winning home-run ball, Ralph Terry isn't let off the hook so easily. Asked constantly about his 1960 slider—or fastball—that wouldn't slide, he continues to answer with grace and humor. Terry, who lives in western Kansas, will autograph photographs of the famous play but refuses to sign a bat or a ball that has already been signed by Mazeroski, a decision misunderstood by many. He says that he doesn't want anyone profiting from the 1960 showdown, except when the proceeds go to charity.

Terry retired from baseball in 1967 and joined the Senior PGA Golf Tour for a successful second career. In an interview with *Post-Gazette* sports columnist Ron Cook, he recalled playing in a pro-am tournament a few years ago in Portugal, when he was pared with a retired steel executive, an Englishman. "As the day progressed and we drank a few bottles of port, this fellow says to me, 'I understand you played a little rounders in your day,' " Terry recalled. "I tell him I did, and he proceeds to tell me he saw one game in his life, in Pittsburgh in 1960. My ears perked up at that."

Apparently, the Englishman was part of a group of U.S. Steel guests visiting Pittsburgh, where on October 13, they played golf in the morning and went to Forbes Field that afternoon to see "a little rounders"—Game 7 of the World Series.

"All this time, I'm thinking that this guy knows who I am and he's pulling my leg," Terry said. "Then I realize he's not because he's getting more and more excited. He says, 'You won't believe what happened. In the final chukker, this bloke hits the ball clear out of the lot and pandemonium breaks loose. We were lucky to escape with our lives.' "

"I just look at him for a second, then told him, 'You know someone had to bowl that ball up here for the bloke to hit? Well, that was me.' What a party we had that night, celebrating the coincidence."

* * *

It was Doug. Just in from Wheeling, West Virginia, and dressed in a Pirates' cap, he had left home several hours before and, while on his way, had made a point to drive by Bill Mazeroski's childhood home. "It seemed appropriate," said Doug as he eyed the scene—some one hundred fellow disciples who had gathered, as they do every October 13, at sacred ground to commemorate what is arguably the greatest moment in Pittsburgh sports' history.

The spot: the lone remaining sliver of Forbes Field's red-brick out-field wall, where on October 13, 1960, the Pirates won it all, thanks in large part to the walk-off home run by that man, Mazeroski. Doug and others gather in reverence every year on this date in front of what is now the University of Pittsburgh Business School, where on a memorable day all those years ago the ball disappeared over the left-center field wall to make the Pirates baseball's improbable champions and set off a celebration of such exuberance in Pittsburgh that the old-timers still talk about.

The ritual isn't advertised. In Pittsburgh, which continues to take its sports seriously, people just know to head to "the wall"—"our wailing wall" as Doug calls it. Some wear suits—businessmen playing hooky—and most dress with some kind of Pirate adornment, caps mostly. One man dons a full Roberto Clemente replica uniform and draws admiring looks. Bob Friend, who pitched that seventh game in relief for the Pirates, shows up, as he does every year: "I wouldn't miss this for the world," he says. "What our team did still means so much to this city. It makes us legends."

Launched in 1985 by a Pirate fan named Saul Finkelstein from Squirrel Hill, the ritual has since grown mostly by word-of-mouth to 100 or so people a year, except for the fortieth anniversary back in 2000, when a crowd four times that big, including Mazeroski himself, showed up. Someone brings a recording of the game and a boom box—and starting at 1 PM, game time in 1960, the crowd takes in every pitch, cheering as if they don't know the outcome. It's the base-ball version of a low-key revival meeting.

Some bring lawn chairs. Most stand. Herb Saul shows up for just a few innings. It is the first day of Yom Kippur, and Saul has stolen a few minutes from synagogue just to attend, armed with a blurry photo of himself storming the field after Game 7 when he was twenty-five. "I was sitting in the reserved section behind the Pirate dugout," Saul recalls of that long-ago day with absolute clarity. "Then I just ran out on the field when Maz hit the home run. It was unbelievable, incredible." Getting into the spirit is Doug, who listens to Saul's memory of the great day and gestures toward the remaining red brick wall where surviving members of Benny Benack's Iron City Six wear skimmers and belt out some schmaltzy tunes.

Saul makes it to the seventh, then hurries back to temple. Nellie King and another former Pirate pitcher-turned-broadcaster, Steve Blass, show up. The schmoozing continues, much of it a lament for the mediocre state of the current Pirates, who haven't been to a Series since 1979 and last had a winning season in 1992, the longest sub.- 500 streak of any team in the four major sports. Two men try hard to remember the names of the Dodgers who comprised baseball's only switch-hitting infield. Clemente's three thousandth base hit is recalled with reverence. "Were you there?" people ask one another. "They were playing the Mets, right?" A construction worker, drilling a gas line just under the old outfield wall, delivers a brick from underground for Friend to sign. Smiling, Friend complies: "My first brick of the day," he says.

Nearby, people smoke cigars—when's the last time you smelled that at a ballgame? One man in a Yankee hat stands his ground defiantly and looks out of place. Another is there with his dog, a striking Lab named Sam. "You mean Sammy Sosa?" asks a bystander. "No, just Sam," the man says. A college student with shaggy hair looks like he'd be more at home at a Phish concert, but he's in the right place: He's wearing a Clemente shirt.

Doug teaches middle-school reading in Wheeling, and uses baseball in his instruction by teaching his students how to keep score. He regrets that more young people don't know about the 1960 Pirates or particularly care for baseball. "Kids are into football and NASCAR these days," Doug says. "Of course, all these losing seasons do not help matters."

Attesting to Doug's point are university students who stride by the proceedings with no clue of the events that happened here. "Who are these people?" asks one. "Was there a bomb scare?" At least somebody connected with the university had a sense of history: Across the road, which is called Clemente Drive, is a mammoth dorm called Posvar Hall, with a bronze replica of Forbes Field's home plate in its original position. On a nearby wall hangs George Silk's famous Forbes Field panoramic shot, framed and signed by Mazeroski.

At the center of the crowd stands Pittsburgh sportswriter Jim O'Brien, whose marvelous books on the 1960 team have made him the unofficial master of ceremonies. "The 1960 Pirates taught me a lesson: through all the hardships and the challenges to never ever give up," says O'Brien, a former sportswriter with the *Pittsburgh Press* and the *New York Post*. "Winning the 1960 World Series is still a magical moment in Pittsburgh sports history. When that home run won the seventh game, everybody knew exactly what they were doing when that ball cleared the wall."

The climatic game hurtles toward the finish, and the crowd hushes, leaning forward in a semicircle to catch Chuck Thompson describe the action. Tied 9-all in the bottom of the nineth, Mazeroski steps to the plate and takes a ball up high. Then he swings at the 1-0 pitch, and the baseball disappears into the Indian summer afternoon—landing perhaps 60 feet from where we stand. The gathering erupts—just as it did all those years ago in the city that will never forget.

Pirates 10, Yankees 9

Thursday, October 13, 1960 at Forbes Field

Yankees	ab	r	h	rbi
Richardson 2b	5	2	2	0
Kubek ss	3	1	0	0
DeMaestri ss	0	0	0	0
Long ph	1	0	1	0
McDougald pr, 3b	0	1	0	0
Maris rf	5	0	0	0
Mantle rf	5	1	3	2
Berra lf	4	2	1	4
Skowron 1b	5	2	2	1
Blanchard c	4	0	1	1
Boyer 3b, ss	4	0	1	1
Turley p	0	0	0	0
Stafford p	0	0	0	0
Lopez ph	1	0	1	0
Shantz p	3	0	1	0
Coates p	0	0	0	0
Terry p	0	0	0	0
Totals	40	9	13	9

Pirates	ab	r	h	rbi
Virdon cf	4	1	2	2
Groat ss	4	1	1	1
Skinner lf	2	1	0	0
Nelson 1b	3	1	1	2
Clemente rf	4	1	1	1
Burgess c	3	0	2	0
Christopher pr	0	0	0	0
Smith c	1	1	1	3
Hoak 3b	3	1	0	0
Mazeroski 2b	4	2	2	1
Law p	2	0	0	0
Face p	0	0	0	0
Cimoli ph	1	1	1	0
Friend p	0	0	0	0
Haddix	0	0	0	0
Totals	31	10	11	10

	1	2	3	4	5	6	7	8	9	R	H	F
New York	0	0	0	0	1	4	0	2	—	9	13	1
Pittsburgh	2	2	0	0	0	0	0	5		10	11	0

Yankees	IP	H	R	ER	BB	SO
Turley	1.0	2	3	3	1	0
Stafford	1.0	2	1	1	1	0
Shantz	5.0	4	3	3	1	0
Coates	0.2	2	2	2	0	0
Terry L (0-2)	0.1	1	1	1	0	0
Totals	8	11	10	10	3	0

Pirates	IP	H	R	ER	BB	SO
Law	5.0	4	3	3	1	0
Face	3.0	6	4	4	1	0
Friend	0.0	2	2	2	0	0
Haddix W (2-0)	1.0	1	0	0	0	0
Totals	9	13	9	9	2	0

E–Maris (1). **DP**–New York 3. **2B**–New York Boyer (2, off Face). **HR**–New York Skowron (2, 5th inning off Law 0 on, 0 out); Berra (1, 6th inning off Face 2 on, 1 out), Pittsburgh Nelson (1, 1st inning off Turley 1 on, 2 out); Smith (1, 8th inning off Coates 2 on, 2 out); Mazeroski (2, 9th inning off Terry 0 on, 0 out). **SH**–Skinner (1, off Coates). **U**–Bill Jackowski (NL), Nestor Chylak (AL), Dusty Boggess (NL), Johnny Stevens (AL), Jim Honochick (AL), Stan Landes (NL). **T**–2:36. **A**–36,683.

ACKNOWLEDGMENTS

HAS IT REALLY been nearly a half century since Game 7 of the 1960 World Series? Visit the site of Forbes Field in Pittsburgh, and the history made there that Indian summer afternoon doesn't seem so long ago. Listen in on the lively airwaves of the more recent, boisterous institution known as New York talk radio, which is where this project started, and this becomes readily apparent.

I was doing yard work at my home in suburban New York City on a Sunday morning in July 2001, listening to caller after caller on a radio show complain that the greatest-fielding second baseman of all time was overrated. It was the day of Bill Mazeroski's induction into the National Baseball Hall of Fame, and Yankee fans were making their opinion known—that he didn't deserve a plaque in Cooperstown—and doing so loudly.

"Pee Wee Reese had a better lifetime batting average than he did," said one caller.

"All he ever did was hit that home run," said another. "Losing the 1960 World Series was a fluke."

Others suggested that Mazeroski didn't deserve election, but that former New York players like Keith Hernandez and Don Mattingly did.

All of this was riling me up. Had any of these callers ever seen Mazeroski play? Doubtful. A fluke? Sorry, baseball teams win occasional games on flukes, but they don't get to a seventh game of the

World Series without significant talent. Keith Hernandez? A great ballplayer to be sure, but a Hall of Famer? Perhaps.

So I resolved to examine what made Game 7 of the 1960 World Series so special, and the results comprise the contents of this book. While much of what those radio callers said was nonsense, their passion for the Yankees and the discussion of a baseball game played long before many of them were born goes right to the heart of what Maury Allen suggests is baseball's uncanny ability: to pass its history and its lore like no other sport from one generation to another.

What I discovered is that the story of Game 7 of the 1960 World Series is filled with drama from its first pitch to its last. So is the story of how that season's Pirates did it, which Pittsburgh author Jim O'Brien covers exceedingly well in his books *Maz and the '60 Bucs: When Pittsburgh and Its Pirates Went All the Way* (James P. O'Brien Publishing, 1993) and *Fantasy Camp: Living the Dream with Maz and the '60 Bucs* (2005). Both are part of O'Brien's "Pittsburgh Proud" series.

As for this book, there are many people to thank for their time in talking with me. Maury Allen, George Berger, Gino Cimoli, Jill Corey, Bob Costas, Joe DeMaestri, Doak Ewing, Elroy Face, Bob Friend, Dick Groat, Stan Isacs, Nellie King, Neil Leifer, Ed McConnell, Gil McDougald, Marvin Newman, Dr. Jean Oertel, Ken Pearlman, Bobby Richardson, Pete Ridge, Ralph Terry, and Bill Virdon all shared their memories of October 13, 1960, with me. A sincere thank-you—and a 15-cent bag of stale 1960 Forbes Field Snax Peanuts—to all for your time.

Tim Wiles, Sue Mackay, Freddy Berkowski, Claudette Burke, and John Horne Jr., at the National Baseball Hall of Fame were there, as always, with authoritative answers to my many questions. Greg Dinkin and Frank Scatoni of Venture Literary are the agents who found a home for this project, and Shaun Dillon of Carroll & Graf is the editor who gave shape and substance to the text. Andrew J. Gasper and Lynn Redmile of the Topps Company were gracious in granting permission to reproduce baseball cards of some of the men who played Game 7 of the 1960 World Series. In Pittsburgh, Paul and Sharon Antis were wonderful hosts. And as always, Frank Fenton was a font of information about the finer points of baseball. Thank you all.

As always, my biggest thank-you goes to my immediate family, Tobie and Julia. You've put up with my ramblings about a baseball game played a very long time ago, and I'm grateful for your patience. For you then, two bags of peanuts—and my love.

BIBLIOGRAPHY

Newspapers, Magazines, and Papers

Baseball Digest

Carnegie Magazine

Carnegie Mellon University Center for Economic Development: The Root of Pittsburgh's Population Drain (2003)

Forbes Field 60th Birthday/Pittsburgh Pirates Picture Album (1969)

National Pastime

Newsweek

New York Daily News

New York Herald-Tribune

New York Post

New York Times

Pittsburgh Post-Gazette

Pittsburgh Press

Pittsburgh Sun-Telegraph

St. Petersburg Times

Saturday Evening Post

Sports Illustrated

Time

USA Today

Books

Alexander, Charles C. *Our Game: An American Baseball History* (New York: Henry Holt and Company, Inc., 1991).

Algeo, Matthew. *Last Team Standing: How the Steelers and the Eagles—"The Steagles"—Saved Pro Football During World War II* (New York: Da Capo Press, 2006).

Allen, Maury. *Now wait a minute, Casey!* (New York: Doubleday & Company, 1965).

Castro, Tony. *Mickey Mantle: America's Prodigal Son* (Dulles, VA: Brassey's, Inc., 2002).

Chieger, Bob (ed.). *Voices of Baseball: Quotations on the Summer Game* (New York: Atheneum Publishers, Inc., 1983).

Cope, Myron. *The Game That Was* (Cleveland: The World Publishing Company, 1970).

Creamer, Robert W. *Stengel: His Life and Times* (New York: Simon & Schuster, 1984).

Fetter, Henry D. *Taking on the Yankees* (New York: W. W. Norton & Company, Inc., 2003).

Gallen, David (ed.). *The Baseball Chronicles* (New York: Galahad Books, 1991).

Gershman, Michael, Pete Palmer, David Pietrusza, and John Thorn, (eds.). *Total Baseball: The Official Encyclopedia of Major League Baseball* (New York: Viking, 1997).

Groat, Dick and Bill Surface. *The World Champion Pittsburgh Pirates* (New York: Coward-McCann, Inc., 1961).

Halberstam, David. *October 1964* (New York: Ballantine Books, 1995).

Hano, Arnold. *A Day in the Bleachers* (New York: Da Capo Press, 1995; first published 1955).

Holtzman, Jerome. *No Cheering in the Press Box* (New York: Henry Holt and Company, Inc., 1973).

Huhn, Rick. *The Sizzler: George Sisler, Baseball's Forgotten Great* (Columbia, MO: University of Missouri Press, 2004).

Keene, Kerry. *1960: The Last Pure Season* (Chicago: Sports Publishing Inc., 2000).

Kuenster, John (ed.). *The Best of Baseball Digest* (Chicago: Ivan R. Dee, 2006).

Lanctot, Neil. Negro League Baseball: *The Rise and Ruin of a Black Institution* (Philadelphia: University of Pennsylvania Press, 2004).

Levenson, Barry. *The Seventh Game: The 35 World Series That Have Gone the Distance* (New York: McGraw-Hill, 2004).

Lieb, Frederick G. *The Pittsburgh Pirates* (Carbondale, IL: Southern Illinois University Press, 2003; first published by G. P. Putman's Sons, 1948).

Lorant, Stefan. *Pittsburgh: The Story of an American City* (Lenox, MA: Authors Edition, Inc., 1964).

Lowry, Phillip J. *Green Cathedrals* (Published by Society for American Baseball Research, 1986, manufactured by AG Press, Manhattan, KS).

Maraniss, David. *Clemente: The Passion and Grace of Baseball's Last Hero* (New York: Simon & Schuster, 2006).

McCollister, John. *Tales from the Pirates Dugout: A Collection of the Greatest Pirates Stories Ever Told* (Chicago: Sports Publishing L.L.C., 2003).

O'Brien, Jim. *Maz and the '60 Bucs: When Pittsburgh and Its Pirates Went All the Way* (Pittsburgh: James P. O'Brien Publishing, 1993).

O'Toole, Andrew. *Branch Rickey in Pittsburgh: Baseball's Trailblazing General Manager for the Pirates, 1950–1955* (Jefferson, NC: McFarland & Company, 2000).

Rosewell, Albert Kennedy. *Rosey Reflections* (Pittsburgh: A.E.P. Kerr Company, 1945).

Schaap, Dick. *Dick Schaap as Told to Dick Schaap. Flashing Before My Eyes: 50 Years of Headlines, Deadlines & Punchlines* (New York: HarperCollins Publishers, 2001).

Smith, Curt. *Voices of Summer: Ranking Baseball's 101 All-Time Best Announcers* (New York: Carroll & Graf Publishers, 2005).

Smith, Curt. *Voices of the Game* (South Bend, IN: Diamond Communications, 1987).

Smizik, Bob. *The Pittsburgh Pirates: An Illustrated History* (New York: Walker & Company, 1990).

Stephenson, Sam (ed.). *Dream Street: W. Eugene Smith's Pittsburgh Project* (New York: W. W. Norton & Company, Inc., & Lyndhurst Books, 2001).

Wagenheim, Kal. *Clemente!* (Maplewood, NJ: Waterfront Press, 1984; originally published by Praeger Publishers, 1973).

Weber, Michael P. *Don't Call Me Boss: David L. Lawrence, Pittsburgh's Renaissance Mayor* (Pittsburgh: University of Pittsburgh Press, 1988).

Interviews

Maury Allen

George Berger

Gino Cimoli

Jill Corey

Bob Costas

Joe DeMaestri

Doak Ewing

Elroy Face

Bob Friend

Dick Groat

Stan Isaacs

Nellie King

Neil Leifer

Ed McConnell

Gil McDougald

Marvin Newman

Dr. Jean Oertel

Ken Pearlman

Bobby Richardson

Pete Ridge

Ralph Terry

Bill Virdon

INDEX
....